THE MORMON
MISSIONARIES

THE MORMON MISSIONARIES

An Inside Look at Their Real Message and Methods

JANIS HUTCHINSON

kregel
RESOURCES

Grand Rapids, MI 49501

The Mormon Missionaries: An Inside Look at Their Real Message and Methods

© 1995 by Janis Hutchinson

Published by Kregel Resources, an imprint of Kregel Publications, P.O. Box 2607, Grand Rapids, MI 49501. Kregel Resources provides timely and relevant resources for Christian life and service. Your comments and suggestions are valued.

Cover and book design: Alan G. Hartman

Library of Congress Cataloging-in-Publication Data
Hutchinson, Janis
    The Mormon missionaries: an inside look at their real message and methods / by Janis Hutchinson.
        p.   cm.
    Includes bibliographical references.
        1. Church of Jesus Christ of Latter-Day Saints—
Missions—Controversial literature. 2. Church of Jesus
Christ of Latter-Day Saints—Doctrines—Controversial
literature. 3. Mormon Church—Missions—Controversial
literature. 4. Mormon Church—Doctrines—Controversial
literature. I. Title.
BX8661.H745   1995   266'.9332—dc20   95-23764
                                                            CIP
ISBN 0-8254-2886-6 (paperback)

2 3 4 5 Printing / Year 00 99 98 97 96

Printed in the United States of America

To my daughter Debra,
whose love for Jesus and the truth
overcame her love for the Mormon Church

Contents

Preface

When I first contemplated writing *The Mormon Missionaries,* I seriously struggled over whether to write it or not. I knew the information contained in the book was needed, yet at the same time I had a reluctance to present the negative side of the Mormon Church—especially after spending so many happy years in it. But now due to the many individuals who have contacted me describing their specific concerns about Mormonism, I finally changed my mind.

Within the pages of this book you will learn about Mormon missionaries. You will see how they present their lessons and what subjects they cover, and by knowing this, have an edge in witnessing. You will discover startling facts surrounding Mormonism's beginnings, receive an eye-opener on where Joseph Smith actually got his doctrines, and find out the shocking motive behind Mormon missionary work. In addition, your own testimony will be strengthened as to the falseness of Mormonism—just in case those television commercials are getting to you.

Furthermore, this book can be used as a witnessing tool. Offer it to individuals who are already taking, or who are considering taking, the Mormon missionary lessons. It will reveal many doctrines the missionaries purposely conceal.

Missionaries of the Church of Jesus Christ of Latter-day Saints are a special group of young men and women. Willingly, they give eighteen months to two years of their lives to preach what they truly believe is the Gospel of Jesus Christ. Of course they are wrong— but their dedication is admirable. Personally, I feel a special endearment toward them in spite of knowing their teachings to be false. This comes from my thirty-four years of devoted activity in the Mormon Church during which time I filled two stake missions, married a returned missionary, and sent a daughter on a full-time mission. I know the missionary mind-set, sincerity, and dedication. As a result, I may be guilty of rendering too sympathetic a portrayal of the two Mormon missionaries in this book.

However, despite my tender feelings, I recognize their clever methods and errors and do not hesitate to point them out. I explain the deceptive way in which they deliver their lessons, expose certain of their hidden doctrines, and compare their presentation of God to orthodox Christianity.

Mormon missionaries never question the tactics they use. Believing they are instructed by inspired leaders, they honestly view their methods as spiritually correct. This is because they consider those who are investigating Mormonism to be on a "kindergarten" level and thus to be incapable of handling anything but the basics. Milk must come before meat—even if it means giving the wrong impression about Mormon beliefs. By not telling all, missionaries feel they are following the Old Testament pattern found in Isaiah 28:10, "Precept upon precept; line upon line . . . here a little, and there a little."

If the missionary dialogue sounds canned, that's because it is. New missionaries often memorize all conversational dialogue. When teaching, some even read directly from the lesson books. However, those nearing the end of their missionary time are well versed and can give the lessons in their own words. The subjects covered in this book are the same as the major topics included in the six lesson books used by missionaries.

One caution is in order. If the reader is successful in bringing someone out of Mormonism, there is an additional responsibility that is often overlooked. When Mormons leave their church to enter Christianity, there is a traumatic aftermath. Emotional repercussions can last as long as three to eight years after they are saved. With no one to help them, they will do one of four things: stay in the church and be miserable, start church-hopping, drop out of church, or return to the Mormon Church.

The sad part is that most Christians, even pastors with all their training in counseling, are unprepared to address the problems that these new converts have. Practically every letter I receive from former cultists testifies to this. Christians may be knowledgeable in how to biblically refute cult doctrines, but as far as giving effective help afterward they are at a loss. Even countercult organizations are ineffective in doing this. While they play their part in disseminating information, their ministries go no further. Therefore, there is a desperate need for Christians to become knowledgeable about the transition process in order to provide needed support.

In view of this, I strongly recommend my book *Out of the Cults and Into the Church* that describes the transitional problems in detail and gives instructions on how to help.

While the dialogue of the characters in this story and the Bible college setting is based on actual experience, the characters are purely fictional and any resemblance to persons living or dead is coincidental.

Unless otherwise noted, all Scripture verses are taken from the King James Version. Mormons recognize no other version.

Acknowledgments

I wish to thank my sister, Carol Foulkes, for her valuable input during the writing of my manuscript.

Also, Pastor George Johnson of Central Christian Church in Snohomish, Washington, for his exceptional editing expertise, and Pastor Gale O'Neil of Memorial Community Church for use of his personal library.

Special thanks to my daughter Debra, a former Mormon missionary, who critiqued, offered advice, and confirmed what I was writing.

Lastly, I must express my gratitude and admiration to Jerald and Sandra Tanner of Utah Lighthouse Ministry for their years of dedicated research on Mormonism, which aided in the writing of this book.

CHAPTER ONE

Surprise on Campus

Encountering the Mormon missionaries

C ome quick!" a student yelled, bursting through the door of the empty classroom where I was correcting papers. Startled, my chair clattered to the hardwood floor as I jumped to my feet. Racing to the door, my mind went through possible scenarios. Was it a student lying on the ground gasping for breath? Frantically I tried to recall my CPR class. *Blow! two, three, four . . .*

Dashing outside the small wood-framed bungalow where I served as teacher of the cults class at a small Texas Bible college, I suddenly stopped short. I couldn't believe my eyes!

There they were! Two Mormon missionaries! And—of all places—at a Bible college!

Like two rabbits cornered by hounds, they had been backed onto the porch of the administration building by eight zealous students eager to try out their third-year polemics. I almost felt sorry for the missionaries.

Both were in their early twenties, had short haircuts, were dressed in white shirts, ties, and dark pants, and wore black plastic lapel pins that stated their last names preceded by "Elder." Underneath their names was "Church of Jesus Christ of Latter-day Saints."

Tucked beneath their arms, they carried a thick black book that resembled the Bible. Nevertheless, I recognized the *Standard Works*. Nicknamed the Four-in-One, it consists of four major works: the King James version of the Bible, with Mormon annotations; the Book of Mormon, which claims to be the history of the ancient inhabitants of the Americas; the Doctrine and Covenants, revelations given to their church; and the Pearl of Great Price, consisting of the Book of Moses, Book of Abraham, Writings of Joseph Smith, and the Articles of Faith.

I knew why the students had sent for me. They expected me, a former Mormon, to convert the missionaries, to denounce them, or to at least send them whirling into a state of inextricable confusion.

Looking like they were fresh off the farm, the two men appeared young and inexperienced. As I walked toward them, I knew I didn't have the heart to be rough on them. I knew they believed they had something precious to offer. In addition, I knew what they felt. I knew their love for God, their zeal, their dedication— I had once stood where they stood. I had served two stake missions (stake missionaries remain at home and hold secular jobs; missionary work is done after work and on weekends). I had married a returned Mormon missionary, who later died, and sent a daughter, now a Christian, on a Mormon mission.

Complying with Mark 6:7, they always went out two by two. Studying them, it was easy to spot which of the two classifications each fell into, *senior companion* or *greenie*. The one longest into his two-year mission, the senior companion, was tall and slender with reddish blonde hair—handsome in a boyish kind of way—maintaining a bold stance. The other, the greenie, as new missionaries are called, was stocky and had brown hair. Unsure of himself, he was letting his companion take the lead.

There are a variety of motives that bring young men like these two on a mission. Some go to better qualify themselves as husbands for Latter-day Saint girls back home. Many consent simply because it is expected. Others go with the sole intent of meeting lady missionaries (called LMs) as future spouses. Then there are some who, living a life contrary to Mormon standards before their mission, are forced by their parents as a last-ditch effort to straighten them out. Of course there are those who, deeply devoted and full of zeal, are genuinely anxious to bring the news of the "restored gospel" to the world.

As I approached the small circle, I quickly glanced to see which of my students were there.

I saw Robert, the overstudious son of one of our college instructors. Sure of himself because of his academic abilities, he nevertheless lacked spiritual sensitivity. Ilya, a Russian student who had fled to America as a result of the civil war in Georgia, Russia, was also there. Then there was Matt, with his blond pigtail and his funny way of walking—like he was keeping time to the beat of some

invisible rock group. There was also Sheri, the *señorita*, affectionately nicknamed Tia by the students because she had a zillion ways
to fix tortillas. Tall and slender, she was a Christian of Spanish de-
scent with snappy, black eyes that flashed with fire when she
danced. She was looking forward to becoming a missionary to Latin
America.

It seemed that my whole class was there. While I made note
of the others, I saw Tia's roommate, Susan, tossing her long
blonde hair so as to catch the sunlight. Her eye-fluttering attention was focused on the senior companion. Humorously, I passed
it off. That was just Susan—she flirted with all the boys.

I was particularly interested in the facial expressions of the students. Some, never having seen a Mormon missionary before,
stared at them in wonderment. Others, assuming more sober expressions, looked like they were just waiting for an opening to
witness. The remaining few, however, exhibited caution as if fearing the missionaries might bite or at least send a demon jumping
out at them.

Finally within hearing range, I heard the greenie (Elder Barrett,
according to his lapel pin) say, "Did you know that, just like the
Bible, God has given us another book that testifies of Christ?"

"Are you talking about the Book of Mormon?" I asked, moving in closer.

"Why yes!" He turned toward me with an eager smile. The students made room for me, and the air was tense with suppressed
excitement.

"I've read the Book of Mormon," I began, "and since it quotes
extensively from the Bible, plus has exciting adventure stories in
it, I do have to admit it's impressive.

"But," I quickly added, looking genuinely puzzled, "the only
problem I can't seem to reconcile is the way it describes God."

"What do you mean?" Elder Barrett asked, confident he could
solve my dilemma.

"Well," I continued, "I know the Mormon Church teaches that
God is an exalted man and that there are many gods. But, why
doesn't the Book of Mormon, which your leaders say contains
the 'fullness' of the gospel, back up your church's teachings? If
the Mormon Church was started by God, then the book you say
He has revealed ought to match its doctrines."

"Uh . . . ma'am . . . ," started Elder Barrett, "there is, of course,
no question that the Book of Mormon is in complete agreement
with our church's teachings."

"Well, then," I hurriedly added, "maybe I've missed something. I'll tell you what. I'll consider joining your church if you can show me in the Book of Mormon where it teaches the *Mormon* God" (I knew I was on safe ground. The Book of Mormon taught the Christian concept of only one God as spirit, which contradicted the LDS Church's present teaching that God, one among many gods, is a glorified man).

One of the students behind me quietly gasped. Elder Barrett quickly looked to his companion, whose lapel pin identified him as Elder Black. He, too, looked nervous. Evidently, they had never had this challenge put to them before. Not having a rehearsed response, they were in trouble—and they knew it. Then, Elder Black did exactly what I expected.

Pulling himself up to full height so he could say what he had to say all in one breath, he looked me squarely in the eye and in a tone of great conviction, began: "I *know*, by the power of the Holy Ghost, that the Book of Mormon is true and was restored by divine revelation to the prophet Joseph Smith . . . that Jesus is the Christ . . . President Gordon B. Hinckley is a prophet, seer, and revelator . . . and the Church of Jesus Christ of Latter-day Saints is the only true church upon the face of the earth!"

There was silence for a split second. I knew most of the students had never heard a Mormon bear testimony before. I was sure they were wondering how I could possibly combat someone's personal conviction.

"How do you know those things, Elder?" I asked.

"I know by a special feeling I have in my heart."

"Well," I quickly responded, "I too have a testimony." A blank look slipped over both their faces.

"I *know* beyond the shadow of a doubt," I began, "that Jesus is the Christ and Savior of the world . . . that He died for my sins and was resurrected. I *know* that I am saved by grace and not by works and will inherit heaven upon that principle. I also *know* that God hears and answers prayer. I *know* all this not only by the feeling I have from the inner witness of the Holy Ghost but by the reliability of God's Word, the Bible, which *declares* it to be so. And, I also *know* that because of my relationship with Christ, Jesus has changed my life and continues to bless me!"

The elders simply stared. I already knew the questions racing through their minds: *How can an outsider say "I know," since only someone who has received the Holy Ghost can use that phrase? How can this person, who isn't a Mormon, even have the Holy Ghost without having received it from someone holding the Melchizedek Priesthood?*

At that point, I deliberately said nothing. Hesitantly, the elders fumbled for words. "That's very nice. We, uh . . . we have another appointment and don't have time to spend right now."

In an attempt to cover up their confusion, Elder Black suddenly forced a Cheshire-cat-like grin on his face. Courageously he said, "But, if any of you would like to know more about the Mormon Church, we can be contacted at this number." He handed his card to Susan. They turned and left but not before I saw Elder Black give Susan a second glance.

Just then the bell rang. Saying that I would cover the situation in class, everyone scattered.

As I hurried across campus, relieved that I didn't have to give CPR after all, I still felt that I had a life-or-death situation on my hands. The missionaries were personable and disarming, and I knew how impressive a verbal testimony could be—even a Mormon's. I recalled Josh McDowell saying he admired a man or woman with conviction and often felt more at home with radicals who could state with certainty what they believed than with wishy-washy Christians.[1] I was concerned. The students couldn't help but be affected by Elder Black's testimony. Then there was Susan. It was obvious she was attracted to him.

☙☙ ☙☙

When the second bell rang, the students were already seated, eager-faced—the word had gotten around.

Glancing about, a tiny alarm suddenly went off inside me—Susan wasn't in her seat! I glanced questioningly at Tia, who sheepishly looked the other way. I then dismissed my feelings. She'd be here soon.

"Today," I began, "we had a little excitement on campus." Everyone laughed. Quickly explaining what happened for the benefit of those few who hadn't heard, I then cautioned them.

"All of you have been studying cults for quite a while, and you probably think that all you have to do is say exactly what I said today, *verbatim*, and you'll stump the missionaries every time. You're foolish if you believe this. Today I was simply fortunate to converse with two missionaries who hadn't encountered a Christian bearing a testimony before. More especially, they'd never been quizzed about the contradiction between their church's present teachings on God and that contained in the Book of Mormon.

"In addition, you may also believe that all you have to do is quote Scripture telling them they're sinners and suddenly they're going to exclaim, 'Wow, I really see that I'm lost!' If so, you're very naive.

"While I encourage you to plant seeds if you should encounter missionaries, remember to plant only positive ones. Keep it simple and don't argue with them. You are not going to convert them—at least not while they're on their mission because they're trained to defend Mormonism. Those who have spent as many as thirty years dealing with Mormons offer the same advice. After their mission, however, there is a chance that one may convert to Christianity, even as my daughter did.

"But, remember these cautions: *Don't* try to take on the Mormon missionaries in a theological debate until you've dealt with the average Mormon and *don't* take on the average Mormon without a thorough understanding of Mormonism!

"I would also add that since it takes years to become well versed in the doctrines and mentality of a single cult, you will be more effective if you concentrate on just one and leave the others for someone else."

Tia raised her hand. "Today you made a faith statement to the missionaries. Christians don't usually say it the way you did, so what were you trying to do? Imitate their testimony? If so, what was there about it that apparently disarmed them?"

"Before I answer that," I replied, "let me explain what a Mormon testimony is.

"As a major rite of passage, every worthy member is supposed to acquire one. That is, a Mormon is expected to reach a point where he or she can stand up in a testimony meeting and say, 'I know my beliefs are true,' as you heard the one elder do this afternoon. They also list certain basic doctrines one by one. This rhetoric is usually declared all in one sentence to illustrate that the witness of the Holy Ghost has encompassed all beliefs as one comprehensive truth.

"Now, admittedly, members are taught from toddlerhood to memorize this testimony. Church leaders especially encourage it, knowing that the verbalization of one's faith tends to give more meaning to beliefs. As children are growing up, they rattle it off as a conditioned response and as an incentive for acceptance and approval. If missionaries don't have one, they are urged, as Elder Boyd K. Packer admonished, to keep stating a testimony until they get one.[2]

"Training Mormon children to memorize a testimony eventually produces an inner conviction that it *really* is true. When this happens, it translates into an emotional experience that becomes personally meaningful. They are told that this emotional 'feeling' is the Holy Ghost confirming their beliefs. Elder Black, you may also recall, said he knew his church was true because of a feeling. You may recall that in my testimony, I stated that I knew my beliefs were true, not only by a feeling, but because God's Word declared them such.

"The testimony is one of the tools missionaries carry with them. They are taught that when they are backed into a corner by Christians, their personal testimony will always render non-Mormons helpless. Since the missionaries couldn't respond to my claim that the Book of Mormon's concept of God contradicts their church's teachings, that's exactly what Elder Black did."

Robert raised his hand. "There was one thing I noticed when you were making your faith statement. You put an unusual emphasis on the words *I know*. It sounded strange. Christians don't say that."

"Those words, *I know*," I replied, "comprise a key phrase that is loaded with implications for Mormons. So also is *I know beyond a shadow of a doubt* and *I bear witness*. Incorporating one of these phrases is the only way a Christian can impress a Mormon with a faith statement. But it must be declared with conviction."

Reaching for a book, I said, "Listen to what John L. Smith, who has worked with Mormons for years, says about witnessing:

> Any indication or hesitation on the part of the [Christian] witness is interpreted by the Mormon as weakness and error. He is used to seeing non-Mormons who are timid and unsure of themselves. He sees the Mormon self-assuredness as an indication of his being "right." Therefore, the fearful, timid, flinching, fainthearted witness has already almost defeated his effort by his lack of "boldness."[3]

"Remember, in the book of Acts," I said, "boldness is what impressed many who listened to Peter and Paul (See Acts 14:13; 9:29). To Mormons, a testimony stated with boldness and conviction signifies that the Holy Ghost is producing that testimony by supernatural revelation.

"Now, while they believe that God can confer a 'temporary' endowment of the Holy Ghost to convince a non-Mormon of the truth of Mormonism, a person can only have the *permanent* companionship of the Holy Ghost by having hands laid on him by an elder in the church.

"What caused the elders to fumble today was their confusion as to how I, who am not a Mormon, could possibly have the Holy Ghost when I had not received it by the laying on of hands by someone holding the Mormon priesthood. In addition, how could I have the Holy Ghost and not be moved to testify about the truth of Mormonism? To them, that is the Holy Ghost's primary function."

Matt raised his hand. "I noticed today, that you said Holy *Ghost* instead of Holy *Spirit*. Isn't that term outdated?"

"Yes, it is. However, when dealing with Mormons, be sure you use it. To them, the Holy *Ghost* and Holy *Spirit* are two different entities. The Holy *Ghost* is the third member of the Godhead, a separate personage of spirit who will some day acquire a body. His job is to confirm truth. The Holy *Spirit*, on the other hand, is a spiritual substance—an intelligent energy that was in the beginning and co-eternal with God. It was the material out of which man and the world was created.[4]

"One last thing. You'll recall in my testimony that I stated that I know God hears and answers my prayers. Always include that statement. It will puzzle a Mormon. He or she believes that only Mormons, members of the only church God recognizes, are privileged to have their prayers answered on a regular basis. That is, they believe that an outsider may genuinely receive an answer when praying about Mormon doctrine, but not in other matters.

"Here's an example. When I was teaching the gospel doctrine class in my ward, I dared to state that Baptists could possibly have their prayers answered. The reaction was startling. Four indignant people immediately got up and marched out. The negative response from all seventy members of my class was so extreme that I thought I'd be stoned on the spot!

"However, if you do share a prayer experience with Mormons, they'll never indicate this bias. They will make a good show, convincing you that they accept your experience. If they are impressed with it, they'll think one of three things. One, God has already picked you and has led you to them, which explains your prayer experience; two, it is of the Devil; or three, they'll be impressed enough about its genuineness to wonder why God gave it to you. If you tell specifics of your prayer experience, it is one seed they will always remember. Coupled with other seeds, it may contribute to their questioning Mormonism in the future."

Tia raised her hand. "You shocked quite a few of us by telling the missionaries you would join their church if they could show you where the Book of Mormon teaches the Mormon God. Would you really go back?"

"Of course not. However, I knew that I was on safe ground. When Joseph Smith first wrote the Book of Mormon, he pretty much believed in the traditional God. Today, however, Mormonism teaches that God is a resurrected man, that Jesus is *not* God and that there are many gods. Listen to this," I said, picking up a Book of Mormon. "In Alma 18:26–28 we read the following: 'And then Ammon said: Believest thou that there is a Great Spirit? And he said, Yea, and Ammon said: This is God.' It also teaches that Jesus is God:

> And now Abinadi said unto them: I would that ye should understand that God himself shall come down among the children of men, and shall redeem his people. And because he dwelleth in flesh he shall be called the Son of God, and having subjected the flesh to the will of the Father, being the Father and the Son—The Father, because he was conceived by the power of God; and the Son, because of the flesh; thus becoming the Father and Son—And they are one God, yea the very Eternal Father of heaven and of earth.[5]

Further, it teaches *against* a plurality of gods:

> Now Zeezrom said unto him: Thou sayest there is a true and living God? And Amulek said: Yea, there is a true and living God. Now, Zeezrom said: Is there more than one God? And he answered, no. Now Zeezrom said unto him again: How knowest thou these things? And he said: An angel hath made them known unto me.[6]

"However, doctrinal changes were gradually made as Joseph Smith advanced in his ideas. For example," I said, picking up a chart, "notice the difference between the original 1830 edition and the present version of the Book of Mormon:

> And the angel said unto me, behold the Lamb of God, yea, even the Eternal Father (1830 edition).[7]

And the angel said unto me: Behold the Lamb of God, yea even *the son of* the Eternal Father (1993 edition)![8]

"But now, I have a surprise," I said, glancing out the window at the tall, willowy figure hurrying up the stone walkway to the classroom. "How would you like to quiz a real live Mormon missionary?" Everyone looked stunned.

Laughing, I continued, "I asked my daughter Debra to come. I believe most of you know that she was born in the Mormon Church and later filled a Mormon mission before she became a Christian. Strangely, it was while she was on that mission that she decided she wanted nothing more to do with Mormonism. When she saw that the objective of the missionary lessons was to convert people to the church, tithing, Word of Wisdom, and Joseph Smith, and that Jesus wasn't mentioned until the sixth lesson, she became disillusioned. And, to top it off, she tells how she kept running into those 'born-again Christians' who would say things that made her think.

"Anyway, I've asked her to speak to you today. However, I think I'll just open it up to questions."

The class looked pleased and all eyes turned to the door. Debra entered, her short, honey-colored hair slightly disheveled from the Texas humidity. I felt a mother's pleasure at her graceful self-assuredness as she smiled contagiously at the students, then at me. More than one person had told me how lovely she was.

"Debra, we've had a little change in plans," I said. "Two Mormon elders came on campus this morning, so I'm sure the class would like to ask you some questions. Okay?"

"Sure," she said, smiling. Dropping the books from her arms into a corner chair, she then walked to the front of the class and said, "First question?"

Five hands shot up at once. "You," she said, pointing to Robert.

"Is there any difference," Robert asked, "between what a female missionary does and what a male missionary does?"

"One difference" she replied, "is that females only serve eighteen months, whereas the men serve two years. However, there is nothing different in the message they preach when knocking on doors. But, there is one major difference that makes itself known when lady missionaries finally get a convert—the priesthood. Females cannot baptize or lay on hands to give the gift of the Holy Ghost. Only men."

Robert looked puzzled. "The only time I ever heard of the

priesthood," he continued, "was in connection with the Catholic Church. Is it the same thing?"

"There is one similarity," Debra replied. "Both churches claim priesthood authority through apostolic succession. Catholics claim that Peter established the priesthood in Rome and it was handed down from pope to pope; Mormons claim that Peter, James, and John, all resurrected beings, personally appeared and restored the priesthood to Joseph Smith.[9]

"To Mormons, priesthood is their one claim to fame, so to speak. It is their authority to act in the name of God. Without the priesthood, they believe no church can officially function. Nor, can one baptize. This is why they emphasize it so much. They feel this is their elite edge over a pastor or member of any Christian church. In fact," she said, "every elder in the Mormon church can trace his priesthood lineage back to Joseph Smith—who supposedly received it from Peter, James, and John, who received it from Christ."

"How," Matt called out, "did Smith claim to receive the priesthood? From some supernatural voice?"

Another student spoke, "I don't believe even Jesus ever laid hands to confer priesthood on anyone, did He?"

"Debra," I interrupted, "these are a lot of questions to answer. Why don't you take them in order by first giving a thumbnail sketch of Joseph Smith's account of receiving the priesthood."

"Good idea," she replied, grabbing one of her books from the chair.

"First," she began, "in talking about Mormon priesthood, we're talking about *two* priesthoods—the Aaronic and the Melchizedek. Mormon elders hold both. Since the Aaronic is the first one Smith claimed to receive, I'll start by telling you that story.

"On May 15, 1829, Joseph Smith and Oliver Cowdery supposedly went into the woods at Harmony, Pennsylvania, to inquire of the Lord about baptism for the remission of sins. John the Baptist, a resurrected personage, suddenly appeared to them in a cloud of light. The following is the account of John's words to them:

> Upon you my fellow servants, in the name of Messiah, I confer the Priesthood of Aaron, which holds the keys of the ministering of angels, and of the gospel or repentance and of baptism by immersion for the remission of sins; and this shall never be taken again from the earth until the sons of Levi do offer again an offering unto the Lord in righteousness.[10]

"After receiving this priesthood from John," Debra continued, "Joseph Smith and Oliver Cowdery then baptized each other. Of course, Jesus never taught that one had to hold the Aaronic priesthood before he could baptize another believer.

"Nevertheless, what is so illogical is that Smith and Cowdery, after baptizing each other, ordained each other to the priesthood. 'What?' you are probably asking. 'Do you mean they *lost* their priesthood within the first few minutes after John the Baptist gave it to them?'"

The class laughed.

"But, even if their story hung together, there's another problem. The Bible says that the Aaronic priesthood was reserved only for the descendants of Aaron. Mormons claim to be of the tribes of Ephraim and Manassah, not Aaron. They believe that until someone steps forth with a legitimate claim to being a descendant of Aaron (which they believe is supernaturally disclosed through one's patriarchal blessing), members of the priesthood can substitutionally officiate in the duties of the Aaronic priesthood. So now, even though they are not descendants of Aaron, they ordain young men and older, newly-converted men to the Aaronic priesthood.

"What is so presumptuous is that in the Bible, God was very strict about who could hold the Aaronic priesthood. Because Christ was of the tribe of Judah, even He couldn't hold it.[11] That means that Mormon men are making themselves more privileged than Christ. That alone ought to refute the Mormon Aaronic priesthood.

"And, further," Debra said, "it's inconsistent with God's Word to continue a priesthood that was done away with. Since all the work of Old Testament priesthood offerings pointed to Jesus as the final Lamb, the Aaronic priesthood was no longer needed after His sacrifice."

Matt spoke up. "If Mormons insist on claiming the Aaronic priesthood, then their priests really ought to offer animal sacrifices!"

"Well, brace yourself," Debra said, grabbing another book. "Joseph Smith taught that animal sacrifice would eventually be reinstated. He says:

> It is generally supposed that sacrifice was entirely done away when the Great Sacrifice [i.e.] the sacrifice of the Lord Jesus was offered up, and that there will be no necessity for the ordinance

of sacrifice in [*sic*] future; but those who assert this are certainly not acquainted with the duties, privileges and authority of the Priesthood, or with the Prophets. . . . These sacrifices as well as every ordinance belonging to the Priesthood, will, when the Temple of the Lord shall be built, and the sons of Levi be purified, be fully restored and attended to in all their powers, ramifications, and blessings. . . . It is not to be understood that the law of Moses will be established again with all its rites and variety of ceremonies; this has never been spoken of by the prophets; but those things which existed prior to Moses' day, namely, sacrifice, will be continued.[12]

Another student spoke up. "How did Joseph Smith get the Melchizedek priesthood? Another visitation?"

"Well, sort of," Debra laughed. "Joseph Smith didn't provide a written account of Peter, James, and John's visitation. Perhaps this is why the story had to be invented by the church six years later. The 1830 edition of the Book of Commandments, the predecessor to the Doctrine and Covenants, makes no mention of either the Aaronic or Melchizedek priesthoods being part of the Mormon Church. But later, when they decided to use them, verses about the two priesthoods were inserted into the first edition of the 1835 Doctrine and Covenants.[13] Sidney Rigdon was behind this, according to David Whitmer, one of the witnesses to the Book of Mormon.[14]

"The reason the Melchizedek priesthood was needed was probably because leaders suddenly remembered their Bible.[15] They knew John the Baptist said he wasn't able to confer the baptism of the Holy Ghost (Matthew 3:11). His authority wasn't enough, so they had to incorporate an additional priesthood. The only one left was the Melchizedek."

"But, I thought," Matt interrupted, "that Jesus was the only one who held that priesthood."

"You're right," Debra continued. "And that's the one fact that destroys the Mormon claim to the Melchizedek priesthood.

"In the Old Testament, the priesthood was passed on from one person to another so that animal sacrifices, which pointed to Christ, could be officially performed for the cleansing of sin. But, now that Jesus fulfilled the sacrifice and lives eternally, there is no longer any need for anyone else to be ordained to the priesthood, or the need for such sacrifices (Hebrews 7:24).

"All New Testament believers became priests of a sort, because they daily offered themselves as *living* sacrifices to God (Romans 12:1). As Christians, we also share Christ's royal priesthood, but it is neither Aaronic or Melchizedek (1 Peter 2:5, 9). While we don't offer sacrifices for others' sins like Old Testament priests did, we intercede for others in prayer so they'll turn to the one High Priest, Jesus, who can assure them of cleansing through His sacrifice.

"Another difficulty with the Mormon priesthood," Debra continued, "is that bishops holding the Melchizedek priesthood are called high priests. But not even the high priest in the Old Testament held the Melchizedek priesthood. To make matters worse, in the Old Testament there was never more than one major high priest at a time. But Mormons have many. Further, the office of high priest was abolished after Christ became our High Priest. This is why there were no high priests in the New Testament church."

"But," Matt interjected, "don't Mormons claim that Jesus gave the priesthood to His disciples?"

"That's right. But, Jesus never conferred priesthood on anyone. However, He ordained, or appointed, individuals to do certain *tasks*.

"Mormons, suggesting Jesus did confer priesthood, quote the King James version of John 15:16, 'Ye have not chosen me, but I have chosen you, and ordained you.' But they go no further. The rest of the verse, which they ignore, says He ordained (or appointed) them to 'go and bring forth fruit.' It says nothing about priesthood. They say the word *ordained* means He conferred priesthood by the laying on of hands. This is *not* what that verse says.

"The problem with Mormons is that they apply the wrong meaning to the word *ordain*. It actually means 'appoint.' If the word *ordain* means 'priesthood,' then everything mentioned in the Bible that God *ordained* means He gave it priesthood. In section 89 of the Doctrine and Covenants it says: 'all grain is ordained for the use of man and of beast.' Marvin Cowan, in *Mormon Claims Answered*, asks: 'Did someone lay hands on the grain and give it the Priesthood?' He says further:

> While it is true that someone can be ordained by "laying on of hands," that is not the meaning of the word. It means to "appoint" or "point out." D. & C. 89 also mentions that herbs and flesh of beasts and fowls are "ordained for the use of man." That context shows that "ordained" means "appointed."[16]

"Mormons get the idea that priesthood must be conferred by the laying on of hands and quote Hebrews 5:4, 'No man taketh this honor unto himself but he that is called of God as was Aaron.'[17] Once again Cowan states:

> Nothing is said in the Bible about "laying on of hands" or ordaining Aaron or anyone else to the priest's office. Aaron was "anointed" (Ex. 40:13), but so was the tabernacle and everything in it (Ex. 40:9–15). Surely this "anointing" was not the "laying on of hands" to give the priesthood, or the tabernacle and everything in it were also ordained to the priesthood![18]

"Here is a chart," said Debra, placing a large poster against the blackboard. "It contains a brief summary of biblical facts about the priesthood. The contradictions between it and the Mormon concepts are obvious."

Bible	Mormon Church
• God ended the Aaronic priesthood since it only served to point to Christ.	• Mormons reinstituted the Aaronic priesthood.
• God was strict about which tribe could hold the Aaronic priesthood. Even Jesus was denied because He was of the tribe of Judah.	• Mormons disregard this restriction. Alleging to be of the tribes of Ephraim and Manassah, they still claim this right.
• Animal sacrifice was ended since it pointed to Christ.	• Mormons anticipate the reinstitution of animal sacrifice.
• There was only one major high priest in the Old Testament at a time.	• Mormons have many.
• Old Testament high priests never held the Melchizedek priesthood.	• Mormon high priests hold the Melchizedek priesthood.
• New Testament believers never had the Aaronic or Melchizedek priesthood conferred upon them.	• Mormons confer both.

- Jesus, after His resurrection, held an eternal, untransferable priesthood. It no longer had to be passed on in order to be continued.
- God said all believers, regardless of race or gender, are priests and hold royal priesthood since they sacrifice to God daily.
- Jesus did not lay hands on His disciples to confer either the Aaronic or Melchizedek priesthood.

- Mormons insist the Melchizedek priesthood is transferable and must be passed on to someone to perpetuate it.
- Mormon priesthood is reserved only for males.
- Mormons lay on hands to confer both priesthoods.

"Therefore," Debra continued, "the Mormon claim to priesthood is in contradiction to the Bible in every respect. The inconsistencies are all the more apparent in light of the Mormon Church's claim that it is a restoration of the New Testament church."

Ilya raised her hand. "Mormons talk about how dey haf sure answers to everyting. Yet, if dey can't take vhat God said in Bible as absolute, I vould call dat a very confusing environment to live in, let alone a faith to stand firm in."

"Only we, as Christians," Debra responded, "are able to see that. Most Mormons, however, don't feel insecure. Their security, albeit a false security, comes from believing that God sent Joseph Smith the Aaronic priesthood by way of John the Baptist; the Melchizedek priesthood by Peter, James, and John; and that Jesus continually revealed privileged truths to Joseph Smith. These so-called truths supply members with answers to mysteries about heaven, creation, and life itself. No, members feel very secure. The only aspect of Mormonism that some members feel insecure about is whether they have made themselves worthy enough to inherit the Celestial Kingdom."

"No wonder," interjected Matt, "the Mormon elders looked so sure of themselves today. Do you think a Christian could ever say anything to missionaries that would make them question their beliefs?"

"I doubt it," Debra replied. "However, this is not to say you shouldn't plant seeds. By seeds, though, I'm not talking about a theological argument that will only repel them. I'm talking about letting the light of Jesus shine forth. You need to let a missionary see that you have something he doesn't have. At least make him or her want what you have. It may be a joyful expression about the Lord or perhaps sharing an answer you received to prayer. It's these kinds of experiences they will remember."

"Debra," I asked, "do you know of any missionaries who ever left in the middle of their mission because they no longer believed Mormonism?"

"No," she replied thoughtfully. "I've never heard of any. I suppose I came pretty close. But, I only had a couple of months left, so I decided to stay and finish it out. But whether I had left then or later, what matters is here I am now, a born-again Christian for twelve years!"

Everyone applauded, pressing to ask more questions. But Debra, saying she had to go to another appointment, promised she'd come back. With a wave to me, she quickly gathered her materials and left.

With the bell due to ring, I decided to draw some feedback from the class.

"I'm sure we all enjoyed Debra's presentation," I said. "But, I'd like to hear what you got out of class today. Matt, why don't you go first."

"Well," Matt began, "today on campus I had a real live encounter with two Mormon missionaries. That was an experience and a half! And now, for the first time, I understand what a Mormon *testimony* is. More importantly, I also have a testimony! I learned what I can say, and that I can combat the Mormon's testimony by sharing mine."

"What else?" I prodded. "Robert?"

"I thought Debra's discussion about the Mormon priesthood was fascinating. I can see why missionaries feel they have an edge over Christians. But, at the same time, I see more clearly how they have absolutely no biblical grounds for their claims."

Tia raised her hand. "I think Debra did a good job of showing how little Mormons understand Jesus' sacrifice—otherwise, they wouldn't have reinstituted the Aaronic priesthood. I think it takes a lot of nerve for a church to assume its members can hold the Aaronic priesthood when even Jesus couldn't hold it. It's also pretty arrogant to assume the Melchizedek priesthood when it was reserved only for Jesus."

"I think," I said smiling, "that we had a pretty good class today." They all agreed.

The bell rang. "Tomorrow," I said, raising my voice over the rustle of papers and notebooks, "we'll continue the subject."

With that, the students scrambled out the door.

Outside, the weather was hot and the humid air suffocating. Filling the air was the loud buzz of the cicadas, a kind of summer locust that infested the trees. Students came pouring out of the other buildings and the campus came alive. Some sought out a cool place under the trees while others gathered around the soft drink machine. Others, in spite of the heat, headed for the small cement slab that served as both basketball and volleyball court.

Although I could hardly stand the San Antonio climate, I did enjoy the Mexican flavor of the city. There was mariachi music playing everywhere, not only at public events, but blasting loudly from the radio of nearly every car that drove by. Then, of course, there was the Alamo and the famous River Walk.

But, even with all that, I still missed my home state with its changing seasons, especially gold and red-orange leaves in the fall. But this is where I chose to be and, overall, I was happy. I enjoyed the students and their myriad personalities, all of which God would use in special ways. Then I thought about Susan, who had obviously skipped class.

Sitting down on a bench near the bungalow, I began looking for her. I finally spotted her seated with Tia on the small cement curb that lined the blacktopped driveway leading in from the street. It was private talk, that much I could tell. I also surmised by Susan's face that it was something about a boy. *What's new?* I thought. But, deciding to chance it, I walked over.

"Susan—missed you in class."

"Well," she explained, "there was this really great opportunity to witness. Under the circumstances, I felt missing class would be okay."

"Oh? Tell me about it," I asked.

"After the missionaries left, I saw them go down to the 7-Eleven, so I dashed down there too. We got to talking and do you know, I think they're really open to hearing about Jesus! Wouldn't that be something—if I won two Mormon missionaries to the Lord!"

"Oh, Susan," I exclaimed, "I wish you could have been in class today. Mormon missionaries don't convert while on their mission. I'm not saying you couldn't say something they might remember, but it will take more than a few comments from one person to bring them out. But since I doubt they'll come back on campus, you won't be seeing them again."

"But, I will," Susan exclaimed. "I told them I'd like to discuss the Bible and they made arrangements for me to meet them at their friend's house."

My heart sank. Susan didn't know what she was getting into.

"Susan, take my word for it. They are only interested in one thing and that's converting *you* to Mormonism. While they'll respond encouragingly to anything you have to say about the Bible, they will privately feel you are on a kindergarten level, compared to their more advanced gospel.

"In addition, they'll use logic that will soon have you agreeing with what they say. They'll not only quote Scripture out of context but also use other methods. Plus, their 'friend' is really a Mormon family called 'friendshippers' who will work on you after the missionaries move on. You're not ready to take all this on, Susan!"

Susan smiled. "I'll certainly consider what you're saying," she said.

As I walked away, I knew she had no intention of giving it up. Also, I felt her so-called dedication had more to do with being smitten with Elder Black than with witnessing.

I began to wonder about the others in my class. While I felt Susan was the only one romantically swayed, I knew they, too, could be influenced for other reasons. I also knew that, if this were so, they certainly wouldn't admit it. Could that be why they were so captivated by the subject? I suddenly felt their salvation weighing heavily upon my shoulders.

What on earth could I present in class tomorrow that might help?

What the Mormon Missionaries Have That We Don't Have

*A look at Mormon media campaigns
and their "sacred canopy"*

Robert suddenly blurted out, "How can that many people be converted to Mormonism? I mean, ninety million by the year 2030![1] Even if they had more than their present 48,000 missionaries in the field, that seems impossible."[2] With brow furrowed, he furiously began scribbling on a piece of paper.

Smiling, I settled back into the chair at my desk and waited for Robert to work his figures. After yesterday's encounter with the Mormon missionaries, the class seemed even more eager to learn. I was especially glad to see Susan in attendance.

"Taking into consideration," Robert mumbled, "their present membership of nine million[3]. . . wow! That's about three million converts a year!"

Suddenly, he looked up. "I hate to ask this, but what have the Mormon missionaries got that we haven't got?"

I knew exactly what they had. They had a multimillion dollar corporate church behind them with an elaborate plan. One that in 1993 alone brought in nearly three hundred thousand converts.[4] Robert had unknowingly introduced today's subject.

"See if you can figure it out," I challenged. But, the class only stared at me with a blank look.

"Here's the first part of the answer," I finally offered.

"The Mormon missionaries have a high-tech public relations machine behind them, the gears of which are moving into action long before they arrive on the scene. This machine functions at three levels: marketing strategy, missionary lessons, and use of friendshipping families. Today, we'll take level one.

"The Mormon marketing strategy," I explained, "is more extensive and expensive than you can imagine. It involves a worldwide public relations enterprise involving electronic broadcasting, space-age technology, print media, telecommunications, motion pictures, and radio—all very costly.

"Seventy-five million dollars was earmarked by Bonneville International, the Mormon Church's powerful communications branch, for satellite dishes in Canada and Mexico. The same goal was set for South America, Europe, Asia, and the Philippines. One source says the Mormon Church's satellite is the largest video network in the world, having the ability to merge into any cable system in North America."[5]

"Man!" Robert interrupted, "I never guessed they were involved in that big a project. All I've been aware of is their advertisements in the *Reader's Digest* and *TV Guide*."

"Vhat kind of response," interjected Ilya, "do dey get from magazine advertisements?"

"As a result of ads," I replied, "tens, if not hundreds, of millions of copies of the Book of Mormon have been issued.[6] Their media campaign is big business. Some say that the Mormon Church expects to spend 'over 100 million dollars in annual advertising in the 1990s to see that their message gets into every home in the United States.'[7]

"But," I added, "the LDS Church can well afford it. Its corporate side consists of a 'mammoth conglomerate . . . diversified into insurance, broadcasting, real estate, agriculture, and many other business avenues.'[8] According to author Anson Shupe, the church's wealth totals more than $16 billion.[9] Daily income from tithing is estimated at $11.5 million."[10]

"Wow!" the class exclaimed.

"Where does the church get all its money," asked one student. "Members' tithing?"

"No," I replied, "from investment portfolios and various businesses it controls. The church takes in about $8 billion per year.

Their income places them about 110th on the Fortune 500 list of industrial corporations, ranking them 'among companies such as Gillette and Chiquita Brands International.'[11] The Mormon Church is one of the most financially prosperous cults in the world. This explains why its missionary program is so pervasive and successful."

"How much of their $8 billion," Susan asked, "does the Mormon Church actually spend on its missionary program?"

"Worldwide," I replied, "it spends approximately $550 million a year."[12]

As the class soaked that in, Robert, who had been busily scribbling figures again exclaimed, "That's about $10 million per week!"

"Man, that's pretty heavy duty," Matt interjected.

"How many of you," I asked, "have heard their radio commercials on the family?" Less than half of the class raised their hands.

"Well, they're impressive," I admitted, "and I'm almost hesitant to tell you this, but I played a part in those radio spots." The class came to full attention.

"When I was a Mormon," I began, "I wrote articles on the family for their official magazine. Later, I found out they were using excerpts from those articles in their radio commercials.[13]

"Water under the bridge," I sighed. "But the deceptive part is that these wholesome messages draw attention away from their unorthodox doctrines.

"Since many of you haven't heard the radio ads, how many of you have at least seen their television spots?" Nearly every hand raised.

"These messages," I began, "are called Home Front. Purposely down-playing religion, they promote outstanding family values and ethics. But," I emphasized, "they're certainly not principles that are exclusive to Mormons. Christians also have these same values. We, too, believe in the integrity of the home and the sanctity of life. The LDS Church has simply taken advantage of the old slogan: *It pays to advertise.*

"Another strategy they use to reach people is their seasonal TV shows: *Mr. Kreuger's Christmas,* a moving story with no Mormon emphasis; also *The Other Wise Man* and *The Last Leaf,* both non-Mormon classics. They also have more direct commercials promoting the Book of Mormon.

"In addition, they receive $60 million in free advertising to use for their public service messages called Times and Seasons.[14] These programs are impressive; in fact, one was selected by the

National Catholic Association of Broadcasters and Communicators as winner of the 1994 Gabriel Award for Public Service."[15]

"I wonder," Susan mused, "how many people really see those TV spots?"

Flipping quickly through my notes, I read, "It's estimated that the total audience reached through radio and television is '2.3 million adults per day [or] 357.4 million people in a single year.'"[16]

Tia raised her hand. "When they exhaust the United States, do you think they'll start in other countries?"

"They already have," I responded. "However, commercials abroad may not be on the family.

"In the Third World, for example, the focus may be on health and hygiene, maybe law and order, or perhaps obedience to authority—whatever is applicable to that country's situation.

"And," I asked the class, "why do you think they put so much emphasis on producing commercials?"

Robert's hand quickly shot up. "To create a public image, which will pave the way for the missionaries!"

"Right. However, the way doesn't open up overnight. In foreign countries the Mormon Church must move slowly.

"As an example, they had to invest ten years of broadcasting in the Dominican Republic before they were able to organize a mission. But it worked. They attributed the first one thousand baptisms to their advance publicity.[17]

"In South America, however, they used a different strategy. They provided free broadcasts of Brigham Young University's basketball games to Chile, Peru, and Uruguay. Five years later they were able to set up missions in Chile.[18] Then, when the Mormon elders began tracting, that is, going door to door proselytizing, they were instructed to look only for houses that had TV antennas.[19] Introducing themselves as BYU students they inquired if anyone in the household had seen the games.[20] It was an automatic door opener.

"'The number of converts in South America, Africa, and the Philippines,'" I began reading from a *Salt Lake Tribune* clipping, "'continues to spiral—quadrupling in South America, up from 12,000 to 70,000 in Africa, and soaring from 43,000 to 293,000 in the Philippines over a 12-year period ending in 1992.'"[21]

Robert's hand went up again. "How do they get into countries that are against missionizing?"

"I know answer!" interjected Ilya in her broken English. "Dey send Mormon Tabernacle Choir and international dance group from BYU!"

"Did you see them when you were living in Russia?" I inquired.

"Da. Der vas ninety-minute TV special in Bucharest, also Moscow. The news said dey perform before very large audiences in Romania, Czechoslovakia, Hungary, and Poland."

"Yes," I agreed, "it was a well set up program. I read that their television documentary spanned eleven time zones, reaching 150 million viewers.[22]

"And, of course," I continued, "we know why they were sent. They served, as one BYU history professor admitted, a 'John the Baptist function' to prepare nations for the Mormon gospel.[23] It was through this method that they penetrated both the Iron and Bamboo Curtains.[24] They've also been successful in the People's Republic of China. And Cambodia recently opened their doors to them.

"Once in," I said, "and after the Mormon Church feels there is sufficient goodwill achieved, leaders who accompany these tour groups pretending to be counselors or chaperons, soon contact government officials.[25] They promise them that if Mormons are allowed to live there, 'future members [will] stay out of opposition politics . . . .'[26]

"Of course," I added, "when they move in, they pretend they are there for other than proselytizing reasons. Operating underground first, they later move into the open. In some countries, the secret police discover their operations and they're deported.[27]

"But in spite of these setbacks, the Mormon Church continues to grow at the rate of '1,500 new members per day.'[28] That's about 45,000 converts a month, 540,000 a year."

"Did they grow that fast," asked Tia, "in Joseph Smith's day?"

"Well," I replied, "not quite as fast but, nevertheless, impressive. They started in 1830 with six people and in no time at all the church gained 35,000 members. This was mainly because the men were willing to leave their families and spend years proselytizing overseas. Later, the church financed foreign converts to come to Utah. Within the next forty years the Mormon population increased by 85,000.[29]

"In our day, however, the Mormon Church brings in more—and faster. Converts have increased in the United States by 7 percent. Missionary activity, itself, has grown by 16 percent through the use of modern media and public relations campaigns."[30]

Allowing the class to catch up on their note-taking, I began pulling more material from my briefcase.

"And now, class, besides the media campaign, the Mormon missionaries have something else going for them."

"Good grief," Tia exclaimed, "what more could they possibly have? It seems like the only thing left is for Jesus Christ Himself to come down and give divine approval!"

"Well, Tia," I laughed, "You're close—closer than you think. Remember the cloud that rested upon the tabernacle as evidence of God's presence? Well, of course, there's no such sacred cloud hanging over the Mormon Church, but they do have a sacred canopy."

While the class looked blank, I added, "Put in more academic terms, they have a *cosmitized* church, and . . ."

"Well, of course," Matt jokingly blurted out, covering up the fact that he had no idea what the word meant. "We all know it's *cosmitized,* we just wanted to see if you knew!" The class laughingly joined in.

Robert's hand began waving wildly. "I know what you're talking about," he said.

"That's no fair, Robert," I said. "You already know your dad is coming to talk on the subject."

"Yeah," he said grinning.

"Robert's father, Pastor Donaldson," I told the class, "is due here in a few minutes. He's going to tell you how the Mormon Church has cosmitized itself and set up this sacred canopy. So, let's take a short break until he arrives."

While the class milled about, I stepped out the door into the summer heat. Glancing toward the administration building for a sign of Pastor Donaldson, I sat down on the bench to wait.

I knew the subject would interest the class. Especially, I chuckled, since I was sure they were all puzzling over how a giant canopy could be hovering over Salt Lake City. I only hoped Pastor Donaldson wouldn't make it too academic.

Then I saw him. Walking down the steps of the ad building was a man of about fifty, tall with slightly humped shoulders and somewhat on the thin side, wearing thick glasses. The students greatly respected him and so did I. Besides nicknaming him "Pastor D," they also enjoyed kidding him over one thing—how he combed his hair—that is, what he had left. Trying to slick the few valuable hairs he had from one side of his head to the other, he always looked as if he were standing sideways in a wind storm. But, I thought affectionately, he sure knows his stuff.

"Hi," I said getting up as he approached. "We're all ready and looking forward to your presentation."

"Well," he said, "I'll do my best. While I don't know a whole lot about Mormonism, I believe we can glean something useful."

As we entered the classroom, the students quickly took their seats.

"Pastor Donaldson," I announced, "is going to explain to you about the sacred canopy. He'll give you the academics and, afterward, we'll see how they apply to the Mormon Church." I then took a seat near the front and nodded for him to go ahead.

"The *sacred canopy*," he began, "is a term Peter Berger introduced to describe the concept of cosmitization.

"But in order to get us to that point," he added, "we'll have to take a little trip around the mulberry bush, so to speak, and brush up on some academics."

The class groaned, but he smiled and continued.

"Unless you understand this term, you'll never understand the canopy. Nor will you understand why cults need to use it. So, now, to the academics.

"From the beginning," he began, "the ancient, uncivilized primitive tribes and pagan cultures, were aware that being born entailed living in a world that was confusing, fearful, chaotic, and often purposeless. They also discovered that if they chose to live outside an organized society, they were confronted with aloneness, meaninglessness, and chaos. In other words, they became 'worldless.'[31] It was, as Peter Berger says, the 'nightmare *par excellence*.'[32] Even thinking about it constituted a powerful threat to one's self.

"Therefore, people found safety in the collective. That is, by belonging to a society, tribe, or clan, with its institutions and established mores, they found safety and purpose.

"But, it wasn't enough to simply form an organized group. The ancients recognized that unless they took certain precautions, their society could disintegrate and they still might find themselves plunged into that world of meaninglessness. They needed to introduce something that would create a stable, secure, and permanent world.

"This is where cosmitization comes in. The word sounds complex, but it isn't. It's from the word *cosmos*, which we generally understand when we picture outer space and the stars.

"The cosmos represents a stable, orderly, harmonious, and systematic universe. In other words, an absolute world that is dependable—the stars shine and the sun always comes up. It is a taken-for-granted world that is always there.

"Therefore, cultures turned to this one observable phenomenon that was predictable—the cosmos. If they could establish a link to that cosmos, they believed its harmony, orderliness, and stability would become theirs also.

"The way to establish this link was to model the cosmos. They established a society and government complete with mores, taboos, and taken-for-granted meanings that, much like the cosmos, was believed to merge with the fundamental meaning of the universe itself.

"They acquired the science of astronomy and studied the heavens. They also established the art of astrology so the stars could guide them. By so doing, life became endowed with purpose and meaning. They were able to answer the mysterious why's of life, and provide a strong sense of assurance in the uncertainties of existence. In other words, they established a cosmic canopy. Their society was now validated by a world more powerful than they. In this way, they could avoid the nightmare of worldlessness."

"Pastor D?" Tia asked. "It sure sounds like everyone was . . . well, neurotic."

"Well, now, don't speak too quickly," Pastor Donaldson replied. "As modern human beings, we have the same basic fears and anxieties as the ancients.

"Do you remember how, as a child in bed, you were afraid of the dark?" The class laughed knowingly.

Then a voice from the back called out, "Yes, but it's just because the shadows on the wall looked like monsters!"

"So, how were your fears relieved?" he queried.

"Well," the student replied, "Mom or Dad would come in and explain that the shadows on the wall were from moonlight shining on the trees outside my window. Or the noise I heard was the rubbing of branches on the side of the house."

"Or," interjected Matt, "the dark figure looming in my bedroom was only a toy sitting on top of my dresser."

"Right! It took an all-knowing person to continually reassure you of the reality of things. Once you understood the reality—that shadows weren't really monsters—you felt more secure.

"Now, while we may grow out of childhood fears, we continue to have uncertainties as adults. Life has its shadows and we still need to be reassured.

"One way the ancients established a stronger reality was by deciding that there had to be a god who created and controlled their cosmic world. Therefore, they came up with a sky god who became their mommy and daddy, so to speak. Their god put their fears to rest and kept reassuring them (as a result of placating the god with sacrifices), that all would be well. While ancient cultures often believed in many gods, there was, nevertheless, always a chief god who ruled over the others.

"It's at this point," Pastor Donaldson said, "that religion enters in and the *cosmic* canopy becomes a *sacred* canopy.

"By appeasing the god with sacrifices that they believed brought them into correct relationship with the sacred, their society acquired a kind of insurance—protection against becoming victims of the nightmare of chaos and meaninglessness.

"Gradually, this concept developed into the idea that the sky god didn't rule earth directly—but ruled through an earthly representative. Only through that individual could justice, truth, and order be established. This, of course, translated into a king or monarch who, thereafter, ruled under the sacred canopy by divine right.

"In many cultures, a ruler was acknowledged as 'son of god' or 'son of heaven.' Japanese emperors, you'll recall, were regarded as such. Egyptian pharaohs also followed suit. A good example is found in a letter written to the king of France by Khan, ruler of the Mogul race, who proclaimed himself 'Genghis Khan, son of God!' Genghis Khan's seal also bore the following inscription: 'One God in heaven, and the Khan on earth.'[33]

"To confirm a divine ruler's heavenly endowment, symbols were used—the throne, scepter, crown, headdress, and staff. These reflected the royal accoutrements of the sky god.

"Since royalty was linked to heaven, the true pattern of government and society, as practiced by the gods, was believed to be transferred to the people through the god's representative. Every institution and law was seen as an extension of the heavenly order, mirroring the world of the gods.

"But, there is more that a sacred canopy produces—sacred literature. We see this in King Hammurabi's famous code, supposedly inspired by Shamash, the god of justice. The Moslems also had their Koran; the Hindus, their Vedas and their Bhagavad Gita; the Confucians, their Yi-King. And, I might add, the Mormons have their Pearl of Great Price, Doctrine and Covenants, and Book of Mormon.

"Since continuous contact with heaven is crucial for any cosmitized society, the next step is to build a temple, palace, or pyramid. The location of this edifice is referred to as the navel, or center of the earth. It is the designated spot where divine power flows down from the god into the society.

"It is at these shrines that sacred rituals serve to remind them of the will of the gods. And, since the rituals are supposed to be revealed from heaven, it also confirms their sacred canopy, and establishes order and control. We see this same purpose fulfilled in Mormon Temples.

"Thus, with the god of the cosmos giving divine approval, a royal representative on earth, a society and government reflecting the heavenly pattern, sacred literature, and holy temples with revealed rituals, society is relieved of life's instinctual fears, acquires stability, and finds purpose and meaning. As a by-product of all this, they come to believe that they are God's favored people.

"This," Pastor Donaldson stated, "is the principle of cosmitization. Or, in other words, religious validation that spreads a sacred canopy over a society.

"Now, cults follow this very same pattern. More especially because they are competing against Christianity's genuine canopy, which consists of prophets and apostles, a God-anointed leader (Jesus), a true church, the Holy Spirit, and a royal priesthood. In addition, an inspired, God-breathed volume—the Bible.

"Cults must produce the same, plus more. They must, out of necessity, pour every effort into projecting a bigger and better cosmitized canopy.

"Mormons, therefore, also claim leaders anointed of God, a priesthood, insist that Jesus started their church, and declare they are God's chosen people. They also have temples like those of old with sacred ceremonies revealed from heaven. Thus, copying the Bible, their sacred canopy is reaffirmed to them.

"When cults follow this pattern, the by-product is always the same. Members believe that they comprise the only true church on the face of the earth, and are convinced they are God's elite.

"Now," he said, closing his notebook abruptly, "at this point, I think I'll quit." He took a seat near the front.

As I got up from my chair, and began thanking Pastor Donaldson, Matt raised his hand.

"Shouldn't Mormons, if they're following the ancient concept of cosmitization, claim a scepter or other royal objects? Pastor D inferred that all rulers acquire some kind of symbols to reflect their authority from God."

"They do," I replied. "Since the scepter is the symbol for authority, the Mormon Church's scepter is their priesthood."

"How about a crown and a throne?" Matt persisted.

"Oh, they have that," I said. "Although most outsiders, even many

Mormons, are unaware of it, five presidents of the Mormon Church were anointed and crowned king.[34] Some believe this practice is still being done privately—especially since they consider the president of their church a king.[35] But, I'll cover that another time.

"However, to answer your first question about royal objects, faithful Mormons are to receive thrones in eternity when they eventually become kings and queens over their heavenly offspring."

Pastor Donaldson spoke up. "And, don't forget one other element the Mormon Church uses to confirm their sacred canopy. Something comparable," he hinted, "to the Code of Hammurabi."

"Oh yes, of course," I said, smiling and waiting to see if the class would remember.

"The Book of Mormon!" three students suddenly blurted out at the same time.

"Yes," I replied. "Like other religious cultures, they too have inspired texts. Which are . . ." I prodded.

"The Book of Mormon," Robert called out.

"The Doctrine and Covenants," Tia said.

"And, The Pearl of Great Price," called out Matt.

"Yes—by direct revelation from their sky god," I said smiling. The class laughed.

"However, time is getting short," I said glancing at the wall clock. "I need to wrap this up.

"Therefore," I began, "in addition to the powerful influence of the Mormon media campaign, what else do the Mormon missionaries have going for them?

The class exclaimed in unison, "A church validated by a sacred canopy!"

"Right," I said, turning to the blackboard.

"And what must a cult do to establish a sacred canopy?" I asked, writing down their answers as they called them out.

1. claim contact with heaven or the cosmos
2. claim God has chosen a leader as His divinely chosen representative
3. give royal or divine status to the leader
4. insist their society mirrors the divine structure of heaven
5. claim to be God's chosen people
6. build temples to practice sacred ordinances
7. produce sacred literature
8. proclaim a bigger and better canopy than Christianity's

"Good," I said. "If a cult can do all that, then it will be convincing.

"Certainly the Mormon Church has done all this. It declares that God and Jesus appeared to Joseph Smith; that God established him as prophet; that the organization of the Church of Jesus Christ of Latter-day Saints is patterned after God's heavenly organization; that the three persons in their First Presidency correspond to the Father, Son, and Holy Ghost; that their Council, or Quorum of the Twelve Apostles, also has a counterpart to the council in heaven; that they are God's chosen people; that their temples claim to be modeled after Solomon's temple; and, lastly, they have sacred literature revealed by an angel.

"Living beneath that kind of canopy, albeit false, produces a strong sense of security and dedication. Whether the beliefs are true or not, is irrelevant. They are real as long as members believe they are.

"However," I said, "if they start doing their homework and begin questioning, they soon lose that world with its special canopy. They are then thrown into the nightmare of worldlessness. This is why ex-cultists converting to Christianity have such a difficult time. They need to find a structured religion that will offer the same number of assurances the cult offered. Often, they are disappointed in Christianity's simple canopy."

Pastor Donaldson interrupted. "Do you mind if I make one more comment before we conclude?" he asked.

"Be my guest," I said.

Standing and facing the class, he said, "There are three ways for a cult to validate its religion and claim a sacred canopy.

"First, explain its world in terms that deny its human production. Joseph Smith did this by declaring that God appeared to him and literally started it.

"Second, it must claim to teach timeless truths that date back to the beginning of time. Since the Mormon Church claims to have the writings of Moses and Abraham and doctrines that date beyond Adam to worlds aeons before this one, this exemplifies legitimization at its best.

"Third, convince members that only its unique society has divine approval. The Mormon's Doctrine and Covenants, containing modern-day revelations from Jesus Christ, is proof enough for its members.

"These three components are used to convince members and convert outsiders."

"Thank you Pastor D," I said.

"Class, we've covered some pretty heavy subjects. But, let me wrap it all up by giving a summary answer to Robert's first question: What have the Mormon missionaries got that we haven't got?

"The Mormon missionaries," I began, "have two things going for them as far as methods on how to appeal to an unsuspecting public.

"The first, is the Mormon Church's high-tech media campaign, which includes an intelligent marketing strategy, sophisticated advertising techniques, electronic broadcasting, satellite dishes, and print media—all of which paves the way for their missionaries and provides contacts for them.

"Their campaign also includes commercials on their church-owned television and radio stations that reach 2.3 million adults a day, 357.4 million people a year. All of this is financed by wealth derived from extensive corporate holdings and investments.

"That wealth, according to author Ron Rhodes, will finance in the nineties, $550 million dollars worth of worldwide advertising a year.[36] That advertising will deceptively downplay their religion, leading many non-Christians to believe that the Mormon Church is simply another Christian denomination.

"The next thing the Mormon missionaries have going for them, is their sacred canopy. The Mormon Church provides an exceptionally impressive canopy and missionaries derive their confidence and personal testimonies from that. As with all cults, they try to make it bigger and better than Christianity's.

"But," I added, "the Mormon canopy is false! Remember, no matter how genuine the Mormon Church claims its sacred canopy is; no matter how high their ethics and standards are; no matter how sincere their missionaries' testimonies; God's Word says, 'if we or an angel from heaven should preach a gospel other than the one we preached to you, let him be eternally condemned.'[37]

"It was Jesus who received a visitation from God, declaring, 'This is my beloved son—hear him'—not Joseph Smith! Only Jesus, as High Priest, was given the Melchizedek priesthood—not Joseph Smith! It is the Bible that is God-breathed—not the Book of Mormon! Only Sanctuaries made without hands are where God dwells—not Mormon Temples!

"God's Word declares that He has already established His sacred canopy. It began when He chose both the Lamb and the Church before the foundation of the world. It continued when He made His covenant with Noah, then with Abraham, Israel, and David. It was renewed when He anointed Jesus. It continued with the church, which the gates of hell never prevailed against.[38] All this provides the complete and only necessary canopy for Christianity today.

"We may not have God's Word on gold plates, but we have historically verified manuscripts available in museums for all to see—not conveniently taken back to heaven by an angel.

"How strongly," I asked, looking intently into each student's face, "do you believe that God's authoritative sacred canopy is over Christianity? Do you believe in it as powerfully as the Mormons do theirs?

"Maurice C. Burrell in *The Challenge of the Cults* says that the zeal of cultists 'challenge us to ask questions about the earnestness of our own Christian witness.'[39]

"Let me present something sobering for you to consider.

"In 1959, Mormon president David O. McKay put out this admonition: 'Every member a missionary!' Within the next ten years, the Mormon Church increased from 33,330 converts to 70,010! In 1974, President Spencer W. Kimball issued a similar challenge, "Lengthen our stride," and converts increased from 69,018 to 192,983.[40]

"Now, if a pastor told his congregation they needed to witness more, do you think the response would be the same?" Everyone slowly shook their heads in the negative.

"What do you think propels Mormon dedication?" I asked. Once again the class looked perplexed.

"The answer," I offered, "is that they so firmly believe in their sacred canopy. They have been so efficiently programmed in this respect that they have no doubt that their church is God's and that their president is His mouthpiece. They *know* God speaks through him. And, who wouldn't obey if one really thought God was speaking through a living prophet?

"In addition, there is a corporate strength derived from everyone acknowledging the same sacred canopy. This produces a sense of solidarity that translates into an intense dedication.

"So, I'm asking you to question the strength of your witness. I'm asking you to analyze how authentically you believe Christianity's sacred canopy. Ask yourself: How does my conviction measure up to the cults?"

As I studied their sober faces, I said, "As students at a Bible college, I know you're here because you want to make a difference in God's kingdom—you want to win the world for Christ. But, it's up to you how dedicated you intend to make yourself.

"Presently there are, worldwide, 9 million Mormons competing against 1.87 billion Christians, although many of those Christians are lukewarm.[41] Nevertheless, numbers don't determine outcome. A strong minority can overcome a majority. Moses said, 'two can put ten thousand to flight.'[42] In other words, *one* person can really make a difference if one is determined! When you evangelize one person, or warn someone about a cult, the repercussions can have far-reaching effects. You may affect *generations.*"

"Therefore, all of you have a serious responsibility. First, know what you believe and why. Second, analyze your commitment level, then do something about it. Third, become more informed about cults. Fourth, warn others before they succumb to the message of the Mormon media. And, fifth, prepare *yourself* against the cults. Maurice Burrell cautions that even 'a well-grounded and spiritually mature Christian . . . need[s] to be on . . . guard.'"[43]

The bell rang as I finished. After again thanking Pastor Donaldson, I dismissed the class. Watching everyone stream out, I particularly studied Susan who had a troubled look. In a way, I was glad. It showed she was at least thinking about the seriousness of her contact with the missionaries.

Then my thoughts turned to tomorrow's class. With so many facets to Mormonism, I struggled over which to cover. I also tried to consider Susan. Her meeting with the missionaries was getting close. Therefore, I needed something that would open her eyes to the fallacies of Mormonism—but, I also needed something for the rest of the class.

Gathering my papers, I slowly headed out of the classroom and walked across campus. Suddenly, I thought of it!

There was one aspect of Mormonism that the class knew nothing about—in fact, neither did most Mormons.

Yes, I decided, that's what I'll present. The *real* reason behind Mormon proselytizing. Boy, are they ever in for a shock!"

CHAPTER THREE

Why the Mormon Church Sends Out So Many Missionaries

Unmasking the underlying motive

It doesn't make sense!" Matt exclaimed at the beginning of class. "Why does the Mormon Church keep pushing for greater numbers when they already have nine million members?[1] Why aren't they satisfied?"

"Matt," I replied, "they're not satisfied and never will be because there is a behind-the-scenes motive—a motive that is generally unknown. It, and it alone, explains why they pump so many dollars into their public relations and electronics campaigns. But," I added, "it is one that you will probably find unbelievable."

All eyes suddenly looked up.

"Matt, you've triggered a subject that not only explains why the Mormon Church pushes for greater numbers, but why we, as Christians, should be concerned about their proselytizing activities . . . in fact, very concerned.

"The *real* purpose behind their proselytizing is based on a conviction promulgated in secret during early Mormon history. While some may say, 'Well, that's something they believed a long time ago,' I personally believe it is still active today but kept from the public eye."

"Tell us!" the class excitedly coaxed.

47

"Yeah, let's have it," said Matt beating his usual rhythm on the desk with his palms.

"Well," I smiled, "it concerns, first of all, a Mormon belief that has two facets.

"The first facet is what I call the *public* one, their church's general theology—especially its belief that Jesus started the Mormon Church and at His second coming will acknowledge the Mormon Church as the only true church—a belief not uncommon to other cults.

"The second facet, which most are unacquainted with, is what I call the *private* facet. Mormon leaders are more obsessed with this facet than anything else. It consists of an intense dynamic that has controlled every president of the church since Joseph Smith. I'm convinced it's the *real* motive for expending so many dollars on their missionary program.

"Here it is . . .

"The Mormon Church plans on gaining a political stronghold in our government. Early Mormon leaders described this goal as a one-world government ruled by their priesthood."[2]

The class suddenly became more alert.

"Now let me add that it's more than a government as we understand it. Rather, it's a government ruled by a *king*.

"But, first, I do need to say this before I get into the details. While one side of me holds a wait-and-see stance, there is another side of me that says, given time, they may succeed. After all, we know there are others in the political and banking arenas who already have the same goal. Therefore, considering the enormous wealth of the Mormon Church, they may secretly have their finger in part of the pie already.

"So, to define it in a nutshell, the *public* facet is the church, the visible structure of the Church of Jesus Christ of Latter-day Saints and its doctrine. The *private* facet is the political machinery, officially named the Kingdom of God, also called the Government of God.

"Now, to us the two titles, *church* and *kingdom*, sound synonymous—but not to those who understand early Mormon history. Joseph Smith set up his 'restored gospel' in two parts. The public front of the church with beliefs everyone is already familiar with, and the private belief, his political kingdom.

"Today, the average Mormon is aware of only the first facet, the visible church structure. As postmillennialists, they believe they have an obligation to prepare the way for Jesus' return by converting as many people as possible. They expect that when Christ comes to usher in the millennium and acknowledge the Mormon Church as the only true church, He will appoint Mormon men and women to be the spiritual leaders.

"The general membership is unaware of Joseph Smith's secret political ambitions. For them, the task of the millennium will be to continue proselytizing the Mormon gospel and offer the rest of the world a last chance to be saved. Again, beliefs no different from other cults.

"But, Joseph Smith certainly had something grander in mind than the promulgation of theology. So did succeeding Mormon presidents. While the general members interpret Daniel's stone (Daniel 2:31–45), which is to fill the whole earth, as the Mormon Church and its theology, Joseph Smith taught that Daniel's stone was a distinct political system, separate from the church.

"To distinguish these two separate organizations, Smith called the visible church and its doctrines the *Church* of God and the political organization the *Kingdom* of God.[3] It is the latter, aided by the church's corporate wealth, that Mormon leaders expect will one day take over as a one-world government.[4] Brigham Young said, 'We are called the State Legislature [of Utah], but when the time comes, we shall be called the Kingdom of God. . . . For the time will come when we will give laws to the nations of the earth.'[5]

"From the *Journal of Discourses*, we read, '[This] means no more or less than the complete overthrow of the nation, and not only of this nation, but the nations of Europe.'[6]

"To keep non-Mormons from becoming alarmed, according to Mormon author Klaus Hansen, church leaders do not publicize this and feel it necessary to 'flatly deny it.'[7]

"It's important to understand that the Mormon's political kingdom is not synonymous with the church—nor was it ever an organization *within* their church. It was a *separate* entity, although it grew *out* of the church and was directed by men holding the Mormon priesthood.

"Governed by a group of fifty men and officially organized March 11, 1844, it was called the Council of Fifty or the Grand Council.[8] It was to become 'the ultimate governing body for all mankind.'[9]

"Thinking to hurry their project along, the Council of Fifty tried to nominate Joseph Smith for President of the United States.[10] Their goal was, as Mormon writer Klaus J. Hansen states, to 'bring the United States Government under the rule of the priesthood.'"[11]

"That's confusing," Robert interrupted. "Since most of the members were priesthood holders, it still sounds like their political kingdom is the same as the church."

"I know," I replied. "But, here's a clarification given by Mormon professor Dr. Hyrum L. Andrus:

> [The church] with its priesthood authority, was the body out of which the political organ[ization] was to be developed, and, since the priesthood was thereafter to have power to name men to political office . . . the government of God could be said to grow out of the Church. But following the appointment of men to political office there was then to be a constitutional separation of powers between Zion [the church] and the political government. In this way the Church and the State were to be separate bodies; for example, in our present Federal government the judicial branch, in a sense, grows out of the executive branch, in that its officers have their origin as judges in the nomination of the President. But following such nominations and a vote of consent by the Senate, federal judges become separate and independent officers, subject only to the covenants and bylaws which govern their actions in office. So also with Zion and her political government: the latter was pictured as growing out of the former body, but thereafter there was to be a constitutional separation of powers between the two organizations.[12]

"The Council of Fifty," I continued, "patterned their constitution after the Constitution of the United States. The latter was seen as a divine stepping stone leading to the establishment of the Mormon political kingdom. However, the Council made one distinct modification. It would not be a government of the people or by the people. There would be no election of officers. Men would be appointed by Mormon revelation."[13]

"Are you saying," Matt interjected, "that the common people would have no say—no voting rights? How would they stand not having a voice in the matter? All power would reside in one small council! How could they tell if laws and appointments were prophecy, personal preference, or political maneuvering? It doesn't sound like a very good constitution if you ask me!"

"Good thinking, Matt. You've hit on the—"

"On the other hand," Matt continued, "maybe we're misreading Joseph Smith's intentions. This was over one hundred years ago and, after all, religions had weird ideas back then."

"Well," I added, "as the old saying goes, the proof is in the pudding. All one has to do is look at how the Council of Fifty implemented their political machinery when they migrated to the Great Salt Lake Valley and see which aspects of it are still practiced by the Mormon church today.

"When the Council of Fifty first established the territorial government called Deseret in the Salt Lake Valley, it was a way to realize, as Klaus J. Hansen says, 'as many of the ideals of the political kingdom of God as possible before affiliation with the United States.'[14]

"Upon arriving in the Great Basin, Hyrum Andrus, another Mormon writer says, the Council incorporated itself into the legislature and immediately became its political government.[15] The Council of Fifty dictated all nominating and appointing.

"Obviously," I continued, "there was no need for parties—"

"Man," interrupted Matt with a sober face and hint of mischievousness, "what a dull lot. No party—no balloons—no nothing?"

While the class snickered, I managed to stifle a grin and shake my head in mock exasperation.

"Be serious, Matt.

"Continuing," I said, "Hansen describes the way it was:

> The Council of Fifty, in creating the State of Deseret [Utah], paid lip service to the doctrine of the sovereignty of the people and the democratic practices of a constitutional convention and free elections. . . . Since the Council of Fifty controlled both the executive and legislative branches of government, the leaders of the political kingdom of God, through the probate courts, could influence the administration of the counties.[16]

"However," I added, "the people did have a *kind* of vote, but not as we visualize it. The names of those appointed were presented to the people for a *vote of consent*."

Susan's hand shot up. "Well, that sounds like the people at least got a chance to say yea or nay. Maybe it wasn't as bad as we think."

"Take another look, Susan, there's more. A vote of consent was not the same as a vote of choice or an election as we know it. When a Mormon raised his or her hand, it simply meant they were confirming God's choice and were faithfully supporting priesthood leaders.

"It's still practiced today in the church and is called the Law of Common Consent. But, again, involves no real choice. Also, like then, no one *dares* to oppose. Listen to how President John Taylor describes this so-called voting privilege. The first part of what he says is deceptive because it sounds like he's extolling the people's free agency. Taylor says:

> The proper mode of government is this—God first speaks, and then the people have their action. . . . They are free: they are independent under God. The government of God is not a species of priestcraft . . . where one man dictates and everybody obeys without having a voice in it. We have our voice and agency, and act with the most perfect freedom . . .

"Sounds impressive, doesn't it?" I interjected. "However, listen to what he adds:

> *Still* we believe there is a correct order—some wisdom and knowledge somewhere that is superior to ours: *that wisdom and knowledge proceeds from God through the medium of the Holy Priesthood* [emphasis mine].[17]

"This kind of rhetoric is typical of all cult leaders. Described in an article in *USA Today* as 'slick-operators' by two authors, each having a Ph.D. in psychology, cults 'emphasize the victim's freedom of choice, after tactfully constraining the alternatives.'[18]

"So, in one breath Taylor proclaimed the free agency of members but explained how it *really* is and what one *ought* to do. Since appointments were supposedly made by revelation, no member, if he or she wished to remain in good standing with the church, would dare vote to the contrary."

"Didn't anyone ever speak out against that?" Tia asked.

"Yes," I answered. "There were a rare few who bravely dissented, but they were threatened with excommunication. Stanley S. Ivins explains:

> Elections were held but they did not mean much. A single list of properly selected candidates would be submitted to the people, who would go through the motions of voting for them. There was no law against voting for someone else, but the balloting was not secret, so that anyone not voting right could be easily identified and branded an apostate. And since apostasy

[*sic*] was just about the greatest of sins, very few wanted to be charged with it.[19]

"However," I added, "to impress both members and outsiders, the church issued a political manifesto stating that 'the Church has never tried to interfere in the affairs of state.'[20] In a way, it was double-talk. By having a separate political organization, church leaders could say the church wasn't involved. But, since the political leaders also held offices in the church, the two were so closely entwined that even members had difficulty distinguishing the difference.

"One of the early apostles, Moses Thatcher, wouldn't sign the political manifesto because, as Abraham H. Cannon wrote, 'he saw it as a misleading statement of the past and present attitude of the church leaders in political matters.'[21] But, when he refused, they threatened him with excommunication . . . the worst thing that can happen to a Mormon.

"Later," I continued, "when Utah was forced to accept a two-party system, the Council still had the last word. They decided who were to be Republicans and who were to be Democrats. Bishops even went so far as to dictate that those sitting on one side of the congregation were to be Democrats and those on the other side, Republicans.[22] Since the Republican party was the political kingdom's favorite, it was understood, as Stanley S. Ivins said, that those 'who were republicans, would [be allowed to] campaign for their party, [but] those who were democrats would remain silent.'[23]

Ilya shook her head. "Dis sounds too political for a church. I haf idea dat Mormons fled to Utah for religious freedom."

"They did," I said, "but there's more to it than that. Most people believe the trek was unplanned, and that Mormons were suddenly forced to leave because of overwhelming persecution. They fail to realize that the Council of Fifty, long before the migration took place, were already talking about a journey westward. The leaders wanted to move to a territory where they could set up a political nation all to themselves. They first discussed Texas, but it was the Salt Lake Valley that eventually materialized.

"Therefore, contrary to historians, the exodus west was a *political* movement, not a *religious* movement, although the general members were led to believe it was the latter.[24] Dr. Andrus confirms this in his book *Joseph Smith and World Government*. He states that the historian Bancroft misunderstood when he wrote that the Mormons in Utah were under the control of the church's clergical leaders.[25] Actually, they were under the *political* control of the Council of Fifty.

"Andrus cites another historian who erroneously saw it as 'a pure theocracy' with a 'complete fusion of church and state.'[26] Other writers believed Utah government was 'merely a "spontaneous government" that grew out of the immediate needs of the settlers.'[27] In all cases, *wrong*. Outsiders just didn't realize what was going on politically.

"Neither does the general membership today. Many of them believe the Mormon exodus was a desperate, spur-of-the-moment decision by Brigham Young to flee for religious freedom. The truth is that it was the Council of Fifty, the political kingdom, that laid the plans and made all major decisions pertaining to the move. Their new government was to be a stepping stone to taking over the United States and eventually the world."

"But," Robert said, "maybe they don't follow that line of thinking anymore. I hear they now teach that a present-day prophet always supersedes whatever former ones taught. And, in addition, they no longer tell members how to vote."

"Well, that's right—to a degree. They no longer dictate to members who they should vote for in government elections.

"When I was a member, I recall when I heard that announcement. At the time, others and myself felt very disheartened. We *wanted* our prophet to tell us who to vote for. We believed he was a recipient of heavenly revelation and would naturally know which candidate God approved of.

"But, in spite of this change in policy, the Law of Common Consent, raising one's hand to confirm those appointed within the church, is still operative. If a Mormon dares vote contrary, he or she is called in for the dreaded *interview*. If the individual doesn't repent, excommunication is inevitable.

"The point is, if the Mormon Church gains any kind of political control in the future, this kind of government I have described will be operative.

"Since 'World government,'" Klaus Hansen confirms, 'was one of the Council's primary missions,' the modern-day church leaders are not going to do away with it. [28]

"Though unable to fully implement this kingdom at present, the Mormon Church awaits the day when they can. They believe it will happen when the world will be in such chaos that it will be more than ready for their theocratic government. They also believe that at that point, world governments will *beg* the Mormon Church to step in.[29]

"This may surprise you, but in preparation for this kingly government, Joseph Smith actually had himself crowned king. He believed that he 'held his political office by divine right and not by sovereignty.'[30] Claiming to be a descendant of Joseph through Ephraim, he felt he should 'rule over all Israel . . . and ultimately the Jews and Gentiles.'[31]

"The practice of being anointed king was carried down through four more church presidents: Brigham Young, John Taylor, Wilford Woodruff, and Lorenzo Snow.[32] I believe this coronation ceremony is still performed."

Suddenly, much to the class's enjoyment, Matt stood up, grabbed a nearby yardstick and with regal bow and swirl of his jacket, stately strode up the aisle with his newly acquired scepter.

"Matt," I sighed, leaning back against the desk, "if you're thinking about becoming a pastor some day, how do you think your congregation is going to respond to these kinds of antics?"

Nevertheless, everyone applauded with enthusiasm as he turned around and headed back to his chair. Slowly and regally, he sat down on his "throne." With majestic flourish and nod of head, he condescendingly said, "You may now continue. . . ."

"Thank you, your majesty!" I said. (I did have to admit that I rather enjoyed his clowning.) After the class settled down, I continued.

Reaching for a book from my desk, I said, "The early church leaders were very serious about their political kingdom.

"The reason I'm emphasizing this is because by seeing what their political philosophy is, we can be on guard. You might be swayed to vote a Mormon into office just because of his clean-cut standards. Listen to what President John Taylor says about their anticipated world rule:

> The priesthood will be the only legitimate ruling power under the whole heavens; for every other power and influence will be subject to it. When the millennium . . . is introduced all potentates, powers, and authorities—every man, woman, and child will be in subjection to the *Kingdom* of God; they will be under the power and dominion of the priesthood of God. . . .[emphasis mine].[33]

"And just how," quizzed Robert, "will non-Mormons be swayed to succumb to this government?"

"By observing the Mormon lifestyle of high standards," I replied. "The membership is continually admonished to set this kind of example to the rest of the world for this very reason. The average church member, however, only looks at it as a means to convert outsiders to their church.

"In addition, when world conditions become so bad that the people have had enough, the Mormon Church expects the U.S. government to ask them to step in and help. Leaders and members continually reiterate Joseph Smith's and Brigham Young's teaching, that one day the Constitution will hang by a thread and 'they will have to call upon the Mormon elders to save it from utter destruction.'[34]

"However, modern church leaders believe it can only happen when they have enough Mormons in key political positions. Through them, Dr. Andrus explains, 'God could then dictate, through revelation, the affairs of His [political] kingdom on earth.'[35]

"If the majority of non-Mormons did decide to join their kingdom, if only for protection and other civil advantages, leaders will also expect them to join the Mormon Church. Recognizing that some may refuse to embrace Mormon theology, Brigham Young describes what he expects church leaders will say to them:

> They [Mormon appointed leaders] will say [to the world's non-Mormons], "We offer you life [meaning Mormon membership and heavenly exaltation]; will you receive it?" "No," some will say. "Then you are at perfect liberty to choose *death*: the Lord does not, neither will we control you in the least in the exercise of your agency. We place the principles of life before you. Do as you please, and we will protect you in your rights, *though you will learn that the system you have chosen to follow brings you to dissolution—to being resolved to native element*" [emphasis mine].[36]

"Once again, cult double-talk assuring free agency, but at the same time telling them the awful consequences."

"What did he mean," queried Susan, "by *dissolution* and *native element*?"

"Brigham Young believed that those who come under the Mormon kingdom's political jurisdiction have Mormonism explained to them, but refuse to join the Mormon Church, will become sons of perdition and be cast into outer darkness.

"Their ultimate fate will *not* be to suffer in hell eternally, but to eventually have their identity annihilated.[37] Their body and spirit will be reduced back to the common element out of which they were created, meaning *intelligence*, the basic nondestructible, eternal material, out of which everything was created.[38] Young often used the example of the potter and the clay to show that when a vessel is no longer useful it is crushed and placed back into the common lump to be molded into something else."

"So," one of the students called from the back of the room, "if I decide the world's situation is desperate enough that I want to live under the protection of the Mormon's political kingdom, but don't want to join their church, I'd be destined for hell, squashed back into my basic essence, lose my identity, and perhaps be made into something else?"

"That's right."

"And," queried Matt, "when their political government or kingdom reigns, where are they going to set up their capital—Salt Lake City?"

"No," I answered. "There will be two political headquarters. Independence, Missouri will be the capital for the Western hemisphere, often called the New Jerusalem or Zion.[39] Orson Pratt explains, 'The law for the government of all nations will go forth from Zion [Missouri], the same as the laws for the government of the United States now go forth from Washington.'[40]

"Jerusalem on the other hand," I said, "will be the capital for the Eastern hemisphere.

"In addition," I added, "anyone living within the boundaries of this kingly government, whether Mormon or non-Mormon, must adhere to an economic policy called the United Order or Law of Consecration. Everyone will be expected to live communally and equally share everything they own.

"It was tried by early Mormons as well as non-Mormon groups throughout history, but all failed. Some of the underground fundamentalist movements today still practice it. While it is a noble endeavor, it is not without its problems. In fact, some of you know that I joined such a group. Leaders become competitive, greedy, power hungry, and end up exerting unrighteous dominion.

"However, there's nothing wrong with the concept. The New Testament saints tried it in the book of Acts. But, unless Jesus Christ Himself ushers the system in, it won't work."

"So," Ilya said, "are you saying dat Mormon Church today has Council of Fifty?"

"Yes, but I can't prove it.

"However, Jerald and Sandra Tanner in their book, *Mormonism—Shadow or Reality?* said they contacted a Mormon who claimed to have spoken with Apostle B. H. Roberts 'in which Roberts claimed that the Council of Fifty was established by revelation and would *always* be a part of the church' [emphasis mine].[41] In addition, Heinerman and Shupe state that the Council of Fifty 'operated openly within Mormonism with aspects of that goal in mind as late as 1945.'[42] They also say the ordination of kings is still practiced:

> Though the ceremony of coronation *continues to this day*, it is not publicized outside the Church. Conducted *privately* with only a few members of the Church hierarchy permitted to attend, it is nevertheless an explicit recognition that the kingdom of God is to be a political and spiritual reality [emphasis mine].[43]

"Today," I said, "there is evidence if you look for it. The leaders promote as many Mormons into government positions as they can. They believe the number of Mormons in political office will snowball until, one by one, they become a majority. Then, all the Council has to do is snap its fingers and they will do exactly as they are told.[44] In addition, as Heinerman and Shupe reveal, they also 'exercise [their] corporate strength as a powerful lobbying force in the nation's capital.'[45]

"Church leaders also have another element going for them. Besides hoping to have Mormon politicians in place, they anticipate that at some time in the future they will change their present policy of not dictating who members should vote for in public elections. When they do, they will expect their worldwide membership to rally behind whatever issues they decide need a majority vote. And leaders can communicate their wishes within a matter of hours."

"How can that be," asked Tia, "when their membership is so widespread?"

"They have a networking system," I said, "that communicates messages with amazing speed. One church leader boasted that by using each Ward's telephone tree '[he] can make sixteen calls, and by the end of the day 2,700 people will know something.'[46]

"But, as impressive as that is, the Mormon Church's Information Systems Division anticipates that via their satellite systems, 'the General Authorities expect the time to come when they will be able to notify as many as 3 million church members throughout the U.S., Canada, and Mexico *in less than an hour!*" [emphasis mine].[47] The Mormon Church will indeed be a force to reckon with, whether it be their projection of 12 to 14 million or 90 million by A.D. 2030.[48]

"When considering the ever-increasing number of converts, Mormon influence in political matters is not unrealistic. It will creep and crawl through the earth until the LDS Church gradually gains their secret objective.

"Non-Mormons in present power who are also trying to establish a one-world government may find the Mormon Church joining hands with them. I dare say that if non-Mormons succeed first, the Mormon Church, if it hasn't already, will probably become part of it because of their connections and wealth.

"Now admittedly," I said, "anyone would be hard pressed to prove that the modern church still has a Council of Fifty. Certainly, if Mormon leaders were asked outright, they would deny it. Hansen states:

> In a logical attempt not to arouse the already excited non-Mormon world further, Church leaders thought it wise to publicize their true aims regarding the political Kingdom of God as little as possible. At times, the leaders felt it necessary to flatly negate political aspirations.[49]

"Heinerman and Shupe state that Mormon leaders' success will be 'directly related to *general public ignorance* about their methods and ends' [emphasis mine].[50] They further state

> that while smaller groups as the Unification Church, the Hare Krishnas, and the Moral Majority continue to dominate the headlines, Mormons are making important strides behind the scenes toward fulfilling the promise of post-millennialism.[51]

"I agree. I believe that within secret councils, church leaders presently follow the same procedure as Joseph Smith and the succeeding four church presidents—that of ordaining every president of the church as head of the Council of Fifty and as king. Since their temple ritual continues to anoint men to eventually become kings, this practice is not out of context.[52]

"If the Mormon Church can convert enough people and gain enough political inroads, their hope is that the political kingdom will be realized *before* Jesus comes. And this is why, Robert, getting back to your question at the beginning of class, they push for greater numbers.

"Now, if there are no more questions, I need to wrap this all up. But, before I do, let's take a two-minute break."

While the students milled about the classroom, I motioned to Susan who reluctantly ambled over to my desk.

"Susan, are you still planning on seeing the missionaries?"

"Yes," she replied, her lips forming a taut line.

I could see her mind was already made up. I also knew if I came down too hard on her, she'd sneak away from campus and still go.

"Tell you what, Susan. Since we're studying about Mormon missionaries, it might be enlightening for the class if you were to report back and," I forced a laugh, "give us a blow-by-blow description of their presentation." Her face suddenly relaxed.

"Better yet," I quickly added, "since you're living on campus and I know you'd certainly be in trouble with the dean of women if she found out, why don't I come along?"

It was a bit of blackmail, but I prayed a quick prayer that she wouldn't resist. After all, I rationalized, I couldn't leave her at the mercy of two well-trained missionaries, one of which she found attractive.

"Yeah—well, okay," she said

"What night and what time?" I asked.

"Seven o'clock, tomorrow evening."

"I'll meet you in front of the Ad building," I said, trying to sound enthusiastic.

By the time we finished talking, her countenance had relaxed. *One step gained*, I thought.

As she returned to her seat I motioned to the class. "Two minutes are up!"

The room resounded with the scooting of chairs and the rustling of papers.

"I believe," I began, "we've pretty well covered Matt's first question: Why does the Mormon Church keep pushing for greater numbers when they already have over nine million members?

"So, let's summarize everything on the board we've covered so you can copy it into your notes:

The Mormon Church contains two facets:

The public facet—the visible Church of
Jesus Christ of Latter-day Saints
"The Church of God"

- Members believe that Daniel's prophecy of the stone cut out of the mountain is the Mormon Church and its theology.
- Members believe Jesus, at His second coming, will acknowledge the Mormon Church as the only true church.
- Missionaries and members are to convert as many as they can to provide a kingdom of subjects for Jesus to rule over.
- The millennium will be devoted to evangelism and temple work. Plural marriage will also be reinstituted, as well as the doctrine of blood atonement.

The private facet—the invisible Council of Fifty
"The Kingdom of God"

- Leaders believe Daniel's prophecy of the stone means their political kingdom.
- The Kingdom of God is a separate organization from the church. Led by a Council of Fifty, it will be ruled by their king, the President of the Mormon Church.
- At the second coming, Jesus will appoint the Kingdom of God to have political jurisdiction over all the earth.
- There will be a one world government, controlled by the Mormon Kingdom, with two capitals. The capital for the western hemisphere will be Jackson County, Missouri. Jerusalem will be the capital for the eastern hemisphere.
- Political leaders will be priesthood holders and rule by divine appointment—not by election.
- The Mormon government will not be a democracy. The Law of Common Consent will be in operation.
- Capital punishment will be enforced.
- An economic policy, called a United Order, will be practiced by those living within the boundaries of Zion.

Present methods for achieving the political kingdom
- Accumulate corporate wealth.
- Acquire worldwide membership as quickly as possible.

- Utilize missionary programs.
- Implement full scale public relations and mass media campaigns.
- Establish Mormons in key political positions.

"Mormon missionaries today," I said, "have no inkling about the political kingdom or the Council of Fifty. But, they are determined to do their part in helping convert the world.

"Next week, I hope to introduce you to their actual proselytizing strategies.

"Their missionary lessons are well planned, but deceptive. Without telling what they *really* believe, they present orthodox concepts of God and Jesus that sound 'Christian.' They smoothly slide investigators into gradual acceptance of Mormon beliefs through logic, personal feelings, and other methods.

"As a result of their strategies, converts are increasing at a rapid pace—totaling over nine million. By the year 2080, it is estimated they will bring in over 265 million members.[53]

"It is a grave matter and Christians need to wake up. We need to examine our own faith, know what we believe, and understand why the Mormon Church should not be allowed to come into power."

The look on the students' faces reflected a seriousness that was impressive. As the bell rang and they filed out of the classroom, I wondered if the information had impressed Susan at all. I glanced quickly in her direction. I knew that once away from the classroom and in Elder Black's presence, she'd probably revert to her emotions. Yes, I was glad I had invited myself along. But, I had another concern.

Besides Susan's attraction for Elder Black and her naiveté of their strategy, I knew she would become personally hooked by at least one Mormon teaching—most investigators are. Would it be the Word of Wisdom, or family values; perhaps eternal marriage or the welfare plan; perhaps the Book of Mormon or ethics and standards? Which would it be for her?

Quickly gathering up my notes, I stuffed them into my briefcase. *It'll be interesting*, I mused, *to see how the missionary lessons have changed from when I used to give them.*

As I hurried out the door, I pondered what it would be like—hearing again that which I had once loved with every fiber of my soul.

No problem for me now, I thought. Yet, as I walked across the campus toward my car, something deeper that I couldn't put my finger on, began troubling me. Why did I feel so uneasy?

By the time I drove across town and arrived home, I knew what it was. It was something I didn't want to admit, certainly not to any of my students, much less to my colleagues.

Despite my conviction that the Bible was right and Mormonism was wrong, I was plagued. Would listening to the missionaries remind me of the happy times I enjoyed with Mormon friends . . . the joy I had teaching in Ward organizations . . . the longing for Mormon absolutes, false though they were? Could I withstand hearing stories from the Book of Mormon—the book I once thought I couldn't live without?

And, what about the missionaries' testimonies—their innocent smiles—their expressions of love and logic? Could I succumb again? Was I setting myself up for something dangerous—more dangerous for myself than for Susan?

Well, I decided, I'd cross that bridge when I came to it. Right now, I had to concentrate on preparing material for tomorrow. Every bit of class time would be needed. It would be my only opportunity to relay to Susan the strategies that would be used on her tomorrow evening.

CHAPTER FOUR

Mormon Proselytizing

Exposing missionary strategies and schemes

I fumed as I hurried into the assembly hall. *Of all days for my class to be cut short*! At staff meeting, the president announced that classes before the lunch hour would be shortened. The full-time missionaries from Mexico were up for a visit and a luncheon fiesta was planned. Since the college had a strong evangelizing thrust, it was not only to acknowledge their labors, but to present the student body with an opportunity to talk with them one-on-one.

While I admitted it was nice to have them here—after all, one was an old classmate—I felt cheated over the lost classroom time. A more lengthy class could help Susan more—at least forewarn her as to the Mormon strategy that would be used on her. I knew that only by a close and careful scrutiny of what Mormon missionaries present could anyone be properly prepared.

Hopefully, I could at least cover the first missionary lesson on God and Jesus. But, for now, it was assembly time and I forced myself to settle back in my seat as the music began.

With a brilliant swirl of green and gold, Tia spun across the stage adorned in her native costume of Spain. With arms above her head, castanets clicking, she kept beat with her heels to the rhythmic music of the small student band. Tambourines, accordions, and horns played furiously while the student body clapped, whistled, and trilled their tongues in the high-pitched Mexican *grito*.

I marveled as I watched her gracefully bend and sway. *No doubt about it, she's good*, I thought. I wasn't even middle aged yet, and already I creaked and groaned. Glancing about the assembly, I spied Susan's beaming face. She was obviously proud of her roommate.

Tia's dance ended in a spectacular finale and was enthusiastically rewarded with a standing ovation. Everyone then quieted down to listen to the missionaries from Mexico who, besides preaching, delighted everyone by playing mariachi music on their accordions. It was an outstanding assembly.

At the conclusion, everyone exited through the large swinging doors. Quickly walking down the cement steps I was greeted with a marvelous sight. Crepe paper streamers fluttered high on wires while Mexican music played over loudspeakers. Groups of students were busily putting up decorations, hanging piñatas, and near the Ad building, four large tables were being pushed together by the cafeteria staff in anticipation of their south-of-the-border food.

I smiled with eagerness. *This will be fun*, I admitted. But, with all the excitement, I hoped my class could settle down long enough to pay attention—especially Susan.

The bell rang as I hurried toward the bungalow. Once inside I made a quick assessment. They were all there—so was Susan. The only exception was Tia, whom I knew was helping in the kitchen—no doubt supervising the tortillas.

"Class," I said, moving to the front and picking up a handful of small booklets, "I'd like to show you the books containing the lessons that Mormon missionaries use."

I held up the six discussion booklets, each measuring about 6" x 9" in size, with covers done in soft pastels.

"You'll note," I said, "that four of the six have pictures of Jesus on the front cover. One with Him coming in the clouds; the second, a head shot; another of Him blessing the children; and the last, being baptized by John the Baptist. The two others show a mother holding her baby and Joseph Smith kneeling to receive his famous 'first vision' in the 'sacred grove.'

"Mormon elders strictly follow the contents," I continued. "Some read from it directly, while those who have been out longer either have it memorized or have reached a point where they can discuss the material in their own words.

"But before we get into the actual lessons, I want to focus on the instructions given in the front of each book. I'd like each of you to take turns reading what missionaries are taught to do with contacts and analyze what's wrong. Who wants to go first?"

Dead silence. But, then, Matt slowly got up and strode to the
front of the class in his usual humorous manner.

"Okay, Matt," I said, smiling, as I handed him the manual, "read
what I've underlined."

Clearing his voice and flashing a silly grin at the class, which
never failed to invoke a giggle or two, he began:

> Missionary Instructions:
> Figure out ahead of time, what you can do to make the inves-
> tigator *feel* the Holy Spirit. Convince the investigator that when
> he or she *feels good* about what is being discussed, it is the
> Holy Ghost confirming the truth. Use the suggested scriptures
> to develop spiritual *feelings*, not to demonstrate a point. This
> will prepare investigators to more easily make commitments
> which will lead them to convert and be baptized [emphasis
> mine. See endnote for method used in quoting from mission-
> ary booklets].[1]

"You mean," Matt said, in mock shock, "that *all* one has to do
is feel good and that's supposed to be God telling you something's
right? Man—life should be that easy!"

As Matt walked back to his seat he quickly quipped, "Mari-
juana makes people feel good, too."

"Okay, class," I said, ignoring his last comment but proud of
him for the lifestyle he had given up, "what's wrong with this?"

"What's wrong is obvious!" answered Robert. "While the Holy
Spirit does give us special promptings and confirmations, we can't
stand on feelings alone. Jeremiah 17:9 says, 'The heart is deceit-
ful above all things, and beyond cure. Who can understand it?'
(NIV). Proverbs 28:26 also says that 'He that trusteth in his own
heart is a fool; but whoso waiteth wisely, he shall be delivered.'"

"Yes, I agree. In addition, the Mormon concept of feeling good
doesn't apply in all of life's situations.

"This idea caused me a lot of grief when I entered Christianity. Trained to believe that feeling good was always the sign
of God's confirmation and that the reverse, confusion, had to
be Satan, I was really bewildered. Trying to undo cult indoctrination and adjust to Christianity had turned me into an emotional mess. This was because I didn't anticipate the
psychological aftereffects I would have to deal with.[2] I kept
asking myself: *Is my upset and emotional struggle in a Christian church God telling me Christianity is wrong?* Surely, I kept

saying to myself, *if Christianity is right I wouldn't be feeling so distraught.*

"Mormon leaders," I said, "should come up with a more sure axiom for determining truth. Something as important as God's confirmation shouldn't be relegated to human feelings alone. The sure yardstick, of course, is God's Word—the Bible.

"On the other hand, if Mormon missionaries were to tell investigators that they should use the Bible to confirm truth, they'd be defeating their own purpose because the Bible won't validate Mormon beliefs."

"How," interrupted Ilya from the back of the room, "do Mormon missionaries get investigators to feel goot during der discussion?"

"Easy," I replied, flipping to the instruction manual. They are told this:

> To create a good *feeling* in investigators, share with them about your home town, schooling, family, and personal interests. Also inquire about these same areas in their life. The more you can establish a relationship through personal rapport and trust, the more this same *feeling* will be carried over and applied to the concepts you teach in the rest of the discussions.

"What Mormon leaders are actually saying to their missionaries is, 'the more they can establish rapport with investigators, the more good feelings there will be. These feelings will then be transferred to the Mormon concepts being taught.'

"At strategic points during their presentation, the elders are told to quiz the potential convert. They will ask, 'How do you *feel* about what we've discussed? Do you *feel good* about what you've heard so far?' If investigators say 'yes,' they are told that *that* feeling is the Holy Ghost confirming the truth. During the first part of lesson one, for example, since it consists of biblical statements about God and Jesus Christ that anyone would accept and feel good about, it's easy to say, 'Yes, we feel good about what you are saying.' When they discuss the Book of Mormon, since it doesn't contain any of their bizarre beliefs, but mostly biblical concepts, it's also easy to feel good about it.

"Therefore, the contagious atmosphere of 'feeling good,' maneuvered through a presentation of orthodox concepts enhanced by a rapport between personalities, makes good feelings continue throughout the remaining lessons. The missionaries are told that if they will do this then investigators will be made susceptible to keeping the kind of commitments that will be asked of them as lessons progress. This will lead to their conversion and saying 'yes' to baptism."

"What are these commitments?" Robert asked.

"The following," I responded, "are always presented as challenges at the end of certain lessons:

- to read and pray about the Book of Mormon
- pray about Joseph Smith
- attend church meetings
- continue with the missionary discussions
- be baptized
- live the law of chastity in speech, actions, and thought
- live the Word of Wisdom (abstain from alcohol, coffee, tea, tobacco)
- obey the law of the fast (give to the LDS poor once a month)
- pay tithing
- prepare oneself for the priesthood (if a man) and temple marriage.

"As each lesson concludes, the investigator is always asked how he *feels* about each obligation.

"Naturally, the requirements of keeping one's body and mind clean, are appealing. If investigators answer that they *feel* good about them, they are once again told that it is the Holy Ghost bearing witness to them about these commitments. No mandates, however, are given to investigators to study the Bible for validation of Mormon extrabiblical revelation or other beliefs.

"Therefore, strategy number one of the their proselytizing system is similar to the world's criteria—If it feels good, it must be right. They are to convince one that *feeling good* is the only confirmation needed to authenticate truth.

"And," directing my question to Susan, "what is the real danger of convincing one that 'feeling good' is the only confirmation needed to authenticate truth?"

"Well," she said slowly, a little upset at being asked, but trying hard to come up with an answer, "if one is convinced that *feeling good* is the ultimate yardstick—Scripture isn't important."

"Good, Susan!" But, I wondered, *is this only her intellect talking*? Nevertheless, I decided it was a step in the right direction. Hopefully, her feelings, which I was sure were revolving around Elder Black, would catch up with her intellect later.

"Now, class, let's get into the first part of the missionaries' presentation on God.

"Susan, will you read one of the first statements of dialogue they make to investigators?"

Susan took the book and began reading:

> Mr./Mrs. (calling the investigator by name), almost everyone believes in God, though it might be under various names. We're going to share how we feel about God. He is kind, loving, and all-powerful. And, because he loves us so much, he sent his son Jesus Christ so we could overcome sin and death.

"Do you see anything wrong with that?" I asked.

The class all shook their heads.

"They're not teaching *anything* wrong," Susan quickly said.

"That's right! They present general statements about God and Jesus that any non-Mormon can accept. But, do they really put God first or is it a ploy? Listen to what the *private* instructions to missionaries say:

> The major aim of this particular lesson is the Prophet Joseph Smith and the Book of Mormon. Don't spend unnecessary time on God and Jesus. This will allow you more time to discuss the restoration of the gospel through Joseph Smith. When the lesson is through, the investigator's strongest thoughts should be of Joseph Smith and the Book of Mormon. This is because we could not understand God and his plan of salvation without them.

"So, is God primary or secondary?" I asked.

"Nevertheless," Susan added somewhat defensively, "At least they say *something* about Jesus."

"Yes. But, let me share my daughter's experience, which proves that Jesus is not really the primary focus.

"At the time Debra went on a full-time mission, the lessons were in a different sequence. When she arrived in the mission field she found, to her dismay, that there was nothing about Jesus Christ in the first discussion. Having decided to go on a mission because she wanted to tell people about Christ, she was shocked and bewildered. Jesus wasn't mentioned until the *sixth* lesson. Eventually she wrote home:

I've discovered that, as a missionary, I'm not out here to convert people to Jesus Christ, but to the Church and President Kimball. And investigators aren't sticking with us long enough to get to the sixth lesson! All I know is that when I come home, I want nothing more to do with the Mormon Church.

"Since then, Mormon leaders wisely decided to place Jesus Christ in the first lesson to gain more converts. It was a clever strategy. So now, when missionaries go knocking on doors, one of their main approaches is: "Hello, we're representatives from the Church of Jesus Christ of Latter-day Saints. We'd like to share a message with you about Jesus Christ. Since then, conversions have increased tremendously."

"Now, while individual Mormons, including missionaries, love Jesus, the real focus of Mormonism is different. As their instruction book illustrates, talking about God and Jesus Christ is only a means to an end—conversion to Joseph Smith, the Book of Mormon and other nonbiblical beliefs.

"Well," Susan said, "they do believe that no one can get into heaven *without* Jesus, don't they? After all, their church is named after him."

"Yes," I replied. "A member must accept Christ to get into *any* of their three heavens. But, the *third* heaven—the highest, called the Celestial Kingdom where only God and Jesus Christ are supposed to dwell—is attainable *only* by accepting Joseph Smith. Jesus isn't enough. Brigham Young makes this clear:

> No man or woman in this dispensation will ever enter into the Celestial kingdom of God without the consent of Joseph Smith . . . every man and woman must have the certification of Joseph Smith, Junior, as a passport to their entrance into the mansion where God and Christ are.[3]

"Those qualifying for the second, or middle heaven, will only have the presence of Jesus, but not God the Father. Those in the first, or lowest heaven, will only have the Holy Spirit.

"So, strategy number two is a false prioritizing of Jesus Christ.

"What does Jesus say about those who publicly claim He is first, but privately teach He isn't enough to get into heaven?

> I tell you the truth, the man who does not enter the sheep pen by the gate, but climbs in by some other way, is a thief and a robber . . . I tell you the truth, I am the gate for the sheep . . . .

whoever enters through ME will be saved. (John 10:1, 7, 9 NIV)
[emphasis mine].

"While Mormon missionaries may honestly believe they are bringing people to Christ, they still don't believe He's enough.[4]

"What is misleading and deceptive to investigators, is that all the time Mormon missionaries are talking about God and Jesus, they make it sound as if the Mormon Church embraces the traditional Christian concept.

"They are told to hold back on revealing deeper doctrines. Many who join, believe they are actually joining another Christian church.

"Now, look at this," I said, picking up the pastel blue booklet and turning the cover toward the class. "What is the title?"

"The Plan of Our Heavenly Father!" they all read in unison.

"The ingenious part of this title," I began, "and their third strategy, is the incorporation of one significant word: *plan*.

"First, let's define *plan*. It is a *devised scheme or long-range purposed intention*. The missionaries' long-range goal is to convert investigators to Mormon doctrine. Therefore, they must convince investigators that Mormonism is part of God's *plan*. To do this they emphasize this word when talking about the Bible. They also incorporate it into their Mormon concepts. This strategy begins in the first lesson by showing, from the Bible, that God had a plan:

- He *planned* to create man in his own image;
- He devised a *plan* where his children could progress and be happy;
- He purposed to send Jesus Christ to sacrifice himself as part of that *plan*;
- He *planned* to establish the New Testament church;
- He *planned* a heavenly reward for the faithful.

"Throughout the lessons, the strategic repetition of the word *plan* is deliberately used. The psychological planting of this word creates a programmed mentality in investigators. They anticipate *more* from God as the lessons move through the various historical periods, from creation to Jesus Christ and from Jesus Christ to the present. This expectation makes them receptive to the idea of a modern-day prophet as a *part* of that same plan. Missionaries will reason with them: 'If God had a plan, would he suddenly abandon it in the middle of human history after Jesus' resurrection? No! God would be continuously unfolding more of His plan so He could provide *more* blessings for His children.'

"Therefore, strategy number three is convincing the investigator that Mormonism is a continuation of God's plan.

"Whew!" Matt exclaimed. "There's a real systematic scheme involved here. Every move has been well thought out. But, let me ask this. Since they begin their lessons by making general statements about God the Father that you say are half-truths, just what do Mormons believe about Him that's so radical—besides the fact that He's supposed to have a physical body?"

"First of all," I responded, "they believe in a plurality of evolving gods, each one having a beginning in time.[5] Can you tell me, Matt, what God reveals about Himself in the Bible?"

"Well," he began thoughtfully, "God says in Isaiah 44:6, 'I am the first and I am the last; apart from me there is no God.' (NIV) That's pretty plain. If He declares there are no other gods, then there *are* no other gods. First Timothy also describes Him as eternal, immortal, invisible, the only wise God. Yep," he mused, "If God Himself makes the statement that He is eternal, then He had no beginning—He *always* existed!"

"Right!" I said. "But, Mormon theology doesn't go by God's Word. It teaches that God is not eternal—He had a beginning![6]

"Now, Mormon missionaries won't tell an investigator this up front, but the real belief of the Mormon plan of salvation is that He is only one of many in an evolutionary chain of gods. A Mormon teaching was formed into a couplet by President Lorenzo Snow, which states: 'As man is, God once was; as God is, man may become.'"[7]

Susan raised her hand. "I still don't get what you mean by *evolutionary*," she said puzzled.

"Let me tell you a story," I said, leaning back on the edge of my desk. "First, I'll tell you what *early* Mormon theology taught, then how the modern church differs today.

"Once upon a time," I began, "on a faraway planet long before this one was created, a man named Joe was born. He grew up and during his life came to believe in the Jesus Christ of that world.[8] He then converted to Mormon doctrine, adhered to all its precepts, advanced in the priesthood, and eventually married Jane in a temple. He also entered the practice of plural marriage.

"When he and Jane both died, Joe and all of his wives qualified for the highest degree in the Celestial Kingdom and were rewarded with *eternal* life, which means 'a continuation of the seed.'⁹ Joe's name was then changed to Michael, and he and his hundreds of wives began to produce spiritual offspring.

"Two of Joe/Michael's children are Jehovah, his firstborn, who later becomes Jesus in mortality, and Lucifer, who later becomes Satan.

"At some point, Joe/Michael is advised that he has enough spirit children to begin peopling a world. He is, therefore, now a God. Soon, he, along with Jehovah (Jesus), go down and create a world—our planet.

"Upon completion of that enterprise, a counsel of gods place Joe/God in the Garden of Eden. They cause a deep sleep to come upon him. When he awakens he temporarily forgets his former world and is given the name of Adam.

"Now, early Mormonism explains that the reason Joe/God condescends to do this is because after begetting his children *spiritually* in the premortal world, he also wants to start them off *physically*.

"Jane also comes into the Garden and her name is changed to Eve. Adam and Eve, therefore, were not created from the dust of this earth but, as Brigham Young taught, were 'made as you and I are made, and no person was ever made upon any other principle,' meaning human procreation.¹⁰ The Bible, Mormonism teaches, is in error. Brigham Young says further:

> When our father Adam came into the Garden of Eden, he came into it with a celestial body, and brought Eve, one of his wives, with him. He helped to make and organize this world. He is Michael, the Archangel, the Ancient of Days! . . . He is our father and our God, and the only God with whom we have to do.¹¹

"Eventually, Adam and Eve are maneuvered into their *upward fall* as part of the *plan*, so that man might be born into the world. From then on, Adam and Eve and their posterity produce physical bodies for the spirits of the children they produced in heaven.

"The advantages of mortality for their posterity is so they can gain experience about life, its opposites and challenges, convert to Mormonism, be married in the temple, enter plural marriage, attain the Celestial Kingdom, become gods, bear spirit children, become Adams and Eves on future worlds, and repeat the process."

"Fascinating," Robert interrupted. "But, if Adam was God, which means he couldn't die, how do they explain away his death in Genesis 5:5?"

"According to Mormonism the Bible is, once again, in error. Adam didn't really die. He was allowed to partake of the Tree of Life, which purged out his mortality, then return to his throne to resume his role as God the eternal Father.[12] He later came back in the meridian of time to impregnate Mary and beget Jesus Christ, having already produced Jesus' spirit body in the pre-mortal world.[13] Brigham Young confirms this teaching:

> When the Virgin Mary conceived the child Jesus, the Father had begotten him in his own likeness. He was not begotten by the Holy Ghost. And who is the Father? He is the first of the human family [Adam]. . . . Jesus, our elder brother, was begotten in the flesh by the same character that was in the Garden of Eden, and who is our Father in Heaven.[14]

"There are additional Mormon references to back this up—in fact, the story involves way more than I'm telling here. Nevertheless, it illustrates how one man and his wife made it to godhood."

Susan spoke up. "What's the church's version today?"

"First, in all fairness, I need to say this. Spencer W. Kimball, twelfth president of the church declared this early theology of Brigham Young's to be *false* doctrine.[15] Yet, in the same breath, the Mormon Church insists on revering Young as a prophet, seer, and revelator.

"But, back to your question. The modern church's belief is pretty much the same, with one exception. They teach that Adam was indeed Michael, but do not teach that Michael was God. Michael, they say, was the archangel who helped to create the world and was chosen to be the Adam of the new world. They also believe him to be the Ancient of Days.[16] However, like their early theology, they do teach that God, whoever He is, was once a man who lived in a mortal world before this one and earned his godhood.

"This is what I mean by God being only one god in an evolutionary chain. It is, in a nutshell, the Mormon *plan* of salvation! Does that clarify things, Susan?"

"Yes," she smiled strangely. "But, while it does contradict the Bible, you have to admit it's sure fascinating."

While everyone laughed, I shuddered. I knew Mormon doctrine was fascinating—hadn't I once been hooked by it?

"What we need to remember," I continued, "is that nowhere in

God's Word does He ever say He evolved from a man. On the contrary, He reiterates over and over that He is *eternal*, will exist from everlasting to everlasting, is not subject to change, and there are no other gods besides Him. If you don't remember any other Scriptures, remember these:

> God is not a man, that he should lie, nor a son of man, that he should change his mind (Numbers 23:19 NIV).

> I am God, and not man—the Holy One among you (Hosea 11:9 NIV).

> I the LORD do not change (Malachi 3:6 NIV).

> Apart from me there is no God (Isaiah 44:6 NIV).

"In addition, Romans 1:22–25 describes exactly what Mormonism has done:

> Although they claimed to be wise, they became fools and exchanged the glory of the immortal God for images made to look like mortal man. . . . They exchanged the *truth* of God for a lie (NIV).

Robert raised his hand. "Since that's what Mormons really believe about God, isn't that lying when they don't tell investigators? I thought they had such high ethics."

"They don't consider this fourth strategy—not telling everything up front—as lying.

"Their reasoning is that milk must come before meat. Leaders know that their theology is complex and use the logic that one can't push calculus onto a first grader. They, therefore, instruct missionaries not to go beyond the basic beliefs of the average Christian. This strategy of not telling everything up front, however, is characteristic of cults.

"Knowing, however, that investigators expect to hear *something* from the Bible, Mormon missionaries are told to use Scripture, but only carefully selected verses—ones that are worded in a way that when isolated from the context can be used later to prove certain Mormon beliefs.

"For example, they quote Genesis 1:26–27, 'God created man in his own image.' This later works for them by implying that God must, therefore, be in man's image, physically. They also quote Matthew 5:48, 'Be ye therefore perfect, even as your Father which is in heaven is perfect,' suggesting that perfection is possible and that God expects us to become like Him—a god. Romans 8:16 is also used, 'We are the children of God.' This lays the groundwork for the belief that the spirits inhabiting our physical bodies are the *literal* offspring of God. But, nowhere in the Bible does it say we are the *biological* offspring of God, only *spiritual*.[17]

"The fifth strategy is clever. It is a technique that will gradually make the investigator believe Mormon scripture and accept Joseph Smith. The way this is achieved is through the *amount* of Bible Scriptures quoted compared to the amount of Mormon scriptures. For example, during the first discussion on God, the missionaries quote four Bible Scriptures but only *one* Mormon scripture. Investigators are impressed.

"However, as the lessons progress, a gradual change is made. When the missionaries cover the section on Jesus Christ, Bible Scriptures are gradually reduced to only *two*, and Mormon scriptures are increased to four. Each lesson subtly diminishes the use of Bible Scripture until, by the sixth and final discussion, Mormon scripture is *all* that is used.

"Therefore, the fifth strategy is to decrease the use of Bible Scripture as lessons progress.

"Now, before the bell rings," I said, glancing at my watch, "let me summarize the five missionary strategies on the board.

- Convince one that feeling good is the only confirmation needed to authenticate truth.
- Falsely prioritize Jesus Christ.
- Convince one that Mormonism is a continuation of God's plan.
- Do not tell all beliefs up front.
- Decrease the use of Bible Scripture as lessons progress and replace them with Mormon scripture.

"Just remember," I added, "beware of anyone who subtly begins to substitute extrabiblical scripture for God's Word. God says in Deuteronomy 4:2, 'Ye shall not add unto the word . . . neither shall ye diminish aught from it.' Proverbs 30:6 reiterates, 'Do not add to his words, or he will rebuke you and prove you a liar.' (NIV)

"Although," I said, "we didn't get into the missionaries' other presentations, the same strategies pretty much apply."

The bell rang not a moment too soon.

While everyone quickly put their papers and books away, I glanced at Susan who looked somewhat perplexed. I tried to catch her eye but she purposely hurried out of the classroom with the others.

Walking to the back of the room hoping to catch her, I stepped outside. My breath caught short as I marveled. The campus had suddenly turned into something quite exciting—a bigger change from what I observed after assembly.

Fiesta music was blaring over loud speakers. Many of the students were wearing brightly colored serapes and sombreros. Children were running around laughing and playing. Small booths were decorated with gourds, and hundreds of crepe paper streamers were snapping in the hot breeze. The lunch area was colorfully outlined with large wicker baskets filled with giant paper flowers and the cafeteria staff was hustling with trays of food. The air was exhilaratingly filled with frivolity and laughter and the scene before me unfolded into something quite tantalizing. I became happily lost.

Spying my old classmate at the edge of the basketball court, I made my way over. Nicknamed Bobbycito because of his short stature, he was dressed in full Mexican regalia. It was hard to imagine that this shy young boy from my college days was now a full-time missionary.

Noticing he was deep in conversation with Robert and Matt, I waited for an opening then walked up behind him, tapping him on the shoulder.

"Bobbycito," I said softly. He turned, grinned, and gave me an unexpected bear hug.

"It's been so long," I said, gasping for breath. "How are you?"

"Fine, just fine!" he replied enthusiastically.

"I see you've met two of my students."

"Yes. Matt and Robert have been telling me about your class. In turn, I've been explaining the difficulties we're having in Mexico due to the influx of Mormon missionaries."

"Problems?"

"Yes, since many of the Mexicans are part Indian, the missionaries are making a lot of headway by presenting the Book of Mormon as the ancient record of their forefathers. Indian legends tell of the white god Quetzalcoatl, therefore the missionaries tie him in with the Book of Mormon's account of the resurrected Jesus' appearance on this continent. Many are converting as a result.

"In addition, their welfare program is appealing because of the prevailing poverty. And it goes without saying that their family values are an incentive to join.

"I wouldn't mind," he quickly added, "sitting in on one or two of your classes."

"Fine!" I exclaimed. "In fact, I'll be covering the Book of Mormon the day after tomorrow. That is, after I give the class a blow-by-blow description of what takes place tonight." I then explained to Bobbycito the situation with Susan and the missionaries.

"Have you eaten yet, Bobbycito?" He shook his head.

"Well, c'mon!" I said. Pulling him into the crowd, we headed for the Fajita grill.

The fiesta proved enjoyable. The atmosphere was exciting, the food spicy, and Bobbycito fascinated me with stories of his encounters with Mormon missionaries. It was a good change of pace from class and worrying about Susan.

As the afternoon eventually came to a close, my thoughts, however, raced to the evening ahead. Searching out Susan I once again confirmed our meeting at 7:00.

"I'll be ready," she said. Then she added in a very self-assured tone, "Your lesson today was very helpful. In fact, I'm sure I can handle anything the missionaries present."

I knew her comment was intended to convince me that there was no need to come along. Well, I wasn't taking any chances— I was going! I'd soon find out how well-equipped she was.

Only three hours to go!

CHAPTER FIVE

The First Missionary Presentation

Examining the "heavenly Father's plan"

That must be it," Susan whispered in a hushed voice as we slowly cruised the residential street.

After peering through the windshield, I glanced down at the slip of paper in my hand. "Yep." I mumbled, "Fifty-six, thirty-one Orchard—that's got to be it." The knot in my stomach twisted tighter.

A large weeping willow nearly hid the small frame house with its lavender and white lilacs. While not an expensive home, the lawn was well kept in spite of the few toys strewn about . . . a red Tonka truck, a tricycle, a skateboard.

I must be crazy, I thought. *I should have tried harder to talk Susan out of this.*

"I see the Elders' bicycles around the side," Susan said trying to quell the excitement in her voice.

Pulling up to the curb I turned off the engine, still perplexed with how to handle things. *Should I let the missionaries ramble on with no confrontation or should I counter every point they make?*

I was more tempted to do the latter since I wanted Susan to pick up on every biblical error the elders would make. But, what if she didn't? Without being sure, I'd have to challenge every statement the missionaries made just so I could bring them to her attention. But, on the other hand, if I caused too much disruption, I could find myself uninvited to future meetings with Susan continuing alone. *I'll just have to wing it with the Lord's help.*

After a short word of prayer, we climbed out of the car and headed up the walk.

"Now, remember," I said, "this first lesson will be deceptive. They'll make a lot of general statements about God and Christ that will sound very Christian. They won't present their deeper doctrines because they consider us on a kindergarten level and not ready for college material.

"In addition, we're going to be in the home of 'friendshippers.' If they do what they're supposed to, they're going to overwhelm us with friendliness and use every possible way to establish a strong bond with us."

"Gotcha," Susan said in a tone that sounded like she was only humoring me.

As we neared the front door, a tantalizing fragrance greeted us.

"Wow! Smells great," Susan exclaimed.

"Yes," I said, "it's the old home-made-bread-fresh-out-of-the-oven trick. We can expect a loaf to take home with us."

Susan eagerly rang the bell, acting more like an Avon lady than someone walking into a lion's den.

The door opened and a rosy-cheeked woman in her late thirties greeted us. She was our friendshipper.

"Hi there!" she exclaimed. Then she called over her shoulder. "Elders, they're here!"

"Come on in," she motioned. "I'm so happy you both could come. My name is Ellen. You'll have to excuse my apron," she laughed, brushing flour dust off. "But, you're just in time for some hot bread and scones!"

The famous friendshipping method—'designed to enhance friendly relations,' I recalled, quoting to myself from my old missionary manual.

Ellen, like many Mormons challenged with the goal of converting one new member a year, would use a variety of methods. That these methods are effective is shown in a study of friendshippers conducted by Stark and Bainbridge. They reported that 'one out of every two' non-Mormon contacts that friendshippers make are successfully converted—a significant statistic outranking those of the full-time missionaries.[1]

Friendshippers focus on two types of potential converts. Their own neighbors and investigators brought in by missionaries.

With neighbors, they are instructed to avoid the subject of religion and concentrate only on establishing friendly ties. This is achieved by supplying homemade goodies, helping with yard work, baby-sitting, driving their children to school, including them on picnics, and inviting them to "Family Home Evenings."

With investigators brought in by missionaries, friendshippers offer the use of their homes for lessons. This gesture is more than just a convenient courtesy. A shrewd motive is in motion.

Concentrating only on promoting congenial ties, friendshippers establish a sociable connection that will continue long after the missionaries finish their lessons and move on. With both neighbors and investigators, friendshippers do whatever they can to establish a strong *nonreligious* bond.[2] If, after a long time of enticement it becomes obvious that there is no prospect of conversion, friendshipping stops.[3]

Therefore, I knew pretty much what to expect from Ellen, and she was throwing herself into the part with great gusto.

After calling to the missionaries again, Elder Black and Elder Barrett came out of the kitchen, each holding a thick piece of buttered bread. We shook hands and were then ushered into Ellen's aroma-filled kitchen.

On the counter were six loaves of hot bread with shiny golden crusts that had been glazed with melted butter. On a nearby plate, scones of all sizes were piled high, each fried to a delicate brown and glistening with sugar and cinnamon. My salivary glands were going crazy.

"Oh," I exclaimed, in spite of myself. "Does this ever take me back!"

As we sat down at the table, Ellen set a plate of sliced bread and some butter and honey in front of us along with the scones. At the same time, two small children burst through the back door.

"Mommy," a girl of about six shouted, "Aunt Helen is here. She's waiting in the car."

"This is my daughter Kimberly, and this is little Isaac," she said, pointing to a young boy of about three who followed close behind. "My sister, Helen, is taking them for the afternoon while the missionaries give their lesson. I'm sorry my husband couldn't be here, but he's out of town." She then pointed through the doorway into the frontroom where a boy of about sixteen sat reading a book. "That's my son Tim," she said. At the mention of his name, he looked up, waved a nonchalant greeting, and then became engrossed again in his book.

"He's pretty quiet," Ellen apologized. "He'll probably continue reading his book while the elders give their lesson.'

Turning to Susan, she said, "I also have a daughter about your age, Susan. Wendy would have been here, but she had another commitment. I'm anxious to have her meet you. I'm sure you both will hit it off great." Susan's face lit with interest.

My heart sank. After everything I had told Susan, she was still blind to what Ellen was scheming. All Wendy had to do was pull her into Ward activities and Susan would soon find the Mormon Church irresistible.

Reaching for a towel on the sink, Ellen wet one corner under the faucet and wiped each of the children's faces. "Off with you now," she said, handing each of them a scone. "Remember to mind Aunt Helen."

"We will," they chorused, scampering out the door.

Susan, after spreading honey on her bread and taking a bite, rolled her eyes. "This is heavenly, isn't it?" Directing her query to Elder Black, her eyes locked with his.

With mouth full, he grinned shyly and nodded.

Ellen immediately responded. "I'm glad you like it. I learned how at Relief Society. All the women are encouraged to gain homemaking skills. The 'prophet' wants us to be prepared to take care of our families in case a catastrophe should hit and grocery stores are without food. The Relief Society also taught me how to make substitute meat by extracting gluten from whole wheat. I even grind my own flour!" she said, proudly pointing to a silver, canister-like machine sitting at the end of her sink.

"Wow," Susan said, impressed.

I was impressed too. I began wondering how one did the gluten thing. Then, unexpectedly, a wave of nostalgia hit. I suddenly missed Relief Society with its camaraderie over quilting frames, informative lessons on literature, crafts, music . . . But, I quickly caught myself. *How easy to be sucked in.*

"Tell me about yourself," Ellen asked, directing her question to me.

Aha, I thought. *Step one: Build relationships of trust by becoming acquainted.*

"Well," I began slowly, "I teach at a Bible college—"

"Oh," Elder Barrett quickly interrupted, "we just love the Bible. I don't know what we'd do without the stories of Jesus."

"Yes," Elder Black added, his voice expressing surprising tenderness, "I really love the Lord."

While Elder Barrett's statement sounded "canned," my heart couldn't help but be touched by Elder Black's genuineness. He reminded me of myself when I was a Mormon. I wondered if he, like me, truly had a relationship with Jesus. Back then, I too loved Christ. How often I became impatient with Christians who erroneously insisted that as a Mormon I loved a different Jesus.

"Well," Ellen continued, "have you always lived in Texas?"

"No," I replied. "Actually, I was born and raised in a suburb of Los Angeles."

"What a coincidence!" she exclaimed. "I lived near there, in Long Beach—went to high school there."

"Really?" I exclaimed.

I began sharing with her how a friend and I would take off every day after school and ride the bus all the way to Long Beach just to spend the afternoon at the beach.

"If I have one passion in life," I laughed, "it's surf, salt air, sand, and sea gulls."

Susan suddenly interrupted. "Well, Texas has a good beach— Corpus Christi."

"Oh, yes," Ellen remarked, "my daughter Wendy loves it down there! I think her church class is planning a trip to the Gulf soon. I know she'd love to have you join them. Would you like to go?"

Susan smiled, hesitated, then looked frustrated, suspecting I would object. She was right.

Before Susan could respond, I pushed my plate toward the middle of the table. "This bread is indeed delicious. But," I laughed, "I just can't let myself gain five pounds all in one afternoon!"

"Well," Elder Barrett interjected, looking at his companion, "shall we get started?"[4]

Elder Black nodded, stuffing his mouth with one last chunk of bread and wiping his hands on a paper towel.[5]

"Let's go in the other room," Ellen suggested. "Although I'm really a kitchen person," she laughed, "the living room will be better. And don't let me forget to give you and Susan a loaf of bread to take home."

Boy, she's good!

The living room had the artistic touch I expected. Handmade pillows, afghans, embroidered wall hangings with sayings, *I am a Child of God . . . Happiness is Family Home Evening . . .* and a Bible verse: *As for me and my house, we will serve the Lord.* Everything worked together to tie in with the picture hanging over the fireplace—Christ kneeling in Gethsemane.

Motioning Susan and me toward the couch, Elder Barrett said soberly, "We'd like to open with a word of prayer if you don't mind." Susan and I nodded and the Elders and Ellen folded their arms and bowed their heads.

After Elder Barrett prayed that the Holy Ghost would enlighten our minds to the truth of the gospel, Susan and I sat down on the couch with Ellen sitting off to one side.

Sitting on two straight-backed chairs, the missionaries pulled out their Four-in-One and lesson booklets from their briefcases.[6] On the coffee table, Elder Barrett placed a spiral-bound notebook resembling a stenographer's pad entitled, "Flip charts." Standing it up inan A-shape position, he flipped the cover over to reveal the first visual aid, a head and shoulder's picture of Jesus. Susan and I were now going to learn about the "Plan of Our Heavenly Father."

Elder Barrett began. "Many people believe in God, although under various names. Elder Black and I have very strong testimonies about God and would like to share our *feelings* about Him with you.

"We know from scriptures in Mosiah that while God is omnipotent, He is also a loving God. How do you *feel* about God, Susan?"

"Well, I also feel He is loving," she replied smiling. Elder Barrett then looked questioningly at me.

"Yes, I agree," I said. "The aim of my whole life is to love God. The Bible tells us that He is worthy to be loved."

As I was saying this, I thought, *The Elders are making it sound like we're all talking about the same God. I hope Susan remembers from class the Mormon belief that contradicts the Bible: "The Father has a body of flesh and bones as tangible as man's."*[7]

Both the Elders gave a big grin. "That's wonderful! That's the way we feel too. He is a mighty God. Mosiah 4:9 tells us that we belong to Him and that He loves us very much. And I know He loves me by the feeling He puts in my heart."

Without clarifying that Mosiah was from the Book of Mormon, Elder Barrett continued, "Genesis 1:26–27 also states that God created man in His own image. Therefore, He is our heavenly Father and we are His children. Romans 8:16 confirms this by telling us that 'we are the children of God.' Acts 17:24-29 also states that 'we are the *offspring* of God.'"

The Acts 17 passage immediately sounded an alarm in me. I knew it was purposely included to lay the groundwork for a deeper Mormon belief—the idea that God biologically produced man's spirit through marital relations with a wife.

In addition, I caught the clever way Elder Barrett had smoothly slipped in the Book of Mormon scripture from Mosiah in conjunction with Genesis, Romans, and Acts. By so doing, he gave it equal status with God's Word. I decided to postpone my comments on Acts 17 and pursue Romans.

"Elders," I interrupted, "you quoted Romans 8:16, which says that 'we are the children of God.' How do you believe we become members of His family?"[8]

"We believe," Elder Barrett replied, "that we don't *become* sons and daughters of God. Since He created us, there is never a time when we were not His children. Romans 8:16 says, 'The Spirit itself beareth witness with our spirit, that we are the children of God.' That seems pretty simple. Paul is telling us that the Holy Spirit confirms the reality that *all* men are indeed the children of God. When we accept Christ we just continue being the sons, or children, of God."[9]

"Yes," I said, "generically speaking God is the Father of all because He created us. But, humanity lost that relationship because of the Fall. So, are you positive that your point of view is what Paul is talking about?"

Although I knew their concept was not what the verse meant, I knew why Elder Barrett pushed it along with Acts 17. In a later lesson, logic would be used to show that God and his wife were no different than earthly parents wanting their children to become like themselves, thus promoting the idea of potential godhood for everyone.

"I'm sure you're aware," I quickly continued, "of the importance of quoting verses in context. So, if you don't mind, let's back up to the verse just before the one you quoted.

"In Romans 8:15, just before commenting that believers are children of God, Paul states that the whole redemptive purpose of the cross was that 'we might receive the adoption of sons.' Only after this adoption takes place, do believers become the children of God and regain their special position as sons or daughters. Paul is not referring to the general creation of man.

"Elders, if you say all mankind are *already* children of God through the creation and that there is no event or process whereby we *become* such, it contradicts the Bible."

Susan interrupted. "Does Paul's use of adoption mean like someone adopting an orphan?"

"No," I said. "Paul means something else.

"Elders, since you asked how we feel about God, may I share with you my understanding of what I believe Paul is talking about in Romans?"

Both elders looked uncomfortable. "Certainly," they replied politely.

It was totally unrealistic of me to expect the Elders to be affected by anything I'd say, since they regarded the Bible as incomplete and mistranslated. I also knew that the only concept of *adoption* that they understood was in connection with their patriarchal blessing. In this instance, similar to a prophetic utterance, blessings are pronounced on members, one's future often declared, and a statement given as to which tribe they descend from. If, however, one is not from the chosen tribe of Joseph, one is then *adopted* into it by a mystical process whereby the Holy Ghost literally changes their blood.[10]

Nevertheless, I felt I needed to pursue the subject of adoption for Susan's sake. With the influence Elder Black already had on her, it would be easy for them to later convince her that Paul's statement doesn't mean what it sounds like and that Mormonism is right about God and His wife literally producing her (Susan's) spirit.

Since the elders remained politely quiet, I continued.

"Paul borrowed the term *adoption* from the Greeks and Romans, the meaning of which was entirely different from what we understand.

"This term was used when a young man came of legal age. When this happened, one's new status was called *adult sonship* and attested by public ceremony. It meant that the son could now enjoy all family privileges and was eligible to receive the inheritance. Those still holding the status of *child*, could not receive any inheritance.[11]

"Therefore," I said, "my understanding of what Paul is saying is this. Since we lost our position and our right to inherit heaven because of Adam's fall, there is no way anyone can belong to God's family and receive an inheritance except through the sonship process.

"Now," I asked, directing my question to both elders, "if Mormons accept the Bible as you say, how do members attain this biblical sonship status?" I doubted if they would come up with the correct answer—faith in Jesus Christ.

"Well, uh," Elder Black slowly began fudging his way through, "if, in Paul's world, parents had the adult son's status proclaimed in a public ceremony, then I suppose the comparable ceremony in our church would be the baptism of a new member by one holding proper priesthood authority. After that," he added, "the new member would need to be obedient to all God's commandments. This means paying one's tithing, attending Sacrament meeting, keeping the Word of Wisdom, being morally clean, going through the temple and being married for time and all eternity, upholding church leaders, and fulfilling positions."

"Elder," I said, "while those are commendable, I don't seem to find Paul mentioning any of those things."

Elder Barrett excitedly jumped in. "Of course not," he said. "This is why the next part of our lesson concerns the *plan* of our heavenly Father. Because God loves His children and wants them to progress, He has revealed a more complete plan of salvation. It consists of precious truths lost from the Bible over the centuries but now restored through a living prophet!"

Suddenly quelling his enthusiasm, he apologized. "Please, go on," he said.

"I firmly believe," I continued, "that the Bible is God's inspired Word. I also believe that, even though we don't have the original manuscripts, what we do have accurately presents the *full* plan of salvation.

"Romans states plainly that one *must* come into this sonship relationship in order to become a legal heir to the kingdom of God. This suggests that we do not have sonship status simply because of our creation. The Bible is explicit that we lost this privilege through the Fall. Paul, rather than saying we attain it through works, indicates that there is only *one way* to come into this relationship—through *faith* in Christ. Galatians 3:26 says, 'Ye are all the children of God by faith in Christ Jesus.'" I felt like adding, *not because we are offspring sexually generated by God,* but decided not to.

"Not by works," I quickly added, "for Paul said, 'a man is justified by faith without the deeds of the law.'[12] It's faith, plus nothing.

"And what does faith do?" I asked. "It brings Jesus Christ into one's heart. Since Jesus already holds sonship position, believers automatically acquire His sonship status when He enters them. And the way God confirms that one has gained this status is explained in Romans 4:6, 'Because ye are sons, God hath sent forth the Spirit of his Son into your hearts, crying, Abba, Father.'

"The *Abba Father* is significant. It is a very intimate term comparable to *daddy* or *papa*. In other words, Christ as son in the believer's heart, enables him or her to call God Abba Father.

"In reality, it is not really the individual who calls out to God as Abba Father, but the Spirit of Christ the *Son* speaking from *within* one's heart. This is the mystery of Christ in us that, Colossians 1:27 teaches is our only *hope* for an inheritance in glory.

"With this new sonship status, believers acquire two privileges they didn't have before. First, a personal relationship as son with God as Abba Father, and second, heirship to His kingdom.

"Thus, like the young man reaching legal age who is given adult sonship status and a right to the inheritance, the believer, through faith, qualifies to inherit everything his Heavenly father has."

There were a few seconds of awkward silence as the elders struggled to respond. I knew that their Mormon-tinted glasses would make them see everything I said as on a kindergarten level compared to what their Mormon gospel could teach me. On such a level, I could only qualify for the second heaven, the Terrestrial Kingdom. Finally the silence was broken.

"We're happy you shared your love for the Scriptures with us," Elder Barrett finally said. "We appreciate the fact that you have faith in Jesus Christ. We, too, have gained happiness through loving Jesus Christ. Having the Spirit of the Lord in one's heart, as you say, is certainly an important essential in the plan of salvation."

I sighed inwardly. Their response was typical. They had no understanding of Paul's sonship adoption. Mormons didn't believe faith justified anyone for anything. Everyone is a child of God through creation, whether they have faith in Christ or not.[13] It was like I hadn't even spoken on the subject. I hope Susan saw how the Elders totally missed the point.

Then Elder Black added, "We love John 3:16 which says, 'For God so loved the world that he gave his only begotten Son.' This is in harmony with Third Nephi in the Book of Mormon that says, 'My Father sent me that I might be lifted up upon the cross.'[14] As a result," he continued, "Jesus' crucifixion brought about a general salvation in which all men, good or bad, will be resurrected."

I sighed. *The only thing that the crucifixion stands for to them, is resurrection.*

"I assure you," he smiled, "everything we believe about salvation can be found in the Bible."

Yeah, right, I said to myself, recalling President Joseph Fielding Smith's statement that there is "no salvation without acceptance of Joseph Smith" and only his name will get a person into heaven.[15]

Would Susan pick up on Elder Black's deceptiveness? Would she remember from class that Mormon beliefs about salvation can't be found in the Bible? However, in all fairness, I knew Elder Black was talking about their first level of salvation, which meant a general resurrection for everyone. Susan wasn't aware they believed in two kinds.

The first level meant resurrection. The next, or higher level—individual exaltation—meant being saved in the Celestial Kingdom where only God and Christ dwell. The latter was achievable only as a result of works and rituals plus Joseph Smith's approval. Mormon salvation was not the Biblical experience of faith in Jesus Christ.

The Elders were doing their usual double-talking, speaking in general terms but knowing underneath there was more to their beliefs. I wondered if they would bring up the subject of exaltation in this lesson.

"But," Elder Black continued, interrupting my thoughts, "God's plan is eternal and He wants His children to enjoy the *fullness* of His plan. This means restoring gospel principles that have been lost and are no longer in the Bible."

Here it comes, I thought.

"There is a higher plan of salvation called *exaltation*. This requires that we follow Jesus, keep His commandments, and be obedient to the laws and ordinances of the Gospel.[16] If we do this, we will eventually become more like our heavenly Father."

Will Susan remember, I wondered, that when Mormons talk about becoming like their heavenly Father, what they really mean is eventually becoming a god?

Susan smiled. "Trying to be Godlike is certainly commendable," she said, failing to comprehend their double-talk. She gave me a smug glance. Susan felt sure Elder Black was practically a Christian already.

Just then, Ellen softly interrupted. "Elders," she said, "since you're near the end, I'm going in the kitchen to start refreshments." With that she excused herself.

Elder Black continued. "We'd like to show you the biblical pattern God always follows in relaying His plan to His children. By understanding it, you'll be able to recognize that everything we present is in keeping with what God has done in the past."

Reaching for the flip charts on the coffee table, he turned to the next page that read:

GOD'S PATTERN
He chooses special witnesses.
The prophets testify about Christ.
The Holy Ghost confirms the truth.
We are invited to obey.[17]

"Our heavenly Father," he began, "wants His children to fully understand the *plan* of salvation which, of course, includes the mission of Jesus Christ. Therefore, in the Old Testament, He established a pattern or method.

"His pattern was to choose *witnesses* to whom He would speak directly. Susan, in the Old Testament, who were these witnesses?"

"Why, the prophets, like Isaiah and Jeremiah," Susan confidently replied, acting like she and Elder Black were on the same wave length.

"Yes," Elder Black affirmed. "Our heavenly Father's plan always includes the calling of prophets. Amos 3:7 says, 'surely the Lord God will do nothing, but he revealeth his secret unto his servants the prophets.' The Book of Mormon, in Moroni 7:31, also says that angels declare 'the word of Christ unto the chosen vessels of the Lord, that they may bear testimony of him.'

"After prophets receive this Word they communicate it in two ways, verbal and written. When they write it down, it becomes Scripture.

"When people hear or read the prophets' teachings, they can know they are true by the witness of the Holy Ghost. For example, that's what happened to the people in Acts 2 when they heard Peter preach. The Holy Ghost fell upon them and they knew in their hearts that what he said was true. As a result, three thousand repented and were baptized."

Looking very serious Elder Black said, "Susan, when we know something is true by the power of the Holy Ghost, the Scriptures always invite us to respond. If you received the Holy Ghost's witness about a truth; that is, *feeling* it was right in your heart, would you embrace it?"

"Why, of course," she said smiling sweetly and fluttering her eyelashes more than was necessary.

Why, I fumed, *didn't she say, "Not by feeling. Only if confirmed by the Bible!"*

"Susan," Elder Black said, "I want to testify to you that I know this is indeed God's pattern. He always chooses special witnesses, called prophets, to teach His truth.

"Susan, do you believe it's important to listen to a prophet of God?"

"Of course," Susan answered.

Uh-oh, I thought. *She doesn't know where he's heading!*

"Well, then," Elder Black continued, "if the Scriptures tell us that God is the same yesterday, today, and forever, and He called prophets in biblical times, isn't it logical that He would follow the same pattern today?"

I saw the change on Susan's face. Suddenly aware of the bind she was in, she knew if she said no, it would sound like she was against God and the Bible. If she said yes, she was laying herself wide open for acceptance of Joseph Smith.

Susan stammered uncomfortably. "Well, uh, that prophet would certainly have to teach what's in the Bible."

Good going, Susan.

"Yes, he certainly would," Elder Black declared. "And I'm here to testify to you by the power of the Holy Ghost that God follows that same pattern today. In 1820, He chose a prophet, Joseph Smith, to whom He revealed the *fullness* of His gospel. I bear you my witness that I *know* he is a prophet, for I have received that special *feeling* and testimony in my heart."

Elder Black then sat back. Elder Barrett took over, quickly turning to the next flip chart. It was an artist's rendition of Joseph Smith praying beneath heavenly rays of light.

"In 1820," he began, "when Joseph Smith was just fourteen, he became very confused. There were many churches teaching different doctrines yet all claiming to have the truth.

"Haven't you been confused, Susan, wondering why today's churches don't teach the same thing? Wouldn't you think that if they had the *truth* they would all be in one accord?"

Susan looked at me. But, I decided it would be good experience for her to handle this alone.

"I never thought about it like that," she finally replied.

"Well, Joseph Smith certainly did." Elder Barrett then picked up his Four-in-One and began reading Smith's story of confusion over which church to join.[18]

After reading the lengthy excerpt he said, "Joseph Smith finally came across the verse in James 1:5 that says, 'If any of you lack wisdom, let him ask of God.' So, he decided to do just that.

"On a beautiful spring day, he went into a nearby woods and began to pray. He asked his heavenly Father which church was true and which one he should join. God answered that prayer. Elder Black, would you read Joseph Smith's testimony?"

Flipping to the page, Elder Black began reading:

> I saw a pillar of light exactly over my head, above the brightness of the sun, which descended gradually until it fell upon me. . . . When the light rested upon me I saw two Personages, whose brightness and glory defy all description, standing above me in the air. One of them spake unto me, calling me by name and said, pointing to the other—*This is My Beloved Son. Hear Him*![19]

"Therefore," Elder Black continued, "because Joseph Smith saw the Father and the Son, he became God's special witness for our day—just like Moses and the other prophets.

"His calling was to restore the kingdom of God on earth, testify to the world about Jesus' divine mission, and reveal the plan of salvation in its fullness. This included doctrines for exaltation, previously lost to the world. All this, so we could return to our heavenly Father and live with Him again."

I could tell that Susan was impressed with the story. *But*, I thought, *she'll change her mind when I show her the discrepancies in Smith's account of his vision. Also, the cover-up by the Mormon Church to keep members from finding out.*

Then Elder Barrett's voice rose to a new pitch. "*I know*, beyond a shadow of a doubt," he said with fervor, "that God did indeed appear to Joseph Smith that day in the sacred grove. That his calling as a prophet was one of the most momentous events in this world's history. Like prophets of old, he was a living witness of the resurrected Christ!

"In addition," he continued, "Jesus Himself testifies in the Doctrine and Covenants: 'I have sent forth the fullness of my gospel by the hand of my servant Joseph.'[20]

"I know that what the prophet Joseph Smith received from the Lord is true because God has given me a special *feeling* in my heart. This is the way the Holy Ghost works."

Elder Black looked at both of us. "We realize all this is new to you. We don't ask you to believe it because we say so, but we ask you to sincerely pray about it.

"Will both of you pray and ask God whether Joseph Smith was a prophet? If you do, the Holy Ghost will bear witness that he was. You will receive a *feeling* in your heart that what we are telling

you is true. Once you have that kind of testimony, the Holy Ghost
will continue bearing witness about other things we will be sharing with you." He waited for a response.

I could tell that Susan was trying to figure out what she could
say to pacify the Elders, yet not commit herself to praying about
Joseph Smith. But, I also sensed that since the elders had presented their concept of a modern-day prophet in such a logical
manner, she was confused. It was time for me to step in.

"Elders, it's getting late and we appreciate what you have presented. But, I'm sure you would like to know any problems I have
about praying about Joseph Smith."

The Elders nodded.

"I feel that to pray and ask whether Joseph Smith is a prophet,
is the wrong way to go about it. If the Bible already contains
God's Word, then it seems to me that the Bible is the first place
one should go to for an answer."

"The Bible," Elder Barrett quickly interjected, "will certainly
confirm Joseph Smith's calling. Remember, Amos 3:7 tells us that
speaking through prophets is God's pattern. However, after one
checks the Scriptures one must, of course, pray about it to get
the added witness of the Holy Ghost. The Holy Ghost will then
put that special *feeling* in your heart."

"But, why," I asked, "would I want to pray and ask God about
something He has already answered? For instance, is it logical for
me to pray about whether to steal or not? Do I need to ask whether
I should hate or love and only wait for a feeling in my heart? Of
course not. God has already revealed His will on these matters.

"However, I understand what you're saying." I said, "and I acknowledge that God called prophets in the Old Testament. But,
the New Testament states something quite different about the continuing role of a head prophet.

"Matthew 11:13 says, 'For all the prophets and the law prophesied until John.' Luke 16:16 states, 'The Law and the prophets
were until John.' In other words, it's saying that John the Baptist
marked the end of the Old Testament era and the need for a head
prophet. This was because the mission of Jesus Christ was on the
verge of being fulfilled, which would establish Him as our only
Prophet, Priest, and King.

"Hebrews 1 and 2, written after Christ had risen and after the
church was in full operation, states very clearly that God *ended*
the pattern of prophets and would now speak to us through His
son: 'God, who at sundry times and in divers manners spake in

time past unto the fathers by the prophets, Hath in these last days
spoken unto us by his Son.'

"Although 1 Corinthians notes the gift of prophecy and various accounts of individuals fulfilling that gift, there is no Scripture that says a particular prophet will act as head of the church
or as sole spokesman for God. Jesus is now our head prophet.

"Therefore, Elders, are you asking me to forget what God has
already revealed and ask Him again?" I waited.

"We understand your confusion," Elder Black said compassion-
ately. "But may I suggest another interpretation for Hebrews 1?
When it says God spoke in times past by the prophets and 'hath
in these last days spoken unto us by his Son,' that verse is simply
stating that during Jesus' lifetime, He spoke the words of God *just
like* the prophets of old. It doesn't mean that the role of prophet
was done away with."

"That's right," Elder Barrett added. "When a passage isn't clear
it's usually because it isn't translated correctly. This is why our
Article of Faith says that 'we believe the Bible to be the Word of
God as far as it is translated correctly.'

"If," Elder Barrett continued, "Hebrews really means what you
are interpreting, one would be hard pressed to explain Ephesians
2:20 that says that the church will be built upon the foundation
of apostles and *prophets*."

"With all due respect, Elder Barrett," I persisted, "if you'll re-
read Ephesians you'll see that it does *not* say 'upon the foundation of apostles and prophets.' Rather, it says 'upon the foundation
of *the* apostles and prophets.' The word *the* infers *specific* apostles
and prophets. God is saying that He built the household of God,
upon the foundation of the words and writings of *the* apostles and
prophets who had already testified of His coming.

"In addition, the Bible doesn't say we should test a prophet by *feeling* but, according to Deuteronomy 18:22, to see if his prophecies come
true. First Thessalonians 5:21 says, 'prove, or test, all things.'"

Ellen, who evidently picked up the tenseness of our conversation from the kitchen, suddenly appeared in the doorway announc-
ing, "Carrot cake and ice cream!"

The moment was lost. But, it was probably for the best. An
argument would have put everyone on the defensive. I only hoped
the Elders' comments were enough to show Susan their lack of
biblical understanding and the smooth way in which they avoided
answering any direct questions.

After a closing prayer, refreshments were served, during which time Ellen and Elder Barrett engaged me in conversation. It amounted to nothing more than social chitchat, telling me about their families and church activities and relaying typical expressions of, "I'm so happy to be a Mormon." They also handed me two tracts, *The Plan of Our Heavenly Father* and *The Gospel of Jesus Christ*, which repeated the information given in their lesson.

Elder Black and Susan, I noticed, were off in one corner talking. My imagination suddenly swelled into full focus. Although missionaries were not allowed to date, I knew there were a variety of prankish ways in which courtship and flirtation took place. Writing letters was one, thus avoiding the mission restriction of personal contact. Another, often jokingly revealed by former missionaries, was: "The manual says we can't hold *hands* with girls, but it doesn't say we can't hold *little fingers*."

This evening, I decided, the Elders had presented a very misleading lesson. They declared general statements about God and Jesus that *sounded* Christian. In addition, they had purposely avoided disclosing their belief that God was an exalted man with a wife who had literally begotten the human race. They talked about being children of God, but had no comprehension of Romans 8:16, which says that only through faith can one become a child of God. They cleverly laid the foundation for a two-tiered unbiblical plan of salvation that denied being saved through faith in Jesus Christ.[21]

Further, they disclaimed Hebrews 1:2 by insisting that God was still calling head prophets today, so as to include Joseph Smith. Plus, they continually emphasized knowledge by *feeling* rather than reliance on God's Word.

As I scraped the last crumb of carrot cake from my plate, I was glad I had come in spite of my fear of succumbing to the old love I once had for the Mormon Church. I realized more than ever how much I loved God's Word. My job now was to educate Susan so she wouldn't be influenced.

Just then, Susan tapped me on the shoulder.

"Elder Black and I have already scheduled the next meeting," she said quietly.

Ellen then did what I expected. She gave each of us a loaf of homemade bread to take home, promising that her daughter Wendy would be in touch with Susan.

Saying our goodbyes, we left, with Ellen and the missionaries standing in the doorway issuing exuberant invitations to return. I glanced at Susan, disappointed at her ecstatic face. I could hardly wait to get her into the car.

"Did you notice Elder Black's sincerity," she excitedly said, shutting the car door. "He said he loved the Lord! They both quoted John 3:16. Can you really say they don't love Jesus?" she challenged.

"No, of course not, Susan," I said, as I pulled the car away from the curb. "Most Mormons do love Jesus and truly believe He is speaking to their church.

"No, the Elders presented nothing deceptive in what they declared about God and Jesus because they were mostly general biblical statements. But, listen closely to what I'm going to tell you, Susan. The deception was in what they *didn't* tell you!"

"Okay," she said defensively, "what *didn't* they tell us."

"Well, for one, they didn't tell us that they believe God is an exalted man of flesh and bone, which contradicts what Jesus Himself said, 'A spirit hath not flesh and bones . . .'[22] They also didn't say that they believe that Jesus' death on the cross only partially saves believers.

"In addition, while the Elders gave a beautiful and impressive story of Joseph Smith's alleged visitation by the Father and the Son, that account is a fabrication. Joseph Smith gave at least three *different* accounts of that same event, two of which the Mormon Church has suppressed for over 150 years. But, I'll talk more about that in class tomorrow.

"Susan, you have to decide which you want to follow. The Bible or another gospel.

"Elder Black is indeed a sweet person. But, take my word for it—you are not going to convert him to Christianity. As Proverbs 4:26 says, you need to 'ponder the path of thy feet.' There is more at stake here than you realize!"

For the rest of the drive back, Susan was silent.

Finally arriving on campus, I drove up the winding driveway to the dorm. As Susan got out, her face was a mixture of resentment, confusion, and pain.

"Susan," I said, "with a little more knowledge under your belt, I believe you'll be just fine. I know it's rough going now, but education is your biggest need right now.

"So," I added, in a lighter tone, "please be sure and attend class. Especially tomorrow," I laughed, "the rest of the class will be dying to know what happened tonight. In fact, I'll plan on letting you be the one to satisfy their curiosity. Okay?"

Susan managed a pathetic smile, then turned and walked into the dorm leaving me to ponder.

CHAPTER SIX

Joseph Smith's Validity as a Prophet

Evaluating his prophetic role

Let's hear it Susan!" the class urged.

"Yeah, how did it go?" Matt roared. "Did you tell them where it's all at?"

Susan nervously made her way to the front of the class.

"Well," she said, looking into their expectant faces, "it was just like what was explained to us in class. The missionaries' presentation sounded biblical, but it sorta' wasn't—not when you knew ahead of time what they really believe."

Hesitantly, she began describing Ellen's house, the friendshipping, especially the homemade bread. Then, gradually gathering energy from the class' enthusiasm, her voice grew bolder—even cocky. Soon she was parroting everything I had said to her in the car. She even threw in Scripture that I had shared with her before class.

The students hung on to her every word as if she were some celebrity who had escaped from the very jaws of hell. No one would have guessed that she was still a very mixed-up girl.

Flipping her hair with a dramatic flourish, she said, "Oh yes, they even tried to make us think they believed in the biblical God. But, we knew they believed God was flesh and bone, which of course contradicts John 4:24 and Luke 24:39.

"The missionaries also quoted John 3:16, but failed to understand from it that salvation is free to all who believe in Christ.[1]

In fact," she said, pulling a piece of paper out of her pocket that I had given to her during assembly, "the President of their church came right out and contradicted Romans 10:9 by saying, 'It is a most serious error to believe that Jesus did everything for men if they would but confess him with their lips.'[2]

"They also refute Acts 4:12 which says, 'There is no other name under heaven given to men by which we must be saved' (NIV). They teach that being saved in heaven rests upon the name of Joseph Smith.[3] I mean, really, did God ever say that salvation rested on the name of his prophets, Moses, Jeremiah, or Isaiah?" The class applauded.

"And," she continued, "I found out something about Joseph Smith's first vision that I never knew before. He wrote *more* than one account, each one contradicting the other. But, I think more detail about that will be given in class." She then looked at me, signaling she was through.

As Susan took her seat, I walked around the front of my desk.

"Today," I began, "as I cover the subject of Joseph Smith, I want you to understand something. I don't do it hoping to instill any kind of antagonistic or belligerent attitude in you toward Mormons. But, I present the material to you for three reasons.

"First, it's my responsibility as teacher of this class. Second, you may some day find yourself swayed by Mormon logic and I hope to save you from that. Third, by knowing the facts, you may help some Mormon who is searching for the truth or prevent someone from being converted to it.

"But, before I tell you the specifics of today's lesson, I'd like to comment briefly about last night.

"What the Elders presented on God and Jesus sounded very Christian. And, while they gave a beautiful lesson expressing how much they loved their heavenly Father, it was, in a way, deceptive. It was deceptive because of what they *didn't* tell us.

"They didn't tell us that they believe God is an exalted man of flesh and bone, which contradicts John 4:24 that says, 'God is spirit.'

"They didn't tell us they believe in a plurality of gods.

"They didn't reveal their belief that Jesus' death on the cross only partially saves believers.

"They didn't tell us that salvation can only be achieved through conformity to Mormon rules and ordinances.

"They didn't tell us their belief that there are some sins that Jesus can't forgive, such as murder and, after the second time, adultery.[4]

"They didn't tell us that they have redefined the Bible's new covenant as temple marriage.[5]

"They didn't tell us that when they talk about wanting to become more like their heavenly Father it is a doublethink statement meaning they anticipate becoming gods themselves.

"Lastly, they didn't tell us that belief in Jesus will not get one into the Celestial heaven—that one has to go through a temple ceremony, learn secret signs and passwords, and wear special undergarments."

"All I hear," Ilya suddenly gasped, "is different gospel zan Bible teaches!"

"That's it in a nutshell," I replied.

Then, glancing at Susan, I said, "When one considers Galatians 1:8, 'Even though we, or an angel from heaven, should preach to you a gospel contrary to that which we have preached to you, let him be accursed,' the consequences of accepting such false teachings are very serious."

Susan looked away as I continued.

"Since Susan and I plan on meeting with the missionaries again, I'll be sure and address each subject as they present them to us.

"But, today we're going to cover Joseph Smith's role as prophet. This will include:

• Joseph Smith's first vision
• Joseph Smith's prophecies
• Joseph Smith's translating ability
• The real origin of Joseph Smith's doctrines

Holding up a picture of Joseph Smith praying in the sacred grove, I said, "Profound importance is given to this first vision, beautifully portrayed here. Its significance is reflected in an astounding statement from James B. Allen, BYU professor of history. He said that Smith's vision 'is second only to belief in the divinity of Jesus of Nazareth.'"[6]

A low hum of disapproval swept through the classroom.

"In addition," I continued, "another reason we should focus on the so-called first vision is because two presidents of the Mormon Church stated that it is the *cornerstone* upon which all of Mormonism rests.

"President David O. McKay said, 'The appearing of the Father and the Son to Joseph Smith is the foundation of this church.'[7] President Joseph Fielding Smith said, 'Mormonism . . . must stand or fall on the story of Joseph Smith.'[8]

"Therefore," I said, "if the foundation of all Mormonism rests upon Smith's vision, then we need to take a serious look at it.

"There is, as Susan indicated, more than one account of Smith's first vision. In reality, there are three, all differing from each other. While there are more accounts, they don't vary much in content, so we'll just concentrate on the three.

"One version was written in 1832; another in an 1835–36 diary; and the last in 1838. Smith's 1838 version states, 'When the light rested upon me I saw *two* Personages . . . One of them spake unto me, calling me by name and said, pointing to the other— This is My Beloved Son. Hear Him!'

"This version is what the church has chosen to canonize in their Doctrine and Covenants. At the same time, they have suppressed the 1832 version and deliberately altered the 1835 diary."

Tia raised her hand. "What did Joseph Smith say in those other versions?"

"In the 1832 version," I replied, "Smith has only *one* personage visiting him, the Son. It is this rendition that Mormon historians now admit is the most genuine. In Smith's own handwriting, he says, 'I was filled with the spirit of god and the Lord opened the heavens upon me and I *saw the Lord* and he spake unto me saying. . . .' [emphasis mine].[9] Notice, there is no mention of the Father.

"In his 1835 diary entry, however, he sees neither the Father or the Son, only angels, 'I received the first *visitation of angels* which was when I was about 14 years old.'[10]

"Since his diary only mentions angels, church leaders altered the account by omitting any mention of them. It now reads, 'I received my first vision, which was when I was about fourteen years old.'[11]

"So, on the singular day in 1820, when he supposedly had his famous vision, we have the following:

```
1832 account ------------ Jesus only
1835–36 diary ----------- Angels only
1838 account ------------ God the Father and Jesus
```

"Smith just couldn't keep his stories straight. To make matters worse, Mormon leaders insist that 'during Joseph Smith's lifetime, he told but one story.'"[12]

Ilya raised her hand. "Now dat everyvun know about three versions, how does Mormon Church excuse it?"

"Their only defense," I said, "is reflected in a statement by BYU professor Marvin S. Hill. He claims that each version became different because Smith gradually 'changed his view of the Godhead.'"[13]

The class snickered as Matt said, "That statement doesn't hold much water. Individuals don't change what they see just because years later they acquire a different understanding of the Godhead. He either saw what he said he saw, or he didn't! How much stock can a person put in a prophet who fabricates?"

"Great observation, Matt. Here's an example. If I were sharing with you that a long-lost relative, Aunt Marie, came and visited me on Tuesday, then later changed my story to insist it was three cousins, then again changed my story a third time to say it was really both Aunt Marie and Uncle Ralph—one could rightly say that something is wrong with my story.

"There's also another problem to consider. The missionaries made quite a point of saying that the first vision establishes Smith as a prophet. Therefore, we need to look at his prophecies.

"Who can tell me what the test of a true prophet is?

"Robert?"

"Deuteronomy 18:22," he responded quickly, proceeding to quote it verbatim, 'If what a prophet proclaims in the name of the LORD does not take place or come true, that is a message the LORD has not spoken. That prophet has spoken presumptuously' (NIV).

"In view of that," I said, "one would expect Smith's prophecies to be fulfilled. But, as we'll see, he doesn't pass the biblical test. He had too many unfulfilled prophecies.

"The Mormon Church, realizing this, came to the rescue by refusing to publish those prophecies that didn't come to pass.

"For example, in section 137 of the Doctrine and Covenants, the church deliberately left out four unfulfilled prophecies:[14] Here is one:

> I also beheld Elder M'Lellin in the south, standing upon a hill, surrounded by a vast multitude, preaching to them, and a lame man standing before him supported by his crutches; he threw them down at his word and leaped as a hart, by the mighty power of God.

"This prophecy never came true because M'Lellin apostatized from the church. Here is another:

> And I finally saw the Twelve [Mormon apostles] in the celestial kingdom of God. I also beheld the redemption of Zion

and many things which the tongue of man cannot describe in full.

"Since seven of the twelve apostatized or were excommunicated, they couldn't possibly end up in the Celestial Kingdom. More especially since Smith had already stated that 'whoso breaketh this covenant after he hath received it, and altogether turneth therefrom, shall not have forgiveness of sins in this world nor in the world to come,'[15]

"He also prophesied that Lyman E. Johnson would be like Enoch so that Satan would tremble before him. But, Johnson also apostatized. Johnson, along with Heber C. Kimball, Orson Hyde, David W. Patten, and others were also promised they would be alive to see Christ's second coming. They all died.[16] Smith further said that he, himself, would be eighty-five years old when Jesus returned.[17]

"Smith further prophesied that a temple would be built by his generation in Independence, Missouri.[18] He also prophesied that the Nauvoo house in Nauvoo, Illinois would be in his family forever. Neither of the two materialized.[19]

"He prophesied in the Book of Mormon that Lamanites (American Indians) who convert to the church will turn 'white and delightsome.' Since, over the last 160 years this miraculous event never occurred, the church altered the phrase to 'pure and delightsome.'[20]

"In another unfulfilled prophecy, Smith and a few of his leaders traveled from Kirtland, Ohio, to Salem, Massachusetts, after hearing that there was treasure concealed in the basement of a widow's house. He prophesied having God say He would give them power over the city of Salem so that gold and silver would be given to them and they could pay their debts. No such treasure was acquired and the leaders returned empty-handed.[21]

"A revelation was given to Smith while in jail, promising him that he would 'triumph over all [his] foes.' But, his foes forced the church from the state eight years later. He was also told that his enemies 'and their posterity shall be swept from under heaven.'[22] This prophecy proved false, because Smith was murdered and his enemies outlived him.

"Smith also claimed that the Lord said that if his wife Emma would not accept plural marriage 'she shall be destroyed, saith the Lord.'[23] She fought against this practice and after her husband's death lived to enjoy a ripe old age and even helped start the Reorganized LDS Church.

"Smith prophesied that W. W. Phelps would not taste of death until Jesus came.[24] Phelps died March 7, 1872.

"He also prophesied that the Lord's coming would be in 1891.[25] This, obviously, never took place.

"Although there are many others, I'll conclude with Smith's Civil War prophecy.[26] Mormons enjoy referring to this one because it was given about thirty years before the Civil War. Members say it is proof of his prophetic calling.

"However, rather than being prophetic, Smith simply produced a revelation that matched current thought. South Carolina, at the time of his 'prophecy,' was already rebelling and newspapers were predicting an impending war between the North and South.[27] Therefore, Smith's 'prophecy' only reflected that expectation.

"However, while the Civil War did come to pass, there are statements within that prophecy that never came to pass. Verses 3 to 6 declared that as a result of the civil war, 'war shall be poured out upon all nations . . . slaves shall rise up against their masters . . . [and] remnants who are left of the land will marshal themselves [against the non-Mormons, and God would bring] a full end of all nations.'[28] These four events never occurred.

"The test of a true prophet," I said, "is whether his prophecies are fulfilled. God never said that a prophet should be judged by a good feeling in one's heart or by praying about him.

"But, now we need to examine another aspect of Smith's role as prophet. Up to this point, we've covered his vision and prophesies. But, what about his translating ability? Let's take a look at the Pearl of Great Price.

"This standard work of their church contains the Book of Moses (received by revelation), Matthew 24 (revised by Smith from the King James Version of the Bible), the Writings of Joseph Smith (portions from his personal history, including his first vision), and the Book of Abraham (translated from an Egyptian papyrus).

"Take the latter," I said. "This was supposed to be a translation of a four-thousand-year-old papyrus that Abraham actually wrote and *signed*.

"Found in the wrappings of a mummy, it fell into Smith's hands in 1835. Since the Egyptian language was in its infancy at the time, no one could challenge Smith's translation of the facsimiles (drawings) or the hieroglyphics.

"The papyrus was thought to have been destroyed in the great Chicago fire of 1871. But, in 1967, the Metropolitan Museum of

Art discovered it in their archives and presented it to the LDS Church.[29]

"Since Egyptology was a well-developed science by then, Marvin Cowan, a Baptist missionary, sent the facsimiles and Smith's translation to the Smithsonian Institute for verification.

"John A. Wilson, Professor of Egyptology at the University of Chicago, and Richard A. Parker of the Department of Egyptology at Brown University both came to the same conclusion.[30] Smith's translation was incorrect. What he had actually translated was a pagan funeral text called the 'Book of Breathings' from the *Egyptian Book of the Dead*. There was nothing about Abraham in it, let alone his signature.

"However, the church, totally unaware of this, was excited about having found the Book of Abraham papyrus again. They turned it over to a Mormon well versed in deciphering Egyptian. But he, along with other scholars, confirmed the two Smithsonian professors' conclusions. It definitely was not the Book of Abraham, but a funeral text.

"Mormon leaders began to make excuses. They claimed that Smith did not translate the *literal* meaning of the lines, but treated the Egyptian text as 'super-cryptograms—that is, writings with hidden meaning.'[31] Others believed that the Egyptian text simply served as a *trigger* for revelation.[32] But, Smith had made it very clear that this was *not* what he was doing.[33]

"The Mormon Church refuses to admit the truth to its members. Why? Because it would discredit the Book of Mormon, which also claims to be a translation.

"The most glaring proof," I continued, "that Smith could not translate was the case of the Kinderhook plates, not to be confused with the Book of Mormon plates.

"A group of men in the 1840s, intent on tricking Smith, falsely forged six brass plates with the help of a blacksmith. Using beeswax and acid, they copied hieroglyphic characters from a Chinese tea chest onto the plates. They buried them in the ground, pretended to find them, and the unsuspecting Smith proceeded to translate them:

> I have translated a portion of them, and find they contain the history of the person with whom they were found. He was a descendant of Ham, through the loins of Pharaoh, King of Egypt, and that he received his kingdom from the Ruler of heaven and earth.[34]

"When these oriental characters were later submitted to Professor Li Hsueh-chih of Academia Sinica and National Taiwan University, he identified the writings as ideographs used by the Lolo tribes in Yunnan Province in southwest mainland China.[35] While he was able to identify them, he could not read them.

"Now," I said, picking up my notebook, "for the remainder of the class I want to cover the *true* origins of Joseph Smith's doctrines. But, before I do, I'd like to say this: Many Mormons are wonderful individuals and love their faith just as we do ours. They truly believe they have the truth and that everything their leaders tell them is factual. The problem is that they don't know the real truth about Joseph Smith and early Mormon history because their leaders have taken great pains to conceal it.

"Why have they done this? Because they know that Joseph Smith was a product of his cultural environment—and they know exactly what that environment was. It was one steeped in magic, witchcraft, the occult, blood sacrifices, magic, masonry, divining rods, seer stones, treasure digging, and superstition.[36]

"Yes, Robert?"

"That kind of superstition," he said, "seems strange for early America. Especially, when one considers that the Puritans were the first ones to settle the colonies. Surely, they wouldn't have brought that kind of stuff with them."

"You're right. So, to find out where all that stuff came from, necessitates a little history lesson."

As the class shot dagger looks at Robert, I laughed.

"Don't worry, history can really be fascinating if you give it a chance.

"We'll need to start our story in early Europe.

"I'm sure you're already familiar with the Protestant Reformers. But, there were other contenders during that time known as Radical Reformers—utopian prophets who felt the need for direct revelation and a literally setting up of God's kingdom. Their concepts would eventually reach America and take hold with Joseph Smith.

"There were also the 'cunning folk' who offered supernatural services to solve personal problems.[37] They claimed the ability to heal, tell the future, protect against the devil, and find lost property and ancient treasure troves. The idea of using occult methods to find buried treasure also had an impact in Joseph Smith's time.[38]

"Then, there were the Hermetic Magi. They were called such

because they took their metaphysical teachings from the *Corpus Hermeticum*. This was a manuscript supposedly containing revelations from the Greek god, Hermes Trismegistus, to an ancient Egyptian prophet older than Moses.[39] Within the *Corpus* was a book called the *Pimander*, nicknamed the 'Egyptian Genesis,' which we'll see played a huge part in Smith's doctrines.

"Along with the *Pimander's* teachings, the Hermetic Magi used a mixture of pagan beliefs from the Kabbalah and alchemy, and fused them into their Christian beliefs.[40]

"Alchemy's main teaching was the belief that base metals could be transmuted into gold.[41] But, there was also a mystical side to alchemy, origins of which came from Greco-Roman Egypt. This school of thinking believed they could use the same principle of transmutation to *divinize* human beings. Through this, man could recover the divine power and perfection Adam possessed before the Fall.[42]

"The popularity of alchemy brought one more person into the picture—the con man. Less interested in changing the human condition, he induced people to make a small investment, promising them gold beyond their wildest dreams. These alchemist con men became the models for con men of nineteenth-century America, as diviners of buried treasures.

"Joseph Smith was also a diviner of buried treasure. But, more than swindling people out of their possessions, he swindled people out of the most precious possession they had—faith in the God of the Bible.

"Now, here's where it really gets interesting," I said. "In Europe, after mystical Hermeticism enjoyed popularity, it died down for a while. But it later revived in 1463 when Cosimo de Medici ordered his court scholar, Ficino, to stop working on Plato and work on a collection of manuscripts found in Macedonia in 1460. This is where the *Corpus Hermeticum* comes in.

"The manuscript produced startling concepts. The *Pimander* introduced the idea of *creatio ex deo*, creation out of God, instead of the biblical *creatio ex nihilo*, creation out of nothing. It also stated that the beginning of matter and the beginning of God Himself, came out of 'primal divine intelligence from which also sprang the entire universe. Divine spirit was . . . the original primal matter.'[43]

"The book also taught universal salvation and emphasized free agency. It portrayed a divinely empowered Adam helping in the creation and voluntarily giving up his divinity to 'mate with matter.' It declared his fall voluntary, therefore, not a sin. The Hermeticists also taught the Kabbalah belief in three heavens.

"Now," I said to the class, "listen to the following and see if anything sounds familiar: divinizing human beings, matter springing from primal intelligence, three heavens, negation of the Fall, and divinity of Adam.

"Yes," Tia exclaimed. "It's Mormonism! Especially the part about Adam voluntarily giving up his divinity. It reminds me of an earlier lesson you gave on the Mormon's Adam-God doctrine. In that teaching, God gave up His divinity to become Adam so He could start His spirit children off physically."

"Right! We'll find that none of Smith's concepts were new. Nor, as he claimed, did he receive them by divine revelation. How he found out about these teachings, we'll soon see.

"The Hermetic philosophies developed throughout Europe and one can recognize additional Mormon concepts.

"In the twelfth century John Saltmarsh pursued the idea of three heavens comparable to the sun, moon, and stars.[44] The Muggletonians taught that 'God was a finite being' about 'five foot high,' complete with body parts.[45] This particular teaching extended to America in the area of Connecticut where Joseph Smith's mother came from.[46]

"In the sixteenth century, Paracelsus carried on the philosophy from Joachim of Fiore's teaching of the twelfth century. He spoke of restoring the primitive church in a new dispensation that would be inaugurated by the coming of the prophets Elijah and Elias . . .'[47]

"Hold on," Matt interrupted. "Didn't Joseph Smith claim Elijah appeared to him?"

"Right. That account appears in the Doctrine and Covenants with not only Elijah appearing in the Kirtland temple but also Elias.[48]

"Further," I continued, "the Anabaptists, in the sixteenth century city of Münster, claimed a New Jerusalem with a sociology that reminds one of Smith's United Order. They also practiced polygamy and instigated a Melchizedek priesthood.[49] John Dee's sixteenth-century hermetic underground sect, House of Love, also taught a 'hierarchy of priesthoods,' which probably influenced Smith's concept of the Aaronic, Patriarchal, and Melchizedek levels of priesthood.[50]

"The idea of ordaining men to the Melchizedek priesthood, as well as Rosicrucian, Masonic, alchemic, and Kabbalistic concepts, was later carried to New England from Europe and practiced by the Zionitic Brotherhood of priests at the Ephrata community in Pennsylvania. This community also practiced baptism for the dead by proxy, which 'spread among the local Germans, surviving into the 1840s,'—Joseph Smith's time.[51]

"Marriage for eternity as the *new covenant* was established by Emmanuel Swedenborg in the seventeenth century.[52] This concept was transferred to New England and continued by the Rhode Island perfectionists, especially John Finney, Jr., who taught *spiritual wifery*, a term later incorporated into Mormon polygamy.

"In conjunction with all of the above, there was the influx of esoteric Freemasonry that contributed heavily to Smith's secret temple rituals and teachings.

"Professor John L. Brooke states that the Radical Reformation in Europe was the 'immediate precursor of critical themes in the popular religion of the early American colonies.'[53] In other words, all the mystical and heretical teachings of the Egyptian Genesis (the *Pimander*), the Kabbalah, the occult, the alchemists, and the Hermetic Magi, were transferred to New England and later utilized by Smith.

"Now, test your memory and see if you can remember the European beliefs that Smith incorporated into his new religion."

Matt called out, "The appearance of Elijah!"

"Good! What else?"

Robert raised his hand. "The preexistence of man, the eternal nature of matter, creation coming from divine primal intelligence, the divinity of Adam, his fall not being a sin, and human beings becoming divine."

"And ve mustn't forget," Ilya said, "polygamy and new covenant of marriage for eternity."

"Also," Tia remarked, "Baptism for the dead by proxy and three heavens comparable to the sun, moon, and stars."

"There's a few more. Matt?"

"The Melchizedek priesthood, levels of priesthood, restoration of the primitive church, and establishing of a new dispensation." He leaned back in his seat looking quite proud of himself.

"Great job!" I said, disappointed that Susan wasn't contributing.

"In addition," I said, "there was the Masonic-Rosicrucian myths of buried treasure in underground vaults. Also, astrology, magic, and use of occult talismans all of which I'll save for our next class.

"Robert was right," I smiled. "This 'stuff' didn't come by way of the Puritans.[54] Rather, it came in the post 1660–1730s migrations of Quaker and German sect survivors of the Radical Reformation.[55]

"The Puritans did, however, bring with them the belief that America was the Adamic paradise. Also, the concept of restoring the primitive church and insisting that only the elect could claim keys to the legitimate church. All these ideas, Joseph Smith capitalized on.

"The Hermetic and Rosicrucian mysteries were mainly spread in America by John Withrop, Jr. and others who were advocates of Paracelsus' concepts. The philosophy of mystical alchemy continued and was even reflected in seventeenth-century New England poets.[56]

"Along with the hermetical philosophies, folk and occult magic was also brought here. That magic included using divining rods to locate buried treasure, animal sacrifices, and magic circles to overpower guardian spirits assigned to the treasures.

"All this played a heavy part in the culture Joseph Smith grew up in, eventually sparking the idea of gold plates being buried in the ground with a guardian spirit named Moroni."

"Are you saying," Tia interrupted, "that the only way these practices continued from Europe to America was by word of mouth and that's how Joseph Smith learned it? Or were there books on these practices?"

"Both, Tia. And, if someone will plug in the overhead, I'll show you what books were available in Smith's time. While it's a rather lengthy list, I'd like you to consider the idea that one day you just might meet a Mormon who will require such information. So, stay with me."

Placing the transparency on the projector, I continued.

"While Joseph Smith had access to these books, many feel that it was really Sidney Rigdon who was more familiar with them. He was more of a scholar than Smith.[57] Nevertheless, let's take a look.

"There were the theological dictionaries containing summaries of the hermetic and Kabbalah teachings. They also included discussions on preexistence, materialism, and three heavens.[58]

"Then, there were the *Theological Astronomies* by Thomas Chalmers and Thomas Dick that described uncreated spiritual material and hierarchies of heavenly spheres.[59] We know that Mr. Dick's work was in the Nauvoo library in 1844, available for Smith to check out.[60] Also, we know that Mormon newspapers in 1836 were quoting Dick.

"Thomas Paine's *Age of Reason* could also have planted the idea in Smith's head of 'worlds without number.'[61]

"There were also short texts of Emmanuel Swedenborg's books in Palmyra where Smith lived, with full translations available in other areas.

"Swedenborg's books taught Jacob Boehme's ideas about three heavens comparable to the sun, moon, and stars; a celestial kingdom; rejection of original sin; and universal salvation achieved through works.

"Another book available to Smith at the Manchester, New York library, also at a bookstore in Hanover, New Hampshire, was *The Travels of Cyrus* by Andrew Michael Ramsay. Published in England in 1738 and republished in Boston and New Jersey in the 1790s, this book told about spiritual preexistence, primal matter, spirit intelligence with God as common father, alchemy, the occult, Freemasonry, ancient mystery religions, and the Egyptian *Pimander*.

"Ramsay's later book *The Philosophical Principles of Natural and Revealed Religion* covered the two spiritual and material creations of preexistence. His works must have been popular in Smith's circle, for Parley P. Pratt, a Mormon contemporary of Smith's, in his work, *Key to the Science of Theology*, used similar terms such as *spiritual and holy fluids* in speaking of divine, preexistent intelligent materials.[62] He could have taken it from Ramsay's book or else picked it up from Joseph Smith who had already read it and was passing it off as revelation.

"Although we'll be covering Masonry in our next lesson, I'll also mention Masonic sources available to Smith.

"There was *Masonry Exposed* by William Morgan, *Inquiry into the Nature and Tendency of Speculative Freemasonry* by Stearn, *Some Beauties of Freemasonry* by Joshua Bradley, *Free Masonry* (an anti-Masonic book) by Henry Dana Ward, and Thomas S. Webb's *Free-Mason Monitor*.[63]

"There were other sources for Smith as well. There was his brother Hyrum, as well as church members who were Masons.

"The occult Masonic books available in the 1780s and 1790s in American lending libraries and book shops" I said quickly placing another transparency on the projector, "were Aristotle's *Masterpiece*, apocryphal Erra Pater's *Book of Knowledge* and *The Complete Fortune Teller*, Ebenezer Sibley's *A New and Complete Illustration of the Occult Sciences*, *The Magus* by Francis Barrett, *Astrology* by John Heydon, Herman Kirchenhoffer's *Book of Fate*, and *Christian Astrology* by William Lilly.[64]

"Lastly," I added, "although this is not an idea that came from Europe, there was a book that provided Smith with the idea that the American Indians were Israelites. *View of the Hebrews or the Tribes of Israel in America* by Ethan Smith was published in 1823 at Poultney, Vermont. It was so popular, a second edition was printed in 1825.[65]

"There was also Josiah Priest's *Wonders of Nature and Providence Displayed*, published at Rochester, about twenty miles from the Smith home, that presented ideas similar to those later found in the Book of Mormon.[66] In our next class we'll examine the subject of the American Indians closer.

"While Smith, possibly with Oliver Cowdery or Sidney Rigdon's help, derived the majority of his teachings from the Hermetic books, it is well to remember that he may have picked up ideas from his immediate environment. For example, the idea of Adam's upward stumble was already prevalent with Freewill Baptists, Shakers, and Universalists.[67]

"In addition, other communities were ordaining men to the Melchizedek priesthood and practicing marriage for eternity, and baptism for the dead by proxy. I should add that Joseph Smith could also have taken the idea of the Melchizedek priesthood from the Masons.

"So," I said, turning to the blackboard, "Which aspect of today's lesson did you find the most interesting? Joseph Smith's first vision? Joseph Smith's prophecies? Joseph Smith's translating ability? Or, the European Hermetic sources for Smith's doctrines?"

Much to my delight Susan raised her hand.

"I enjoyed the different accounts of Joseph Smith's vision—actually thought they were funny. I wonder if the Mormon Elders know about them?"

"I doubt it," I replied, wishing she had offered a more serious response.

"Yes, Matt?"

"What blew me away," he began, "were Smith's unfulfilled prophecies. You'd think that if any Mormon took the time to find out what the biblical test of a prophet is, then checked Smith's prophecies out, one would see that he couldn't possibly have been called of God."

"I found his translating attempt," Robert said, "more fascinating. I mean, what an actor! You said that the European con man who fooled people into thinking he could turn money into gold was the model for all later con men—well, Smith sure takes the cake, pulling off that thing with the Egyptian mummy!"

"Those are interesting comments," I responded. "But, weren't any of you impressed with *where* he got all his so-called Mormon ideas?"

"Yea," one student said. "All that was good, I guess. It's just that it's pretty heavy stuff."

"No, it vasn't too heavy," Ilya quickly chimed in. "It vas very goot."

"Thank you Ilya."

"Out of all this information I've given you," I said, "here's what I think is significant.

"Besides Smith's making up his first-vision story, his prophecies failing to come true, and his translating ability exposed, what impressed me the most was his borrowing from Radical Reformationist ideas.[68]

"He copied the Egyptian *Pimander's* teaching on preexistence, spiritual matter and primal divine intelligence, as well as adopted its idea of *creatio ex deo* instead of the biblical *creatio ex nihilo*.

"He applied alchemic teachings to divinize and transmute human beings into gods.[69] He promulgated the idea of Adam's divinity and his fall as an upward stumble. He followed the practice of baptism for the dead by proxy, Melchizedek priesthood ordinations, polygamy, marriage for eternity, three heavens, and a celestial kingdom comparable to the sun. He also claimed direct revelation, an appearance by Elijah, and a literal setting up of the kingdom.

"He plagiarized the Masonic myth of finding a treasure beneath the ground, in his gold plates, and continued the prevalent idea of American Indians being Israelites into his Book of Mormon.

"Lastly, he inherited the cunning folk's occult and superstitious practice of divining for buried treasure and using seer stones.

"However," I added, "although all these concepts were available to Smith in books and in his cultural surroundings, he actually committed no crime by teaching them.

"What he was guilty of, however, was passing them off as God's revelation and claiming they were a restoration of what Jesus and His apostles taught to the primitive church.

"But, now," I said, "we're out of time. In tomorrow's lesson we'll see how Joseph Smith put all the above together, along with Masonry, magic, and the occult, to form one of the most influential, fastest-growing religion of our times.

CHAPTER SEVEN

Magic and Masonry

How Joseph Smith put it all together

Abracadabra!" came the eerie voice from the classroom.

I walked up the steps and paused in the doorway. Matt stood at my desk waving a yardstick over two salad plates, obviously borrowed from the cafeteria. Placing the plates inside an upturned sombrero, he tilted it toward the class.

"Now you see them . . ."

Pausing midsentence, he covered the hat with his jacket, his hands fumbling beneath. Then, with an elegant flourish, he flipped his jacket off, exhibiting the empty sombrero . . .

"Now you don't!" he said triumphantly.

Suddenly, a plate slipped out of the hood of his jacket and went clattering to the floor. His sleight-of-hand discovered, Matt nevertheless took his bows graciously while the class applauded. Then, noticing me, he gave a sheepish grin.

"What on earth is going on?" I asked as I walked to the front of the room.

The class snickered while Matt proceeded to explain. "I'm demonstrating our lesson for today," he said.

"I'm afraid you've lost me, Matt," I said, laying my briefcase on the desk.

"Can't you guess? I'm Joseph Smith!" he grinned. "I miraculously produced some plates, then made them disappear. You said he had a magic hat. Isn't that the way he did it?"

As Matt cockily swaggered back to his seat, I smiled. "Matt, you know Joseph Smith didn't pull the plates out of a hat—although," I hesitated, "now that I think about it, maybe he did."[1] The class looked alert.

"Smith, instead of translating directly from the plates, looked into a seer stone placed inside his hat.[2] It was a practice," I explained, "known as crystal gazing or scrying. And although Smith didn't say 'abracadabra,' his mother admitted the family practiced this magic incantation. Here's what Smith's mother says." Reaching into my briefcase, I pulled out a book and began reading:

> Let not the reader suppose that . . . we stopped our labor and went at trying to win the faculty of *Abrac*, drawing magic circles, or soothsaying, to the neglect of all kinds of business. We never during our lives suffered one important interest to swallow up every other obligation [emphasis mine].[3]

"What exactly is the *faculty of Abrac*?" Matt interrupted.

"*Abrac*," I continued, "is a Jewish Kabbalistic word. It comes from *abracadabra* and *abraxis*, words used on amulets to work magic.[4] The first four letters are acrostics[5] taken from the first letter of four Hebrew words; *Ab*, meaning Father; *Ben*, meaning Son, and *Ruach* and *Adsch*, meaning Holy Spirit. When written in a triangular form on parchment and hung around the neck, it acted as a charm to heal toothaches and other ailments.[6] Because Smith's brother was a Mason, the family probably learned about it from him, although they could have picked it up from any of the available books on magic.[7] But, we need to move on.

"In yesterday's lesson, I told you how magic and metaphysical teachings were popularized in fifteenth-century Europe and later transferred to New England.

"Today, we're going to see what kind of magic and Masonic practices were prevalent in Joseph Smith's time. Especially, we'll see the role they played in his story about the Book of Mormon plates."

Looking purposely at Matt I smiled. "While we may view Joseph Smith's fascination with magic and the occult as humorous, we do need to understand the climate of his culture. Belief in magic was not unusual. Mormon historian, B. H. Roberts, while acknowledging that Smith's family believed in 'fortune telling . . . warlocks and witches,' added that 'to be credulous in such things was to be normal people.'[8]

"The family's involvement in witchcraft was confirmed by Fayette Lapham who, after visiting the Smiths, wrote: '[Joseph's father] was a firm believer in witchcraft and other supernatural things; and had brought up his family in the same belief.'[9]

In addition," I said, "Joseph's father also used seer, or peep, stones. Placing them in a hat, he received revelation on the location of buried treasure. Known as a money digger, Smith's father hired out to locate these caches. An affidavit by David Stafford confirmed that 'the general employment of the Smith family was money digging and fortune telling.'[10]

"Since Joseph naturally followed in his father's footsteps—he also used peep stones.[11] Even before he claimed to translate the Book of Mormon, he was finding buried treasure and deciphering ancient writings. In one instance, he gazed into his stone and translated an unknown language, supposedly telling where Captain Kidd buried two pots of gold and silver.[12]

"Trained by his father, Joseph also learned how to use a divining rod to detect metals. Often called a mineral rod, it was similar to dowsing for water with a hazel branch. This practice, we'll eventually see, was carried into Smith's religion and later used in his temple.

"Smith, however, used peep stones more often than the divining rod. It was through a peep stone, according to Brigham Young and Martin Harris, that Smith located the gold plates using a stone found in the well owned by Mason Chase. This particular stone, in Mormon history, is referred to as the *brown* stone as opposed to the *white* stone called the Urim and Thummin.[13] This is, of course, contrary to Smith's later story that an angel told him where to find the gold plates.

"Joseph also used his peep stones to read palms.[14] I believe the Mormon practice of giving patriarchal blessings today is an outgrowth of Smith's fortune-telling practice."[15]

Susan interrupted. "Don't you think Smith gave all that up after he started his church?"

"I'm afraid the answer is no. The use of divining rods and peep stones continued after the Mormon Church was established.

"According to James Collin Brewster, the Smith family 'anointed the mineral rods and seer stones with consecrated oil, and prayed over them in the house of the Lord in Kirtland.'[16] The ritual consisted of putting on temple robes and asking yes or no questions of the rod. If the rod moved, it meant yes. If there was no movement, it meant no.[17] To validate the church's continued use of a divining rod, Joseph gave a revelation to Oliver Cowdery:[18] 'Now this is not all, for you have another gift, which is the *gift of working with the rod*: *behold it has told you things*: behold there is no other power save God, that can cause this rod of nature, to work in your hands' [emphasis mine].[19]

"Since this later proved embarrassing to the church, the revelation was changed to read: 'You have another gift, which is the *gift of Aaron.*' Nevertheless, the new phrase was still an occult term, since a divining rod was also called a *rod of Aaron.*[20]

"Robert?"

"Smith's mother mentioned magic circles along with the faculty of abrac. Did she mean the same kind witches use?"

"I'm afraid so," I replied. "Here's an example. Joseph said there was a buried chest of gold watches guarded by an evil spirit. To appease the spirit, he ordered stakes set up in the form of a circle. He then sent a man to obtain a long knife, or sword, and to march around the spot with drawn weapon to guard against any satanic assaults.[21]

"Joseph and his father worked together. Often, while his father was performing the circle activity for customers, Joseph would be in the house using his peep stone to keep track of what the evil spirit was doing. William Stafford gives an account:

> Joseph, Sr. first made a circle, twelve or fourteen feet in diameter. This circle, said he, contains the treasure. He then stuck a row of witch hazel sticks, around the said circles, for the purpose of keeping off the evil spirits. Within this circle he made another, of about eight or ten feet in diameter. He walked around three times on the periphery of this last circle, muttering to himself something which I could not understand. . . . [He then] asked leave of absence, and went to the house to inquire of young Joseph the cause of our disappointment. He soon returned and said that Joseph had remained all this time in the house, looking in his stone and watching the motion of the evil spirit—that he saw the spirit come up to the ring and as soon as it beheld the cone which we had formed around the rod, it caused the money to sink."[22]

Tia raised her hand. "You said something about animal sacrifice. Did Smith really do that?"

"Yes. Animal sacrifice was part of the treasure divining business. It was believed that there were both good and bad spirits guarding treasures. According to magic books, 'white animals [were] sacrificed to the good Spirits and black to the evil.'[23]

"Therefore, in one instance, Smith procured a black sheep, claiming it was the only way to appease the evil spirit of a particular treasure. They were to cut its throat and lead it around in a circle while it bled.[24] Smith even sacrificed a dog on one occasion.[25]

"Mr. Stafford, the owner of the sheep, was later asked by M. Wilford Poulson if Smith stole a black sheep from him. Stafford's response was, 'No, not exactly . . . he did miss a black sheep, but soon Joseph came and admitted he took it for sacrifice but he was willing to work for it. He made wooden sap buckets to fully pay for it.'[26]

"Smith carried this ritual magic into his new religion. For example, he refused to let a man be ordained an apostle unless a lamb was first sacrificed in the temple.[27] Joseph's preoccupation with animal sacrifice led him to make the statement I read to you in a previous class—that animal sacrifice in connection with priesthood duties would be reinstated.'[28]

"Did Smith use tea leaves and tarot cards," Matt grinned.

"No, Matt," I said smiling, "not that I know of. However, he did use magic medallions. When Smith was killed, a Jupiter talisman was found on his body.[29] The talisman was shaped like a silver dollar and carried the sign of the spirit of Jupiter. Made of silver or tin, it mostly contained Hebrew characters.[30] Former director of the LDS Institute of Religion at the University of Utah, Dr. Reed C. Durham, Jr.[31] identified it from a magic book available in Smith's time.[32]

"Since, astrologically speaking, Jupiter stood for many of Smith's personal ambitions, he probably selected the talisman for that reason. The power of Jupiter consisted of 'high positions, [having] one's own way,' achieving status, and acquiring the 'dignity of a natural ruler.'[33]

"Dr. Durham tried to lessen the negative impact of Joseph's having it, by confirming its appropriateness:

> It carries the sign and image of Jupiter. . . . And in some very real and quite mysterious sense, this particular Table of Jupiter was the most appropriate talisman for Joseph Smith to possess. Indeed, it seemed meant for him, because on all levels of interpretation: planetary, mythological, numerological, astrological, mystical cabalism, and talismatic magic, the Prophet was, in every case, appropriately described.[34]

"Dr. Durham further explained that the magical 'purpose of the Table of Jupiter . . . was to be able to call upon the celestial intelligences, assigned to the particular talisman [and] to assist one in all endeavors.'[35] By invoking the names of these inscribed gods, he said, it guaranteed the possessor of 'riches and favor, and power, and love and peace . . . honors, and dignities, and councils . . . [and to] obtain the power of stimulating anyone to offer his love to the possessor of the talisman.'[36]

"Certainly, he would need this kind of help in his money-digging ventures, not to mention his spiritual-wifery doctrine where he had to convince a woman to become his plural wife while she was still married to her husband.[37]

"Smith's brother, Hyrum, also practiced magic.[38] He possessed parchments containing pentagrams and pentacles used in gaining power over spirits.[39] He also had a Masonic pouch to hold these parchments and a dagger with the seal of Mars.

"Yes, Robert?"

"After Smith died," he asked, "did succeeding church presidents continue in occult practices?"

"Some of them did. Brigham Young wore a chained bloodstone about his neck for those occasions 'when [he went] into unknown or dangerous places.'[40] He also used Oliver Cowdery's divining rod to decide where the Salt Lake temple should be built.[41]

"In addition, when Young and Taylor supervised the making of a woodcut seal for the twelve apostles, they copied occult symbols from Jacob Boehme's *Theosophical Works*—a book used for two hundred years by Christian Kabbalists and Rosicrucians."[42]

Susan raised her hand. "How do present-day leaders respond to all this?"

"Well," I said, "they mostly try to suppress incriminating evidence. But, when it does leak out, the rationale is to justify it as did Arturo de Hoyos. He writes:

> One cannot help but wonder the reason why the Prophet Joseph Smith, and his brother, Hyrum, the Patriarch would possess articles such as they did unless they actually believed that these items did possess some sort of supernatural power, or that they were a "key" to receiving power or protection. *Is it possible that just as the Masonic ritual, which Joseph termed the "apostate endowment" retained principles of truth, that these Pentacles which have come down through the ages to be asscociated [sic] with witchcraft, black magic, and the occult as a whole yet contain elements of truth which were recognized by the Prophet*? [emphasis mine].[43]

"Not a bad rationalization for a Mormon," I smiled.

Matt impatiently called out, "I heard there was a 'bloody ghost' in Smith's story. Let's hear about it!"

The class laughed but perked up with interest.

"The bloody ghost," I began, "was a Spanish spirit who guarded the Book of Mormon plates. Treasure spirits were usually considered evil and were thought to have the power to kill a person unless appeased by magic circles and blood sacrifices. So, here's the story.

"Smith said he had a dream in which he was shown the location of an iron box containing gold plates.[44] He went there, found the spot, but claimed he was knocked down three times while attempting to remove the stone that covered the treasure.[45] He described his experience to two individuals who later published it in the *Amboy Journal*. Quoting what Smith told them, the article describes his frustration:

> "Why can't I get it?" . . . and then he saw a man standing over the spot, which to him appeared like a Spaniard, having a long beard coming down over his breast to about here. (Smith putting his hand to the pit of his stomach) with his (the ghost's) throat cut from ear to ear, and the blood streaming down, who told him that he could not get it alone; that another person whom he, Smith, would know at first sight, must come with him, and then he could get it.[46] [parentheses in original]

"Smith also told the same story to his father. He related how the ghost told him the valuable treasure contained information soon to be revealed to the world.[47]

"As the story developed, however, the bloody ghost soon became a nameless angel, then an angel called Nephi, finally, Moroni."[48]

"Where does Masonry fit into all this?" Susan inquired.

"As Smith learned more about Masonic beliefs," I replied, "he began to weave them into his buried-treasure tale. He borrowed heavily from a Masonic myth called the Legend of Enoch.[49] The parallels are obvious.[50]

"But first, who can recall Smith's story as told by the church today?"

Ilya raised her hand.

"He vas told dat buried in hill Cumorah vas box covered by stone. In box ver gold plates with engraved characters. Also Urim and Thummin and breast plate of high priest of Israel. He vas told dat more plates ver in an underground cavern in hill. On plates vas story of a migration from Tower of Babel. Another migration coming from Jerusalem, guided by a metal ball as compass. . . ."

"Good, Ilya. Now, class, remembering what she said, listen to the Masonic Legend of Enoch.[51]

"The lore begins with God giving a secret doctrine to Adam in a dream. He is shown a gold plate engraved with unknown characters. Among these characters is the tetragrammaton, the holy name of God. Adam makes a similar plate of gold and copies the sacred characters on it. He hands it down to his son Seth who guards it carefully and then passes it on. Finally, it reaches Enoch.[52]

"Enoch then receives a vision of the future. He foresees a world-destroying flood and that the holy treasure will eventually be kept in a secret cavern inside Mount Moriah.

"Therefore, he proceeds to build an underground cavern to preserve the treasure from the flood. He places a stone door over the cavern and erects two pillars, one of marble, the other of brass. On the marble pillar he engraves the story of the treasure and the history of the Tower of Babel in Egyptian hieroglyphics.

"On the second pillar of brass he engraves the history of creation and the principles of Masonry. On the top of the brass pillar he places a metal ball that miraculously solves problems and gives direction. The legend concludes by stating that the treasure will be found by one of Enoch's Israelitish descendants.

"Now, we need to jump from Enoch to the future King Solomon—after the flood.

"Solomon's masons, while building the king's temple on the hill Moriah, come across pieces of the treasure, although not yet the gold plate. They turn their findings over to the king. Solomon then places the treasure in a secret underground vault beneath the temple, just as Enoch saw in his vision. Solomon instructs the three men to go back to the ruins and see if they can find more treasure.

"Upon doing so, they come across the stone that covered Enoch's cave. After three attempts to descend into the cave, they finally obtained the gold plate, noticing that 'the brilliancy of the plate and jewels are of themselves sufficient to give light to the cavern.'[53]

"Delivering the gold plate to the king, Solomon places it in his underground vault along with the breastplate of the high priest of Israel and the Urim and Thummin. Solomon then changes the status of the vault from secret to sacred and allows only a few to see the plate.

"Now," I said in conclusion, "who can see similarities between this legend and Joseph Smith's story?"

"Easy," Matt offered. "Enoch's gold plate was found inside a hill and so were the gold plates of the Book of Mormon."

"Very good. Yes, Tia?"

"Enoch's cavern was covered with a stone and so was Smith's box of gold plates. In addition, both Enoch and Smith claimed their treasure contained the breastplate of the high priest of Israel and the Urim and Thummin."

"Right. Joseph Smith also considered himself the predicted Israelitish descendant who would find the treasure. Incorporating that idea into the Book of Mormon, he even went so far as to give himself the code name of Enoch in revelations.[54]

"But now, let's look at the parallels on the overhead:

Masonic Legend of Enoch	Joseph Smith's Story
• Enoch is shown the hill Moriah in a vision.	• Smith shown the hill Cumorah in a vision.
• Enoch is shown a hidden treasure.	• Smith is shown the gold plates.
• Enoch's treasure includes a gold plate with engravings.	• Smith's gold plates are engraved.
• Enoch's marble pillar is carved with Egyptian hieroglyphics.	• Smith's plates are engraved in reformed Egyptian.
• Enoch's marble pillar tells the story of the treasure.	• Smith's Book of Mormon tells the story of the gold plates.
• Enoch erects a brass pillar that tells the history of creation.	• The Book of Mormon includes brass plates containing the five books of Moses.[55]
• Enoch writes the history of the Tower of Babel on the marble pillar.	• The Book of Mormon contains the book of Ether, a history of a migration from the Tower of Babel.
• Enoch's brass pillar has a metal ball on top that has the power to direct.	• The Book of Mormon tells of a brass ball, the Liahona, that acts as a compass.
• Enoch predicts that after the flood, an Israelitish descendant will find the treasure.	• The Book of Mormon foretells an Israelitish descendant, having the same name as Joseph of Egypt, who will find the treasure.
• Three masons obtain the treasure after three attempts.	• Smith tries to take the plates and is only successful after three attempts.
• Three masons are witnesses to the treasure.	• Smith also arranges for three witnesses: Martin Harris, Oliver Cowdery, and David Whitmer.
• Solomon's treasure contained the gold plate, a brass pillar/record, the high priest's	• Smith's treasure consisted of the brass plates, gold plates, the Urim and Thummin, the

breastplate, the Urim and Thummin and a metal ball. It also contained the Tetragrammaton, the name of God.

- The three masons note that the gold plate gives off enough light to illuminate the cavern.
- Enoch's treasure is first hidden in his own cavern, then later transferred to the hill Moriah.
- King Solomon allows only a few to see the treasure.
- Enoch's cavern is covered by a large stone with an iron ring.
- Enoch is called by God to preserve the knowledge of the treasure.
- King Solomon changes the status of his underground cavern from *secret* to *sacred*.

breastplate, and a metal ball called the Liahona. The plates were claimed to be from God.

- Smith claims the Book of Mormon plates light up the cavern in the hill Cumorah.
- The Book of Mormon plates are first kept in a hill called Shim, then transferred to the hill Cumorah.
- Smith allows only a few to see the plates.
- Smith earlier claimed the plates were in an iron box, but later said it was stone.
- Smith is called by God to preserve the knowledge of his treasure.
- Mormon leaders claim the temple ceremony is not *secret* but *sacred*.

A student's hand shot up. "Was Smith's only objective in producing the Book of Mormon to promote the Legend of Enoch?"

"No," I said. "I believe he had three other motives.

"First, Smith simply loved to con people and put his imaginative powers to work. His mother told how Smith would often entertain the family for hours, relating stories of how the ancient Americans dressed and acted, about their cities, warfare, and religion long before he came up with the idea of writing the Book of Mormon.[56]

"Further, affidavits by Smith's contemporaries report how Smith enjoyed fooling people. For example, after a rain shower, Smith discovered some white sand. He 'tied up several quarts of it [in his "frock"] and then went home.' His family was eager to know what he had. Smith later told Peter Ingersol how he responded: 'At that moment I happened to think about a history found in Canada, called the Golden Bible; so I very gravely told them it was the Golden Bible. To my surprise they were credulous enough to believe what I said.'[57]

"Second, he wanted to answer the big question of the day— are the American Indians transplanted Israelites?

"This was a hot topic. As early as 1634, Joseph Mede was questioning the origin of the American Indians. By 1650, writer Thomas Thorowgood decided they were the lost tribes of Israel. In 1775 and 1816, Elias Boudinot and James Adair brought the idea to the forefront again.[58] Newspapers in Smith's locale also speculated on the origin of the American Indians. Then, in 1823, Ethan Smith wrote *View of the Hebrews* in an attempt to handle the absence of a recorded history of the American Indians.

"Although Smith borrowed much from Ethan Smith's book, his idea for the Book of Mormon in the first place was probably triggered by a magician named Walters:

> [Walters] had an old copy of Cicero's Orations, in the Latin language, out of which he read [in] an unintelligible jargon, which he would afterwards pretend to interpret, and explain, as a record of the former inhabitants of America, and a particular account of the numerous situations where they deposited their treasures previous to their final [destruction].[59]

"Joseph, therefore, influenced by Walters and using Ethan Smith's book, hit on the idea that he would be the one to provide the recorded history.

"But, this required some thought. If his story was going to cover Lamanite settlements in South America and Nephites in Central America, how was he going to get their sacred records to New York, three thousand miles away, for him to find? Obviously, he had to invent a character who would carry them there.

"Common sense, however, asks why the character Mormon, or his son Moroni, would travel three thousand miles *on foot* when they could have buried the plates closer to home. In addition, how could they have transported as many heavy gold plates as Smith described?

"Third, the Book of Mormon provided Smith with an outlet for his fascination with Masonic mysteries—though it was more than just fascination. Smith admits, in a letter to John Hull, that he really wanted to produce a truer and higher level of Masonry.[60] Not just for the United States, but worldwide.[61] Intrigued with the concept, he began using Masonic vocabulary in his sermons, such as the *nail in a sure place*, which was to become part of his temple ceremony. He interjected the motif of sun, moon, planets, and stars. He also took from Masonry the idea of the political kingdom, consisting of a Council of Fifty, a constitution—even the crowning of himself as king.[62] Smith also believed 'the whole earth was compared symbolically to a Grand Masonic Lodge, the counterpart of which was the Grand Lodge in the eternal regions of Glory.'[63]

"There is also the Masonic all-seeing eye that Mormons today erroneously believe is Jehovah's eye. Occult literature, however, reveals it as the Diva, or the Cyclopean Eye, the ancient third eye of spiritual insight used by the Chaldeans, Egyptians, Greeks, and other pagan religions.[64]

"On the temple walls one can also see the beehive, the compass, clasped hands, stars, and the phrase 'Holiness to the Lord.'[65] Even the weather vane of the Nauvoo temple, with its small angel, exhibited the square and compass.[66]

"In the St. George, Utah tabernacle (not the temple), there still remains, on a mock fireplace, a round circle resting on the horizontal arm of a cross. Occult writer Madame Blavatsky explains in her *Secret Doctrine* that this is the 'Venus looking-glass,' a symbol of human procreation and also the 'sacred cross of Egypt' as carried in the hands of the gods, the Pharaohs, and the mummified dead.[67]

"In the Mormon temple ceremony itself, there is the apron, special handshakes and penalties, the five points of fellowship,[68] special garments with markings of the square and compass, and the giving of a new name—all taken from Masonry.

"Probably the most astounding admission on the subject by a Mormon, is made by Dr. Durham:

> The Mormon ceremony which came to be known as the Endowment, introduced by Joseph Smith to Mormon Masons, had an immediate inspiration from Masonry. This is not to suggest that no other source of inspiration could have been involved, but the similarities between the two ceremonies are so apparent and overwhelming that some dependent relationship cannot be denied. They are so similar, in fact, that one writer was led to refer to the Endowment as Celestial Masonry.[69]

"While members of the Mormon Church believe that every jot and tittle of Mormonism, including the temple ceremony, was received by revelation, one is reminded of Dr. Durham's admission about the similarities: 'To explain them only as coincidence would be ridiculous.'[70]

"Smith, to disguise any Masonic connection to his new religion, used *clangs*. These are word inventions intended to mask other words. For example, according to the Tanners, it is believed he incorporated 'the first three letters of Moriah (M-O-Riah) . . . and the last three letters of Solomon (SoloM-O-N),' to come up with *Mor-mon*, which is both the name of his sacred book and the name of its main character.[71]

"Another clang is *Mahonri Moriancumer*, the name of another Book of Mormon character. According to Dr. Durham, the last name, Moriancumer, could easily be 'a compound of "Moriah," the sacred hill where Solomon stored Enoch's treasure—and "Cumorah," the sacred hill where the new Enoch [Smith] found his treasure plates.'[72]

"Moriancumer's first name, Mahonri, according to Walter F. Prince, is clang for Masonry.[73] This is achieved by replacing the *s* in Masonry with an *h* and changing the y to *i*. Therefore, Mahonri Moriancumer, 'divested of "clang" is *Masonry Moriah Cumorah*.'" [emphasis mine].

Robert raised his hand. "Why do you think Joseph was so caught up with Masonry?"

"Because," I quickly replied, "Joseph believed the Masonic ceremony contained rituals practiced by the ancient Eleusinians and the Greek mystery religions. The reason he was attracted to them was because he was convinced they contained secrets handed down from Adam.[74] Dr. Durham also acknowledged this by saying that Joseph Smith accepted Masonry because 'he recognized true Ancient Mysteries contained therein.'"[75]

"If Smith was so sold on Masonry," Robert persisted, "why didn't he simply stick with the Masonic lodge instead of trying to start his own?"

"He became convinced," I said, "that Masonry's teachings handed down from the Hermetic Magi, Babylon, Chaldea, Egypt, and the Kabbalah had been distorted over time.[76] He felt that further back there was a purer Masonry. Dr. Durham further confirmed this by saying that Smith 'believed he was restoring Masonry's original pristine brilliancy, and re-creating the original Mysteries of the ancient Priesthood.'[77]

"I think Joseph's objective was to get to the very root of things and have a religion he could claim contained the most primordial doctrines—ones that originated as close to the beginning of time as possible. He therefore incorporated ideas from the ancient Eleusinian mysteries, gleaned from the *Encyclopaedia Britannica* and other available sources in 1837.[78]

"These cultic mysteries claimed to be rituals handed down from the beginning of the world and revealed only in secret ceremonies. Believed to be revelations from God, the rites could only be passed on to those made worthy through a ritualistic ceremony.

"The rituals included washings and anointings, oaths and penalties, a new name, special garments, covenants of chastity, achieving godhood, and special passwords in order to pass by the sentries who guard the gates of heaven. In addition, most of the ceremony has the initiates watching actors in a drama. Not much different from the Mormon temple ceremony.[79]

"In a way it was a noble endeavor," I said, "however, as I mentioned earlier, the deceit of the whole matter was that Smith passed these ideas off as revelation inspired by the Holy Ghost.[80]

"The following concepts, for example, are believed by members to have been received by revelation:

> [In the beginning] the head God called together the gods and sat in grand council to bring forth the world . . . The mind or the intelligence which man possesses is [co-eternal] with God himself . . . God . . . is an exalted man . . . we have got to learn how to be gods . . . the same as all gods have done before.[81]

"These new insights were first declared at the funeral of a man named King Follett. But, Smith's diary admits that a year before the funeral he studied with a Jewish convert, Alexander Neibauer, who had an extensive library on Jewish mysticism. Smith gleaned many of his complex ideas from him."[82]

"I thought," Robert said, "that Joseph Smith was supposed to be uneducated?"

"Smith's uneducated background," I said, "is often promoted by the LDS leaders, but he was no dummy. He may have been illiterate in the beginning, but he was an avid learner. He had Latin, Hebrew, German, and Greek New Testaments. Whether he could read them all is debatable; however, LDS history says he could read the German New Testament.[83]

"Yes, Susan?"

"All this may be true about Joseph Smith. But, look at the LDS Church today—it doesn't believe all that superstitious stuff now. They have high morals, excellent ethics . . ."

"That's all true, Susan. No one knows that better than I. But, you're missing an important point.

"For example, will you please read Deuteronomy 18:9–14 to the class."

Susan reluctantly flipped the pages of her Bible and began reading in a monotone voice:

Let no one be found among you . . . who practices divination or sorcery, interprets omens, engages in witchcraft, or casts spells, or who is a medium or spiritist or who consults the dead. Anyone who does these things is detestable to the LORD.

"Well," Susan said defiantly, "Mormons *do* believe in Christ!" At the tone of her voice, the students stared in surprise. Susan became flustered.

"Well, I mean," she said with a nervous laugh, "don't they believe in Christ?"

"Even the most radical cults preach Christ," I said. "Therefore, it's always important to examine the foundation. The foundation, in this instance, is Joseph Smith.

"Susan, one could easily be tempted to say, 'Well, let's not hold Joseph Smith against the Mormon Church, look how far they've come. They no longer believe in divining rods, and present-day leaders don't engage in occult practices. But the issue is not that they don't practice them anymore. The issue is—*that* is what their church was built upon!

"A true church," I said, "must line up with *all* of God's Word. In particular, God's true prophet must live a godly life. Can you imagine God allowing his Old Testament prophets to indulge in occult activities? Smith's reputation was so bad, in this respect, that he was refused membership in the Methodist Church.

"When Joseph Smith asked to join, the preacher was unaware of his occult activities and put his name on the rolls.[84] Eventually, however, a board member, Joseph Lewis, heard about it and objected. He said, 'Joseph's manner of life rendered him unfit to be a member' and Smith was asked to withdraw unless he wanted to recant, confess, and reform himself. Smith refused.[85] Later, in the *Amboy* paper, Lewis, along with a local preacher, Joshua McKune, explained:

We thought it was a disgrace to the church to have a practicing necromancer, a dealer in enchantments and bleeding ghosts . . . his occupation, habits and moral character were at variance with the discipline [and] his name would be a disgrace to the church.[86]

"Susan, it makes no difference whether Mormons have good ethics or profess a belief in Christ. If the foundation is not what it claims to be, it's a lie."

"Well," Susan said, somewhat more subdued, "you've made your point. But, I wonder why Mormon leaders don't wipe the slate clean, tell the truth to their members, gradually get rid of weird beliefs, and continue to build their church around their ethics and belief in Jesus?"

"Mormon leaders," I replied, "find themselves between a rock and a hard place. Knowing, as they do, the facts about Joseph Smith, they realize that if they admit to them, they chance destroying the faith of their members. Therefore, out of necessity they have to continue whitewashing the image of Joseph Smith and extolling the divine foundation of the church. As a result, Mormons are deceived.

"No individual who knows the truth about the Mormon Church's occult background could possibly follow Joseph Smith as a prophet or embrace his teachings. It would be a futile faith—like trying to build a house on a foundation of shifting sand.

"But, now," I said, "our time is running out, so let's quickly run over what we've covered.

"Today, we learned four ways in which Smith was directed to the gold plates. His associates said Joseph found them through a brown seer stone. Smith, however, claimed to be directed to them by; first, a Spanish ghost; second, a dream; then finally, an angel.

"In addition, he was involved in ritual magic, the occult, blood sacrifices, divining rods, and peep stones. He also incorporated Masonic rituals and ancient religious ceremonies into his new church, passing them off as revelation. He then conned people into believing they were requirements for salvation."

"Do you think," Susan interrupted, "that Smith really had any gold plates?"

"Well, if he had any," I replied, "they couldn't possibly have been gold. With the measurements being 7" x 8" x 6" and with gold weighing one and a half pounds per cubic inch, they would have weighed nearly two hundred pounds if solid. Even allowing that they weren't solid and deducting some of the weight to allow for spaces between sheets and the hollowed-out engravings, it isn't possible. There is no way Joseph, according to his mother's story, could have tucked them beneath one arm, walked home, jumped over a log and run a mile from would-be attackers.[87] Neither could his Book of Mormon characters carry them on foot three thousand miles from Central America to New York."

Suddenly Matt changed the subject by asking, "When are you and Susan meeting with the Mormon Elders again?"

"Tomorrow night," I said. "Their lesson will be on the Book of Mormon. They'll no doubt quote Isaiah 29:14 and Ezekiel 37 and probably throw in Meso-American archaeology for good measure.

"But, don't worry," I laughed, "Susan and I will report, so you won't miss out on anything."

With a few minutes to spare I quickly gave the class their assignment and dismissed them. Susan, for some reason, hurried out of the classroom before I could talk to her. Tia, I noticed, hung back.

Fussing with papers on my desk, I gave her an opening. When the classroom finally emptied, she walked over.

"Interesting lesson," she said. "I'm looking forward to hearing about South American ruins—I'm sure it's something I'll have to deal with when I become a missionary."

Then her face clouded. "I thought maybe you ought to know something," she hesitantly began. "Wendy, daughter of that fellowshipping family, called Susan and invited her to a Ward basketball game tonight."

"Did she accept?" I asked, already surmising the answer.

"Yeah, that's why she left so quickly. I tried to talk her out of it," Tia said defensively. "But, she said there was nothing wrong with going to a simple basketball game. But, I know she's hoping the missionaries will be there."

My heart sank as I plopped into my chair. "She still doesn't know what she's getting into," I sighed.

"Well," Tia continued, "I'm concerned over something else. She's really got it bad for Elder Black—I mean, he's all she talks about. She's convinced that because Elder Black loves the Lord, he'll give up his religion for her.

"I'm not supposed to tell you this, but she received a letter from him. It was a real nice letter, talking about how he loved the Mormon gospel. He also said he only has a few months before his mission is over and hopes to see her after that."

I shook my head disapprovingly. "Has Susan talked at all about the biblical errors the missionaries made in their lessons? Has she indicated that *anything* we've discussed in class is changing her mind?"

"Yes," Tia replied, "and she has times when she really gets down in the dumps over it. I've even heard her crying at night."

"Well," I said, "Elder Black may be interested in her. But, if she thinks he's going to give up Mormonism," I shook my head sadly, "she's in for a hard blow. I wish you could have tried harder to talk her out of going."

"I tried, but you know Susan—she even invited me to come along."

"Tia, you're her best friend—you've got to do what you can. Try to make her see that Wendy's friendship has only one purpose—to convert her to Mormonism. Elder Black's objective is the same.

"If Elder Black pursues a romantic relationship with her after he's released he'll, of course, insist on a temple marriage. Then, Susan is going to be faced with a heavy dilemma. She'll have to choose between the Bible and a false faith. Will she be strong or will she give up her faith in Jesus for faith in Joseph Smith? Not an easy decision when one is young and emotions are involved," I smiled grimly.

Walking out of the classroom together, we paused beneath a large mesquite tree. For another fifteen minutes I continued talking, trying to provide Tia with ways to help Susan.

When we parted, I wondered if my efforts with Susan were really doing any good. Maybe I'd made a terrible mistake by not reporting her to the dean in the beginning. But, knowing how headstrong Susan was, she would have sneaked and gone anyway. Well, I rationalized, at least she wasn't attending their lessons alone.

Walking toward my car, I contemplated the next missionary meeting. If I was going to get through to Susan, I decided, I'd have to quit being so polite with the Elders and confront them head on.

Perhaps, by my challenging them more, Susan would see the fallacy of their beliefs. More importantly, see where Elder Black truly stood and the futility of pursuing a relationship.

CHAPTER EIGHT

The Second Missionary Presentation

The Book of Mormon as another testament of Christ

The crashing of cymbals and beating of native drums filled Ellen's darkened front room. Egyptian music in all its strange disharmony rose in ever-increasing crescendos. Colorful scenes of ancient America flashed on the screen before us—esoteric pyramids, dense jungles, feathered serpents—all glaring down from stone colonnades. The mystery of the ruins mesmerized us as Susan and I were transported two thousand years into the past.

Then, flutes, soft and eerie, began a slow oriental melody and a resonant voice began:

> The Indians of North and South America were descendants of an unknown people dating before Columbus. Their remains testify to the greatness of their civilization.
>
> Scholars, unable to translate their inscriptions, have wondered about the secret of their origin.
>
> If only these ancient inhabitants had left a record we would know who the ancestors of the Mayans and Aztecs were. Many traditions have survived. In particular, the two-thousand-year-old legend of the white bearded God, Quetzalcoatl.
>
> Hernando Cortez, landing near Mexico City, was surprised when he was honored as a deity by Montezuma. When Captain James Cook landed in the Hawaiian Islands, the natives welcomed him, as if expected. Why?

The natives believed these two men were Quetzalcoatl, the great white God of their forefathers who promised to return.

Who was this white god, Quetzalcoatl? Why had he left such an indelible impression? Is it possible that Jesus Christ visited the Americas?

Could Jesus have been speaking of these ancient inhabitants when he said in John 10:16, "Other sheep I have which are not of this fold. Them, too, I must visit"? The answer is, yes.

Christ came to the Americas shortly after his resurrection. He came to his other sheep who were descendants of the house of Israel. The account of how they were led from the Holy Land to America can be found in the Book of Mormon.

This ancient record of the Western Hemisphere tells of their civilization; also about prophets who foretold Christ's ministry on the Eastern Hemisphere. They prophesied that he would eventually appear to them in the New World, after his resurrection . . .

Ethereal music began to play gently in the background. The deep, rich voice of the narrator paused then continued as dramatic scenes of Third Nephi began to unfold:

Shortly after Jesus' resurrection, these early Americans were gathered around their temple when they heard a voice from heaven: "Behold my Beloved Son, in whom I am well pleased, in whom I have glorified my name—hear ye him."

Looking up, they saw a man dressed in a white robe descending from heaven. He said: "Behold, I am Jesus Christ, whom the prophets testified shall come into the world."

He then ministered, taught them, and set up his church. This great event was recorded in their sacred record. Mormon, the last warrior prophet, passed this sacred record on to his son, Moroni, who hid them in the ground for future generations.

Centuries, after Moroni hid the sacred record, Joseph Smith was divinely led to the stone box and translated it by the power of God!

The filmstrip then focused on a picture of the Book of Mormon:

The Book of Mormon, as a companion to the Bible, is a second testament that Jesus is the Christ. It is Ezekiel's other "stick" which was to become one with the stick of Judah, the Bible. It is also the fulfillment of Isaiah's sealed book, God's marvelous work and a wonder!

A large Bible hovered over the map of the Holy Land and a Book of Mormon over North and South America. Voices of the Tabernacle choir swelled, as the narrator made his dramatic conclusion:

> The Book of Mormon is another testament to the world that Jesus is the Christ!

Cymbals once again clashed, a picture of Christ appeared, and the choir's voices rose to a grand and thrilling crescendo. Then, THE END abruptly appeared.

Ellen flipped on the lights while Elder Barrett attended to the projector.

Pretty good production, I thought to myself. *I hope Susan remembers it's all fiction.*

"I'm so glad I found this old filmstrip!" Ellen exclaimed. "Missionaries don't usually show these anymore—they use VCR tapes instead. I was lucky to find it in our Ward library. Since our TV is being repaired, I didn't want us to miss it."

"Very interesting," Susan said with a polite smile, trying not to let on to me that she was impressed. Then I noticed her flash a demure smile at Elder Black who eagerly returned it.

I groaned inwardly. Between Susan's infatuation with Elder Black and her new friendship with Wendy, was I making any headway?

Hoping to talk with Susan before the meeting, I had been disappointed. A late faculty meeting had forced us to come in separate cars.

Elder Barrett then asked, "Did you have any special feelings while watching this film?"

Feelings again.

"Well," Susan offered, trying to avoid admitting to any, "it did portray a dramatic story. If it were true," she laughed, "it would certainly be the message of the century."

Elder Black exhibited a wide grin. "Well, we're here to tell you that it is. Indeed, it's the greatest message since the birth of the Savior!"

Elder Barrett then began reiterating the history of the Book of Mormon. He told of three migrations, one led by Lehi in 601 B.C., the Mulekites about 589 B.C., and the Jaredites, a colony from the Tower of Babel who were fortunate not to have their language confused.

I doubted that the elders knew that Smith got his idea of God's preserving the Jaredites' language from Masonry. It taught that at the time of Nimrod, who as Grand Master and builder of the Tower of Babel, God favored all the masons, allowing them to retain the universal language.[1]

Hmmm, I thought, *then the Jaredites would be Masons.*

"Do you have any questions?" Elder Barrett asked.

We shook our heads as I wondered which part of this lesson I was going to jump in on—archaeology or Scripture.

Quickly reaching into his briefcase, Elder Barrett pulled two black books out and handed them to us.

"Here's a Book of Mormon for both of you," he said proudly.

Briefly leading us through the title page, he read aloud its statement that it was for "the convincing of the Jew and Gentile that Jesus is the Christ."

Then he turned to the testimony of the three witnesses, whom he boasted never recanted their testimony. Finally, to Joseph Smith's story about the angel Moroni and a list of Bible references contained in the footnotes.

"I'd like to share a favorite passage of mine," Elder Black offered. It's about a great king who lived about 120 B.C. His example has always been an inspiration to me. "Will you turn to the book of Mosiah on page 148?" After giving us a moment, he continued:

"Shortly before he died, King Benjamin called his people together and spoke to them:

> Behold, I say unto you that because I said unto you that I had spent my days in your service, I do not desire to boast, for I have only been in the service of God.
> And behold, I tell you these things that ye may learn wisdom; that ye may learn that when ye are in the service of your fellow beings, ye are only in the service of your God.[2]

"King Benjamin stated a wonderful principle," Elder Black said, "You'll find that the Book of Mormon presents many Christlike teachings.

"Before the Book of Mormon was translated," he continued, "the Bible was the only book declaring the plan of salvation. But, now we have the Book of Mormon as *another* testament of Jesus Christ containing the *fullness* of the everlasting gospel.

"Now, Elder, will you read 2 Corinthians 13:1?"

Elder Barrett quickly thumbed through the pages of his King James Version and began reading, "In the mouth of two or three witnesses shall every word be established."

"This is a law that God set up," Elder Black explained.

"However, because the Bible is only *one* witness of Christ, God had to provide a second witness.[3]

"And why is a second witness so important?" he asked rhetorically. "Let me give you an example.

"If you wanted to hang a door, you wouldn't try to hang it on only one hinge. Why? Because one hinge makes the door unstable. However, two hinges make the door more secure.

"It's the same with the Bible and the Book of Mormon. Both are like two hinges. Together, they more firmly establish the truth of the Gospel of Jesus Christ."

I glanced at Susan whose expression indicated she was at a loss in the face of this logic. *Time to jump in*, I decided.

"So, Elders," I said, "what you are really saying is the Bible, like one hinge, is unstable all by itself?"

After a long pause, Elder Black finally said, "Of course not. It's just that the more confirmations one receives, the stronger one's testimony. God wants us to be thoroughly convinced that His gospel is the only true Gospel.

"After all, we know there are parts of the Bible that have been copied and translated so many times that they contain mistakes and deletions. That's why our Articles of Faith declare that we believe the Bible is the Word of God only as far as it is translated correctly.

"But, on the other hand," he added, "the Book of Mormon is the pure word of God, having only been translated once. Therefore, Book of Mormon scriptures are more correct than what we have in the Bible.

"Notwithstanding that," he quickly added, "we do love the Bible and reverence Jesus Christ."

"Well, now," I interrupted, "I'm afraid I have a problem with your statement that the Bible contains many errors. You're familiar with the discovery of the Dead Sea Scrolls, aren't you?" They nodded, but looked vague.

"When this discovery was first announced," I began, "LDS scholars felt it would finally vindicate the Book of Mormon. After all, the Dead Sea Scrolls were a thousand years older than the oldest manuscript of the Bible then in existence.[4] They felt the Isaiah scroll, in particular, would validate the section of Isaiah contained in the Book of Mormon. But, two surprises came out of that study.

"The first was that the Old Testament of the King James Bible had been well preserved after all.[5] Ninety-five percent of the words from the Isaiah scroll were identical with the Hebrew text in our present Bible. The other five percent, consisted of minor 'slips of the pen and variations in spelling.'[6]

"The second surprise was that it did *not* validate the Isaiah text in the Book of Mormon.

"Further, a BYU student, in his master's thesis, also compared the Book of Mormon version of Isaiah with the Dead Sea Isaiah and was also forced to the same but disappointing conclusion. There were, he stated, 'no noteworthy instances of support for the Book of Mormon claims.'"[7]

"But," Elder Black interrupted, "he was only a student, certainly not an authority on the subject."

"Well," I said, "you might be right on that. However, let me ask you this. If someone on the faculty of BYU produced a study, would you accept what he said?"

They half nodded, fearing what I was going to spring next.

"Well, Dr. Sidney B. Sperry came to the same conclusion as the student," I said.[8]

Elder Barrett spoke quickly. "I have no doubt that more evidence will eventually come to light that will substantiate the Book of Mormon. However," he added, "there is one validation that is superior to physical evidence!"

Here it comes, I thought.

"It is the witness of the Holy Ghost," he declared. "Both Elder Black and I have received that witness. We *know* that the Book of Mormon is true and that it contains the Word of God even in the face of evidence that appears contradictory."

"In spite of the *facts*, Elder? Facts can also be a testimony."

"I can only go by the testimony that God has given me," he stated. "Also, the testimony he gives to others. For example, the witnesses to the Book of Mormon.

"Do you remember that 2 Corinthians 13:1 says that God requires two or three witnesses to establish a truth? Well, God saw to it that He provided *eleven* for the Book of Mormon!"

Quickly turning to the front of the Book of Mormon, he pointed to the testimony of the three witnesses. "They heard God's voice declaring that the plates were translated by the power of God."

"Elder Black," I gently began, "I understand that both of you revere the testimony of those men with all your heart. However, since your own Dr. Hugh Nibley at BYU stated that the Book of Mormon '*should* be tested,' [emphasis mine].[9] I'm sure you won't mind some questions?"

They both nodded.

"Do you believe," I asked, "that viewing an object in real life is the same as seeing it in a vision?"

"No," Elder Black replied, "naturally there's a difference. However," he added, "the vision might indeed be from God."

"Well," I began, "what if I were to tell you that I had a vision where an angel showed me the rod Moses used. What if I described it as having the shape of a bull's head at the top, with the rest of the staff carved in Greek letters?"

"Could you say to me that you believe my vision without any reservation? Could you testify with certainty that you know Moses' rod looked *exactly* like that?"

"No, of course not," Elder Barrett said. "How would I know but what you conjured the vision up out of your own head? I might believe it, but there would be no real proof unless the rod was actually found. That is . . ." he hesitated, "unless the Holy Ghost witnessed the truth to me."

"But," I asked, "if archaeologists did indeed find Moses' rod, then which would you say would carry more weight—my vision or seeing the actual rod?"

"Obviously seeing the real thing. But," he added, suspecting where I was headed, "concerning the Book of Mormon plates, the three witnesses actually *saw* the plates in broad daylight."

"Are you sure?" I asked.

"Why of course," he puzzled, pointing to the page. "It says so, right here."

"According to LDS history," I offered, "this printed testimony doesn't tell *how* they saw the plates." The Elders looked perplexed.

"In the LDS *Church Almanac*," I continued, "it states that the three witnesses 'viewed the plates in a vision.'[10] That means it was similar to my vision of Moses' rod."

Pulling a small piece of paper from my purse, I said, "Martin Harris, after being asked 'Did you see those plates with your naked eyes?' told John Gilbert, the printer of the Book of Mormon, 'No, I saw them with a *spiritual* eye.'[11] Harris later answered the same question of an attorney who came to Palmyra. He said, 'Why, I did not see them as I do that pencil case, yet I saw them with the *eye of faith*. I saw them just as distinctly as I saw anything about me—though at the time they were *covered over with a cloth*.' [emphasis mine].[12]

"Now, Elders, if they were covered with a cloth, there's no way he or the other witnesses could actually see them. The only alternative is a vision.

"And if it was a vision, how can I be sure it wasn't conjured up out of their own mind because they wanted so desperately to obtain a witness?

"But," Elder Barrett said firmly, "the other eight witnesses actually *hefted* the plates."

"Well, now, they could have been *hefting* something else," I suggested. "It would have been an easy thing, especially since Oliver Cowdery had been a blacksmith, to make a set of metal plates.[13] And since they were covered with a cloth, the makeshift plates wouldn't have needed much detail—only the necessary weight.

"Elders," I said, "I guess my main question is this: If Martin Harris admitted it was really a vision and all indications seem to point to this, why isn't this made clear in the published statement printed in the Book of Mormon?"

As I watched the Elders' confusion, I suddenly felt sorry for them. Here I was destroying two young men's faith. Nevertheless, I felt this was the best way to get through to Susan—she had to be my primary concern.

Elder Black spoke up. "While we understand that it's normal for you to have questions, it's well to remember that many enemies of the church have made statements about the witnesses to the Book of Mormon that aren't true—even going so far as to sign affidavits slandering the prophet, Joseph Smith."

"But, Elders," I interrupted. "I didn't quote *enemies* of your church. I quoted Martin Harris himself, Brigham Young University, and the LDS Church's own *Almanac*." [14]

"Then we feel," Elder Barrett insisted, "that you have taken isolated statements which, if quoted in full context, would probably clarify the matter. This is why a *testimony* of the gospel is so important. If, for example, the Holy Ghost gave you a special testimony of your vision of Moses' rod, then that would settle it."

"Even," I asked, "if the vision portrayed *Greek* letters on his rod?"

They nodded, without realizing the absurdity of Moses using Greek.

"Both Elder Black and myself," he continued, "have received a special testimony that the gospel is true.[15] We *know* that Joseph Smith translated the plates by the power of God. Further, God went beyond His requirement of two or three witnesses and provided eleven! Yes, a testimony given by the Holy Ghost is the *surest* witness."

Elder Black turned to Susan. "Did you pray about whether Joseph Smith was a prophet, like we suggested?"

"No," she replied shyly.

"We hope both of you will do this," he said. "John 14:26 says the Holy Ghost will give you this testimony—so also does 1 Corinthians 2:9–16. And, remember, the influence of the Spirit is always a good and peaceful *feeling*.

"We further suggest that you start reading the Book of Mormon and compare its truths with those in the Bible. As your prayers are answered, the Holy Ghost will let you know that what we are telling you is true. We then hope you will want to follow Christ by being baptized."

Turning especially to me, he said, "It's obvious you've read a lot about our Church. However, we respectfully suggest that instead of concentrating on history, that you focus on receiving a spiritual confirmation.

"Here is a pamphlet listing Scriptures to read, both in the Book of Mormon and in the Bible.[16] After you do that," he said, turning to Moroni 10:4, "we'd like you to prayerfully consider this promise:

> And when ye shall receive these things, I would exhort you that ye would ask God, the Eternal Father, in the name of Christ, if these things are not true; and if ye shall ask with a sincere heart, with real intent, having faith in Christ, he will manifest the truth of it unto you by the power of the Holy Ghost.

"Will you do this by next Thursday?"

While Susan nodded out of desperation, I marveled at how quick they were to ignore everything I had pointed out.

I had proved the accuracy of the Bible by showing evidence from the Dead Sea Scrolls. I had told them a BYU professor concluded the Isaiah text in the Dead Sea Scrolls did *not* back up the Book of Mormon. I had challenged them on the fallacy of their two-hinged door analogy that suggested the Bible could not stand by itself. I had pointed out that the testimony of the three witnesses was a vision and that this important fact was purposely left out of the statement in the front of the Book of Mormon. But, in all that, they still relied on their *testimony*.

I decided there should be a plaque hung over the door of every Ward chapel, *Pray—never mind the facts!*

Elder Black's voice suddenly broke my musings. "Since there are parts of the Bible that *are* accurate," he said, "we'd like to show you the ones that tell about the Book of Mormon. Susan, would you look up Ezekiel 37:15–19?" Susan quickly complied and began reading:

> Moreover, thou son of man, take thee one stick, and write upon
> it, *For Judah*, and for the children of Israel his companions:
> then take another stick and write upon it, *For Joseph*, the stick
> of Ephraim, and for all the house of Israel his companions:
> And join them one to another into one stick; and they shall be-
> come one in thine hand [emphasis mine].

Elder Barrett then dramatically held up both the Bible and the Book of Mormon in one hand.

"These are the two sticks! The prophecy of Ezekiel is fulfilled!"

Sadly I thought, *How can I burst their bubble? But, burst it I must for Susan's sake.*

"Elders, that Scripture is certainly impressive. However, would you please tell me what your interpretation of *sticks* is?"

Obviously pleased that I was finally asking a question they could answer, Elder Barrett jumped in.

"In ancient times parchments, or records, were rolled up on a stick and used for writing. These scrolls were called *sticks*.

"In this passage, God is prophetically foretelling that two sticks, or scrolls, are to be brought together and used as one."

"Elder," I asked, "have you ever looked up the Hebrew word for *stick* or *scroll*?" They got that uncomfortable look again.

"The word for *stick*," I offered, "is *'ēs* or *ets*, meaning 'cut wood.' This is exactly the word Ezekiel used. Nowhere, in the Hebrew is *stick* or *'ēs* ever used to indicate a *scroll*. Whenever Ezekiel referred to a roll of the book, as in 2:9, he used the correct word, *megillah*. If he had chosen to use the more specific word, *scroll*, as in Isaiah 34:4, he would have said *cepher*. Therefore, the two sticks, *'ēs*, in Ezekiel 37 refer to neither a scroll or a roll of a book but plain wood.

"In fact, one of your own members, author Everett Landon, in *The Book of Mormon Foundation* confirms this and cautions Latter-day Saints to stop saying sticks are scrolls![17]

"But," I said, "for the sake of argument, suppose *'ēs* did mean scroll. Could the Book of Mormon be the record of Joseph through Ephraim? The answer is no—because the Book of Mormon itself states that it is a history of the descendants of Manasseh, not Ephraim.[18] In addition, the Book of Mormon was never a scroll, not even a stick of wood, but metal plates."

"So," Elder Black interjected, hoping by a polite inquiry to stump me, "what do *you* think Ezekiel 37 is about?"

"After King Solomon's death," I began, "the kingdom of Israel was divided in two—the north and the south. The two tribes of Judah and Benjamin were in the south under Rehoboam and were called the kingdom of Judah. In the north, under Jeroboam, were Joseph, Ephraim, and Israel, the collective name for the ten tribes.

"Thus, we have ten tribes in the north and two in the south—twelve divided tribes.

"Now, if you read verses 20 and 21 of Ezekiel 37, God explains that He intends to gather the northern and southern kingdoms of Judah and Israel (also called Ephraim) back to Palestine and 'make them one nation again.'

"The reason God had Ezekiel write on these two sticks: 'For Judah,' and 'For Joseph/Ephraim,' was simply to present a visual aid to the people. By seeing it vividly illustrated, they would understand God's message."

"Well," Elder Black began, "I believe we simply have a difference of interpretation here. We *know* that Ezekiel is prophesying of the Book of Mormon. *Our* leaders who are prophets, seers, and revelators have said so. We also have been given a special testimony in our heart.

"However, our eleventh Article of Faith states that we allow all men the privilege of worshipping how, where, or what they may. Therefore, we must respect your interpretation."

I sighed . . . was this even worth it? Secretly I had hoped the blinders would come off, but no such luck.

Elder Barrett continued. "There's one more Scripture we'd like to read. It so strongly points to Joseph Smith and his calling to translate that we feel you will have to agree. Would you please turn to Isaiah 29:11–14?"

I began reading:

> And the vision of all is become unto you as the words of a book that is sealed, which men deliver to one that is learned, saying, Read this, I pray thee: and he saith, I cannot; for it is sealed: And the book is delivered to him that is not learned, saying, Read this, I pray thee: and he saith, I am not learned. Wherefore the Lord said, Forasmuch as this people draw near me with their mouth, and with their lips do honour me, but have

removed their heart far from me . . . Therefore, behold I will proceed to do a marvelous work among this people, even a marvelous work and a wonder: for the wisdom of their wise men shall perish, and the understanding of their prudent men shall be hid.

"Who," asked Elder Barrett, "is this *learned* man and who is the *unlearned*? And where is the sealed book? It certainly isn't the Bible."

Before I could answer, he pressed on.

"We testify that the learned man was Professor Charles Anthon of New York City. Martin Harris took a copy of the Book of Mormon characters to him for validation.

"Professor Anthon, in turn, gave him a certificate stating the translation was correct.[19] But, when he found out an angel delivered it, he tore it up. He then asked Harris to bring the plates to him for translation. After explaining that part of the plates were sealed, Professor Anthon replied, 'I cannot read a sealed book,' thus fulfilling Isaiah 29:11!

"Next," Elder Barrett asked, "who was the *unlearned* man?"

"Joseph Smith," Elder Black offered enthusiastically, "an uneducated youth! He translated the record and it became God's marvelous work and a wonder!"

Looking quite pleased, both Elders waited, certain I could not possibly dispute the remarkable parallel.

"If you'll allow me, Elders, I'd like to back up and look at verse one. Can you tell me who God is talking to?" Silence.

"Susan?"

"Ariel, the city of David, or Jerusalem" she replied.

"Isaiah," I continued, "is speaking to Jerusalem, telling them that because of their transgressions God is going to use the dreaded Assyrians as a chastening rod by allowing them attack Jerusalem. Why?

"Because both their *learned* and *unlearned* had removed their hearts far from God and were listening to the precepts of men. Further, they rejected God's omniscience. That is, in the midst of their evil doings there were saying in verse 15, 'Who seeth us? and who knoweth us?' Verse 16 explains that what they were doing was turning things 'upside down'—as if they were the potter and could mold and shape their lives anyway they saw fit. But God as their true potter both saw and knew them and reminds them that He is the potter and they are the clay, not the reverse.[20]

"As a result, the hearts of the Jews were hardened to the point where the divine message of the prophets was meaningless to them—like a *sealed book* that they couldn't read.

"Because of their self-chosen blindness and deafness God decided, as a just judgment upon them, to give the 'book of prophecy' to them *sealed*. In so doing, He caused the wisdom and understanding of their wise men to perish.

"But," I said, "here comes the *marvelous work and a wonder*!

"In spite of the Jews' blindness and deafness to His Word and in spite of God's pronouncement of punishment, He intended to redeem Jerusalem!

"In verse 18 He explains that at some time in the future, as a result of the work God would perform, He will cause their blind eyes to see out of 'obscurity and darkness' and their 'deaf ears' to once again hear the words of the figurative book. The marvelous work of God's chastisement would be acknowledged and Jerusalem would turn to Him and once again 'sanctify His Name' (v. 23).

"Therefore," I concluded, "Isaiah's prediction is *not* about a literal book in a land that no one in that day had ever heard of. Nor is it about a professor in New York City."

As I waited for their response, the doorbell suddenly startled everyone. Ellen got up and opened it, only to find Wendy who had forgotten her key. The moment was lost and the missionaries, I decided, were saved by the bell.

I turned my attention to Wendy. She was a delightfully exuberant girl with long auburn hair. Waving a friendly hello to Susan, she apologized for interrupting. Ellen, obviously grateful for the timing, said we were already through.

Refreshments were quickly served and Wendy and Susan moved off to one corner to chat, leaving me with the Elders.

They made awkward conversation, asking how I knew so much about their church. My role as a college teacher seemed to satisfy them. But, I sensed that if it weren't for Susan whom they believed was more of a potential convert, they would have point-blank questioned my continuing.

Ellen, on the other hand, was her usual cheerful self—but, that was her role. She gushed over me as if nothing had happened.

Leaving the house, frustrated, I walked toward my car. I had hoped to corner Susan before I took off, but she and Wendy were intent on chatting. All I could do was pray that the Lord would provide the right time to have a serious talk with her.

As I thought about the evening's lesson, more especially the filmstrip, I was disappointed there had been no opportunity to talk about archaeology. Well, tomorrow Bobbycito would be in class. I was sure he'd bring up the subject.

CHAPTER NINE

Archaeological Ruins of the Americas

So-called proof for the Book of Mormon

The door of the classroom burst open as a man in a bright striped serape of yellow and green stood in the entrance. With a swarthy face grinning from beneath a large sombrero, he adjusted accordion straps about his shoulders. Then, with an explosion of arpeggios, his fingers deftly ran over the keyboard, filling the room with music as his arms pumped with gusto.

Startled, but delighted, the class quickly joined in with whistles, *gritos*, and stomps. With a thunderous chord that rattled the windows, he ended with an artistic flourish.

"Bobbycito, please come in!" I laughed.

"Class, I asked our ambassador from Mexico, Pastor Bob, to share his concern about Mormon missionaries south of the border."

Quickly slipping the straps from his shoulders, Bobbycito set the accordion down and walked to the front of the room.

"I am *muy* happy to be here . . ." The class interrupted with laughter. He grinned, looking somewhat embarrassed.

"I am *very* happy to be here," he said. "I don't know how many of you are planning on being missionaries, but I would like to tell you what's happening in Mexico and other parts of Latin America.

"Mormon influence is growing. In 1980, there were only seven hundred thousand Mormons in Latin America. By 1993, membership had grown to 2.7 million, an increase in thirteen years of two million![1]

"While the Mormon missionaries have great appeal because of their church's family values, there is another attraction—the Book of Mormon. When Mormon Elders present it as a record of the Indian's ancestors, it naturally invites interest."

Robert raised his hand. "What do the missionaries actually say?"

"It varies. They may call attention to the great pyramidlike structures, stating that the Book of Mormon people built them. Or, they will say, 'No one has been able to discover the origin of the Indians until the Book of Mormon was translated.'

"They may further tell of carbon dating and Mayan calendars that correspond closely to the time of the Jaredites and Nephites.

"They also bring up the Indian legend of Quetzalcoatl—the bearded white god who once ruled their ancestors.

"They may also call attention to the Tree of Life stone found in Peru, claiming it was carved in memory of Lehi's dream recorded in the Book of Mormon.

"These are just a few of the claims they make. While I firmly believe that the Book of Mormon is an invention of Joseph Smith's, I'm still at a loss as how to refute their statements. Maybe my good friend," he said turning and smiling at me, "can provide some insights."

Anxious to address one of my favorite subjects, I quickly joined him at the front of the class.

"Years ago, as a Mormon," I began, "I constantly devoured Mormon publications about archaeological finds. I was convinced beyond a doubt that South American ruins validated the Book of Mormon.

"I even helped perpetuate the rumor that the Smithsonian Institute used the Book of Mormon as a scientific guide."

Bobbycito interrupted. "What would help me refute Mormon claims are some hard archaeological facts."

"Okay," I said. "That's exactly what we'll do.

"Class, pretend that missionaries are trying to convince you that South American ruins validate the Book of Mormon. What kind of archeological evidence would be helpful in disproving their claim?"

The class was silent for a minute, then a few hands raised slowly.

"Robert?"

"The first thing that comes to mind is language. Since the Book of Mormon is supposed to be written in reformed Egyptian, I'd

need to know if archaeologists had found any Egyptian hieroglyphics in America"

"Okay," I said, writing *language* on the board, "what else?"

A student called out, "Have any names of Book of Mormon
cities been uncovered?"

"Great!"

Ilya quickly raised her hand. "Since Book of Mormon's major
migration came from Jerusalem, is der any vay to prove racial connection between Indians and Jews?"

"Good question, Ilya," I said, listing it on the board with the
others.

"Explain Quetzalcoatl!" Susan challenged.

Thank goodness she's listening, I thought, *I'd better answer this
one for sure.*

The questions then came more rapidly.

"What about special artifacts mentioned in the Book of Mormon?" another asked. "Have any been found?"

"Has anything Jewish been uncovered?" another called out.

"Does the Book of Mormon use any Old Testament terms that
Joseph Smith didn't know about?" Tia asked.

"What do non-Mormon archaeologists say about the origin of
the Mayans and Aztecs?"

"Okay, we've got enough." Starting to read from the blackboard, I said, "We have some good subjects here:

- Language—evidence of reformed Egyptian?
- Names of cities—Book of Mormon names unearthed?
- Jewish findings?—evidence of Jewish worship among
  Indians?
- Artifacts—any found verifying Book of Mormon
  products?
- Incorrect terms used by Joseph Smith in the Book of
  Mormon?
- Quetzalcoatl—was he Jesus?
- Racial connection—between Jews and Indians?

"We won't list what archaeologists state," I said, "since those
will come out during our examination of the questions.

"So, let's start with language first."

Robert raised his hand. "I just got to thinking . . . How come Smith
said that the Book of Mormon was written in Egyptian? If his characters were from Jerusalem, wouldn't they have written in Hebrew?"

"Good observation, Robert. This is one weakness of Smith's book.

"When Lehi left Jerusalem in 600 B.C., no Jew spoke Egyptian. One author points out how preposterous it would have been for Lehi and his family to use Egyptian in any form. They were pure Hebrews—had lived there all their lives, were surrounded by people who only spoke Hebrew, and their people hadn't spoken Egyptian since they left Egypt under Moses.[2]

"If Moses, trained to speak Egyptian, chose to speak and write in Hebrew—as well as the whole nation of Israel after having lived in Egypt for four hundred years—why, then, as author Anthony Hoekema asks, 'should Nephi, who apparently had never lived in Egypt, write in Egyptian?'[3] Further, since the Jews hated the Egyptians, it would have been an insult for Lehi to have used that language.

"Here's another problem. The Book of Mormon says Lehi's family brought brass plates with them containing Old Testament Scriptures. But, in Egyptian? This truly staggers the imagination.[4]

"Who would have written them in Egyptian in the first place? Certainly no self-respecting Jew—especially since Egyptian script is nonalphabetic. Hebrew writing, which is alphabetic, would offer a higher capacity to convey shades of meaning."

"Then, I wonder," Robert mused, "what made Smith decide to say it was reformed Egyptian?"

"I believe," I replied, "that it was a precaution he took to avoid being proved wrong. Since there's no such thing as reformed Egyptian, no one would have been able to check his translation. But, without realizing it, he actually compounded the problem.

"Martin Harris, you recall, took a sample of the characters to Professor Anthon in New York City. Harris claimed that Anthon said they were a combination of four languages: Egyptian, Chaldaic, Assyriac, and Arabic.

"Although Anthon later published a statement that Harris' story was false, that's quite a combination—four different languages rolled into one! Anthony A. Hoekema makes an excellent observation about this:

> If we assume, now, that "Assyriac" stands for Assyrian, and that "Chaldaic" stands for some form of Aramaic, we may note that the professor [Anthon] is reported as saying that characters representing four different languages would provide a readable kind of writing!
> The matter is still further complicated when we observe that

the cuneiform script used by the Assyrians, though it did employ syllabic signs and vowels, never became an alphabetic script, that none of the three types of Egyptian writing [hieroglyphic, hieratic, demotic] were alphabetic scripts, and that both Aramaic and Arabic were written in alphabetic scripts.[5]

"Class, can any of you see the problem this author is suggesting?"

Robert raised his hand. "Well, I would think that if you have four different languages rolled into one, two in alphabetic scripts and two in symbols, it wouldn't even be decipherable!"

"Very good—the exact point Hoekema makes. He says, '[It] would be like trying to write a sentence by putting letters from our own English alphabet next to some Hebrew consonants, some Japanese characters, and some Chinese characters!'[6]

"Even Mormon historian B. H. Roberts," I said, "questioned reformed Egyptian. He looked at the varieties of dissimilar languages and dialects found in the New World, especially the time necessary for their development, and concluded that there was no way they could have originated from the single Hebrew-based language Joseph Smith attributed to the Book of Mormon people.[7]

"However, let's give Smith the benefit of a doubt. Say that reformed Egyptian was indeed some kind of readable mixture of Egyptian and Hebrew. Since Smith portrayed it as being the universal language of North and South America, one would expect archaeologists to uncover something written in it. But, they haven't.

"The three books of the ancient Mayas in existence, written during the same time period of the Nephites, have been closely checked. So have carvings on ruins of the two oldest cities in Central America, Copan, and Palenque. Absolutely no reformed Egyptian has been found!

"In addition, a comparison between pictures of Mayan inscriptions and Harris' characters of Egyptian, Chaldaic, Assyriac, and Arabic show no match.[8] The Smithsonian Institute also confirms that no Egyptian or Hebrew hieroglyphics have been found in the Americas. Richard A. Parker, professor of Egyptology at the University of Chicago, emphatically states, 'From our standpoint there is no such language as "reformed Egyptian."'[9]

"In spite of these authoritative statements from the scientific community, some will go to great lengths to prove them wrong—even to the point of forging.

"For example, in 1870, two stones, dubbed the Newark Stones, were discovered in an Ohio burial mound. Consisting of one carved stone encased by another, they supposedly contained Hebrew writing and a picture of Moses:

> Over the head of this man were the Hebrew characters for . . . the ancient name of Moses; while on each side of this likeness, and on different sides of the stone, above, beneath, and around about were the Ten Commandments that were received on Mount Sinai, written in the ancient Hebrew characters.[10]

"Excited Mormons began claiming it proved the divine authenticity of the Book of Mormon. While the writing was not in reformed Egyptian it, nevertheless, established a link between the New World and the Old World—exactly what they were hoping for.[11]

"However, their bubble burst when it was discovered that an 'enthusiastic archaeologist' after finding no evidence to support his thesis that the lost tribes of Israel were the ancestors of the mound builders forged the two stones himself.[12]

"This example, however, is not to put Mormons down for believing it. These stones were considered authentic at the time. It was only natural to be excited over something that could validate their faith. If the stones had proved genuine, Mormons would have had something to crow about.

"However, Mormons are now bragging about a more recent find—the Tree of Life Stone known as Stela 5, also nicknamed the Lehi Stone. Pastor Bob mentioned it briefly at the beginning of class.

"Discovered in Izapa, Chiapas, Mexico,[13] Mormons, more especially M. Wells Jakeman of BYU, claim that it contains both Hebrew and Egyptian markings and a pictorial carving verifying the Book of Mormon."

"What kind of a picture is it?" Robert interjected.

"A large tree with fruit, two figures hovering in the air, and an old woman and old man. The old man appears to be speaking to four younger men seated on the ground, one of which is holding a pointed object some claim is a writing stylus. Significant to Book of Mormon believers, there is also a wavy line and a narrow double line running straight to the tree.

"Mr. Jakeman explains the stone as the account of Lehi's dream as related in 1 Nephi 8. The hovering figures he interprets as angelic; the old man as Lehi; the woman as Sariah, his wife; and the other four their sons Nephi, Sam, Laman, and Lemuel. He didn't bother to explain why Lehi's two other sons, Jacob and Joseph, aren't in the picture.

"The wavy line is supposed to be the river of water described in Lehi's dream, signifying the love of God. The narrow double line has two meanings. One line is the narrow path of righteousness. The other is the rod of iron, the handrail, depicting the word of God.

"However, Dr. Hugh Nibley, also of BYU, says, 'Mr. Jakeman's study is nothing but an elaborate syllogistic stew.'[14]

"Regardless, this interpretation caused quite a stir in the LDS Church. At the time I was teacher of the Ward Gospel Doctrine class, I was supplied with color transparencies of the Lehi Stone, along with impressive lesson materials.

"Now, admittedly, archaeologists do say the carving suggests a Tree of Life motif. But, this is a common symbol in many cultures. For example, in Central and South America there is a popular belief in a 'tree of nourishment and of life.'[15] This is probably what the Stela 5 Stone is replicating.

"Sounds pretty convincing for the Book of Mormon," Susan muttered softly.

"Yes, it does," I said. "That is, until one does their homework.

"After I left the Mormon Church, I wrote to the BYU Department of Anthropology and Archaeology asking them to verify Mr. Jakeman's interpretation. This," I said, pulling a paper from my briefcase, "was their response:

> The glyph above the head of Lehi is the cipactli glyph, which identifies the person beneath it as Lehi. . . . Likewise the glyph above Nephi's head is the name glyph of the Egyptian grain god, Nepri. Once again, Dr. Jakeman explains how this exactly identifies the person as Nephi.
>
> As for Sariah, the symbol, the headgear she wears could hardly be called a glyph. But since this headgear is such as was worn by royal Egyptian females, queens and princesses, it probably identifies her as Sariah, mother of Nephi the first king.[16]

"I then wrote to the Smithsonian Institute, enclosing a copy of BYU's letter, asking that someone validate or invalidate their interpretation. In addition, I asked them if there was any Hebrew on the Tree of Life Stone.

"My letter was forwarded to a scholar at a Texas University.

She said that the language was probably an 'early form of Mayan or of Mixe-Zoque, but *it certainly was not Hebrew.*' She also added, referring to BYU's interpretation, that 'the suggestions you sent to me in the quotation are *not valid.*' [emphasis mine].[17]

"Two Mormon missionaries, sincerely believing Jakeman's interpretation, submitted an article on Stela 5 to the *El Paso Times*, which read as follows:

> [the] three name glyphs on the carving have been translated as 'Lehi,' 'Sariah,' and 'Nephi,' prominent names in the Book of Mormon, and the study shows a detailed symbolization of a crucial scene in the book termed 'Lehi's Vision of the Tree of Life.' It may be one of the most important finds in the history of archeology . . .[18]

"However, if this interpretation had been correct, the Smithsonian would *not* have come out with the following:

> Reports of findings of ancient Egyptian, Hebrew, and other Old World writings in the New World in pre-Columbian contexts have frequently appeared in newspapers, magazines and sensational books. *None of these claims has stood up to examination by reputable scholars.* [emphasis mine].[19]

"It sounds to me," Tia said, "that it would be less embarrassing for BYU scholars if they were more cautious about jumping to conclusions."

"Well," I said, "in more recent years, they are.[20] But, it's the membership that I feel sorry for. They're very missionary-minded and would like proof such as this to convert others. But, at the same time, understand that the lack of proof will not affect their *testimony.*

"This leads us to another item on our list: Have the names of any Book of Mormon cities been discovered?

"The answer is obvious. No.

"This lack of evidence has unsettled Mormon scholars. Therefore, they must resort to rationalizations as to why this is so.

"One explanation they give is that God purposely disallowed evidence to be uncovered because He wants people to accept the Book of Mormon on faith.[21] But, if so, then why hasn't God kept all biblical evidences hidden?

"Fletcher B. Hammond, a Mormon, adds a second rationale.

The reason nothing can be found, he says, is because 'the entire face of the land of Central America [was] changed' due to the great destruction of earthquakes recorded in Third Nephi [at the time of the crucifixion].'[22]

"However," I said, "this is illogical. Book of Mormon history continued for four hundred years *after* the supposed destruction, providing archaeologists with *stable* strata. Even Mormon Thomas S. Ferguson, founder of BYU's New World Archaeological Foundation, agrees:

> Innumerable excavations . . . in the time span [of the Book of Mormon] (3000 B.C. to A.D. 400) reveal great undisturbed architectural structures, extensive relatively undisturbed ancient strata . . . right through the time of the crucifixion.'[23]

"But," Tia asked, "how do we account for the ruins?"

"We don't need to account for them," I said. "We just need to accept them. As far as where these people came from, the Smithsonian Institute tells us:

> The ancestors of the present Indians came into the New World—probably over a land bridge known to have existed in the Bering Strait region during the last Ice Age—in a continuing series of small migrations beginning from about 25,000 to 30,000 years ago.[24]

"This is *long* before the Book of Mormon people arrived on the scene.

"Mormon authors, playing on the needs of the members, still try to establish a link to the Old World by compiling books with pictures of the ruins. Some have even gone so far as to photograph the tower at the palace at Palenque, giving the impression it is one of the very towers mentioned in the Book of Mormon.[25] They neglect to mention that it was built in the seventh century, three hundred years after the Book of Mormon story ends.

"The city of Macchu Picchu has also been pictured as a sample of Nephite workmanship. But, in reality, it's an Incan construction built during the late 1400s—one thousand years too late for the Book of Mormon![26]

"What about the ruins in Monte Alban, Yagul, and Mitla?" Bobbycito asked. "I've heard Mormon missionaries claim that archaeologists have verified that they coincide with the time of the Jaredite and Nephite migrations." [27]

"Not quite," I responded. "BYU anthropologist Dr. Ross T. Christensen admits that this is another invalid claim.[28] These cities were built *after* the Book of Mormon time period ended.[29]

"Most Mormons don't bother to verify writers' claims, especially if the claims validate their beliefs. One such example of wild claims is given by the author of an LDS book, *Mormonism and Masonry*. Although out of print, it is typical of others.

"In this book the author presents a lengthy quote from an 1886 writer, Le Plongeon, giving the impression to the reader that Le Plongeon is a qualified archaeologist. Instead, he was a writer of mysticism. More importantly, he was trying to prove that the Indians practiced Masonry.

"Le Plongeon describes a Mayan ruin in which he claims to have found Masonic and Egyptian symbols, including a cornice with rings intended to hang curtains for a Holy of Holies. He also stated that the symbols were comparable to those found in the Old World:

> Inscriptions in the Mayan language [are] identical with and [have] the same meaning and value as those carved on the temples of Egypt. . . . These symbols are precisely the same that we find in the temples of Egypt, Chaldea, India and Central America.'[30]

"On the other hand, a highly-skilled Egyptian scholar, Dr. James H. Breasted of the University of Chicago Oriental Institute (now deceased), contradicted him. After Breasted laboriously researched the ruins, Frank H. H. Roberts of the Smithsonian stated:

> I was at the Maya city of Chichen Itza in Yucatan in 1932 when Dr. Breasted spent two weeks studying the ruins and inscriptions at that location as well as at several other cities in the area, and at the end of the period he was very emphatic about the total lack of evidence for any Egyptian influence.[31]

Tia raised her hand. "I almost feel sorry for the Mormons," she said. "Their faith is at stake and they can't find anything to validate it."

"Yeah," Matt called out. "It's sorta' sad. Look at those missionaries—giving two years of their life for something they can't prove."

"Yes," I said, "especially sad when so much archaeological

evidence has been unearthed for the Bible. Can any of you list some of them?"

Robert raised his hand. "From Abraham's birthplace, over seventeen thousand written clay tablets were found.[32] Also, the Israelite/Canaanite city of Lachish left inscriptions from 590 B.C. telling about the reign of Zedekiah, last King of Judah."

"Also," Ilya called out, "in Jerusalem, writings haf been found validating name of King David. In Egyptian museum at Cairo, der is also Merneptah stele, dating to 1224–1214 B.C. confirming name *Israel*."

"Very good!" I said. "There was also the 700 B.C. written account of eight military campaigns written by Sennacherib, King of Assyria. And, we mustn't forget the famous Siloam Inscription of 700 B.C., confirming King Hezekiah's tunnel. Then, of course, the Dead Sea discovery and the Isaiah Scroll—we could go on and on. Just look how much has been unearthed, verifying biblical names of cities and people.

"So, we must conclude that absolutely *nothing* has been found confirming Book of Mormon language, cities, or geography.

"Now," I paused, studying the list, "we still have five more subjects to cover. So, let's take a five-minute break."

Chairs scooted and papers rustled. A few dashed outside, while others ambled to the back of the room to examine pictures of South American ruins I had brought.

Noticing Bobbycito scribbling away on his note pad, I motioned for him to come outside with me and take a break.

Sitting on the bench with me, he said, "Whew, this is heavy-duty stuff, but they're good hard facts that I can use."

"Well, I'm glad for that, Bobbycito. I'm sure you'll help your people understand Mormonism's false claims. At least you won't have someone falling in love with one of the missionaries."

"Oh yeah," he said. "You mentioned that . . . Susan?"

"Yes. I'm really praying all this information will help her. But, you know how it is when a young girl's emotions are involved."

Just then I spied Matt ambling over in our direction looking rather serious. *That's unusual*, I thought, *he's not walking his special strut.*

"Hi!" he said as he walked up. "Pastor Bob, I enjoyed your accordion playing." Then, shifting somewhat uncomfortably, he looked at me.

"You know, there are a few of us who are kinda concerned about Susan. Rumor has it that she's really stuck on this missionary.

There's no chance she might convert is there? I mean, she'd be expelled from school."

Before I could answer, he continued. "I guess what I'm saying is I'd like to help if there's any way."

"Matt, that's great! However, the only thing I can think of is
to take advantage of opportunities. Show her where LDS teachings conflict with God's Word. But, avoid running the missionaries down—she'll only come to their defense."

"Well, I'll sure do what I can," he said. "I'll try to, uh, spend
more time with her . . . maybe ask her to go somewhere? Some
of us are going down to the River Walk after school. . . ." At that
point, he was at a loss for words.

Matt tongue-tied? Well, what do you know, I thought to myself. *Matt likes Susan!*

"I think that would be great, Matt. And you know, I believe I
heard Susan say once that she hadn't been to the Alamo yet. It's
right across the street from the River Walk—why don't you take
her over there. Afterward you could even take her on one of those
horse-and-buggy rides. It would," I said, trying to look serious,
"present a good opportunity for sharing."

"Well, I just might do that," he said. Turning, he headed back
up the steps into the classroom, his special strut resumed.

"Nice fellow, that Matt," Bobbycito said.

"Yes, he wants to be a pastor someday. C'mon," I said, glancing at my watch. "Time's up."

Reentering the classroom, I urged the students back into their
seats. After waiting a few seconds for their chatter to quit, I
glanced up at the next subject on the blackboard: Evidence of Jewish worship among Indians.

"There is none," I said. "But, from the Mormon's view, there
ought to be because the Book of Mormon claims to be a record
of Jews who left Palestine. More especially because their first
king, Nephi, says that they kept the Law of Moses: 'And, notwithstanding we believe in Christ, we keep the law of Moses.'[33]
'And they were *strict* in observing the ordinances of God, according to the law of Moses; for they were taught to keep the law of
Moses' [emphasis mine].[34]

"Obviously," I said, "Smith wasn't well-versed on Israelite
law. The Book of Mormon makes no mention of Sabbath ob-
servance, Jubilee years, tithing, circumcision, sacrifices, Passover, Feast of Unleavened Bread, or any of the festivals. As noted
by the Tanners, 'there is not even one case where a Jewish feast

or festival was celebrated . . . !'[35] Very strange for a people claiming to be strict Jews.[36] Neither does the Book of Mormon's appearance of Jesus have Him explain to the Nephites that the Law of Moses has been fulfilled and to stop sacrificing.

"Tia?"

"How about Nephite artifacts? Although," she quickly added, "I don't see how artifacts can prove or disprove the Book of Mormon. Like every other ancient race, they probably left behind the same kind of pottery and tools."

"But," I smiled, "Joseph Smith mentioned such unique items that, if found, would stand out like a sore thumb. The Book of Mormon mentions linen, silk, carriages, wheels, chariots, compasses, cement, and glass. None of the ruins offer any evidence for these.[37]

"In addition, BYU's Stuart Ferguson established four tests for the Book of Mormon, all of which failed: plant life, animal life, metallurgy, and script. He then became convinced that Smith's book was fiction.[38] Let's look at plant life first.

"The Book of Mormon mentions olives, barley, figs, grapes, and wheat. But, soil excavations, as well as an examination of artwork, carvings, murals, and ceramics, have produced nothing. Even at the great cave at Tehuacan, Puebla, Mexico, where diggings go down to the 5,000 B.C. level, nothing—no olives, no barley, no figs, no grapes, no wheat.[39]

"Next, we'll look at animal life. The Book of Mormon lists donkeys, cattle, sheep, goats, horses, oxen, pigs, elephants, chickens, dogs, and others. Again, nothing!"[40]

"What about metallurgy? Smith's book lists bellows, brass, chains, copper, gold, iron, molten ore, plows, silver, and swords. But, in the Book of Mormon region, none of these artifacts appear until the ninth century A.D.[41]

"The last test is script. The Jaredites who came over at the time of the Tower of Babel would have used cuneiform.[42] The Nephites of 600 B.C. would have used Hebrew. But, no Cuneiform, Hebrew, or Egyptian has been found. That is, except for two items: A seal with Egyptian script was found at Tlatilco, near Mexico City, containing a Hebrew name— Hiram; and in Chiapas, Mexico, a seal with three glyphs on it was discovered, supposedly Egyptian, but 'seriously questioned by scholars.'[43] They indicate that these two items are too minute to use as proof of anything. Therefore, the Smithsonian continues to state:

No reputable Egyptologist or other specialist on Old World archaeology, and no expert on New World prehistory, has discovered or confirmed any relationship between archaeological
remains in Mexico and archaeological remains in Egypt.[44]

Robert raised his hand. "What about my question: Does the
Book of Mormon use any Old Testament terms that Joseph Smith
couldn't possibly have known about?"

"Well, it would have been in his favor if he had, but no. However, he did get himself into hot water over something close to it.

"Similar to the contrived introduction into his story of artifacts
like glass and linen, he unnaturally introduced Greek words into
the Book of Mormon, which the Nephites certainly would not
have known about.

"For example, he used the Greek name for Jesus, *Jeshua*, and
the Greek word for anointed, *Christ*.[45] To make matters worse,
he inserted a French word, *Adieu*—a language that didn't exist
until A.D. 700." [46]

In addition, Smith plagiarized from the Bible in order to make
his text sound more authentic. He borrowed the terms *Alpha* and
Omega, the first and last letter of the Greek alphabet, from the
book of Revelation.[47] All this, in spite of the fact that Joseph Smith
stated, 'There was no Greek or Latin upon the plates from which
I . . . translated the Book of Mormon.'[48] 'Well over a hundred quotations from the New Testament have been found in the first two
books of Nephi alone.'[49] Another author counted twenty-seven
thousand words copied from the King James Version of the
Bible.[50]

"So, the obvious question is, how can characters, writing in 600
B.C. be quoting from Bible sources that weren't written until six
hundred years later?[51]

"Smith also capitalized on John 10:16, 'Other sheep I have
which are not of this fold, them also I must bring; and they shall
hear my voice; and there shall be one fold, and one shepherd.'[52]
This was an ingenious way to get Jesus over to this continent.

"Which brings us to Susan's challenge—explain the great white
God, Quetzalcoatl.

"Yes, Susan?"

"Maybe Jesus really did come here after His resurrection," she
laughed nervously. "Since the Indians are a *dark*-skinned race,
their tradition of a *white* God seems to be a strong point in
Mormonism's favor."

"Well, Susan, at first glance it might sound credible. But, as far as Quetzalcoatl's being white, tradition doesn't always show him as such.

"He is usually portrayed with a dark-hued body emblematic of rain clouds. This is because in many traditions he is the god of rain and wind. However, when he is portrayed as white, it's because *whiteness*, a symbol of deity, is associated with the sun and moon from which they believed gods originate.

"This may explain why the natives hailed Cortez as the returning Quetzalcoatl. They probably looked at Cortez and his men's shining white armor and immediately concluded they were deity.[53]

"However, let me tell you what little I know about Quetzalcoatl. Mostly mythological, he is described as an old man with a beard. The beard, typical of other Mexican deities, is a symbol of descending rain, pollen, or fertilization. Since it is not unusual for a plumed serpent to also symbolize deity, in some traditions he is also called the feathered serpent.[54]

"Of significance is the fact that unlike Jesus, he approved of human sacrifice.[55] He was also a 'penance-inflicting god' and, according to accounts, his companions were 'dwarfs and humpbacks.'[56]

"A popular tradition says that Quetzalcoatl was ruler of the Kingdom of Tollan, but driven away by evil magicians. Defeated, Quetzalcoatl departed across the eastern sea on his serpent raft to Tlapallan, land of plenty, promising to return.

"Quetzalcoatl, after landing, kills himself as a sacrifice 'and from his ashes rose birds with shining feathers (symbols of warrior souls mounting to the sun).'[57]

"However, the strongest argument against Quetzalcoatl's being Jesus is that the time frame doesn't match the A.D. 34 Book of Mormon appearance of Christ.

"The known period of worship of Quetzalcoatl is about A.D. 750 to A.D. 1500. This was nearly seven hundred years *after* the Book of Mormon account of Christ's visit to the Nephites."[58]

"So," Matt said, "Quetzalcoatl is either a myth or someone who really existed. Any ideas?"

"Scholars tell of sporadic visitors from other continents before Columbus.[59] There were small Jewish colonies as well as Phoenicians, Japanese, Europeans, North Africans, and Pacific Islanders who arrived by boat. Quetzalcoatl could easily have been one of them.

"A point worth remembering is to notice what the natives were expecting in Quetzalcoatl's return. They weren't looking for him to come down from the sky as one would expect of a deity, but, rather, in a boat. The legend I mentioned said that after Quetzalcoatl's defeat by evil magicians he left on a raft. Therefore, they naturally expected him to return in like manner. No wonder they revered Cortez and Captain Cook.

"The only way Quetzalcoatl could have been Jesus is if, after His Resurrection, He left the Holy Land and sailed to America in a boat, then left the same way. A pretty primitive mode of transportation for God!

"Now, to Ilya's question: Can any racial connection between the Jews and the American Indians be proven?

"A remarkable book is now available that took sixteen years to complete. Entitled *The History and Geography of Human Genes*, it is written by three geneticists, one a Stanford professor.[60] Synthesizing fifty years of research, it is the first genetic atlas of the world or, in other words, a global family tree.

"The study's importance to the Book of Mormon is significant. First, it confines its research to only those groups that were in their present locations as of 1492. This would include the American Indians.

"Second, the team examined the *genetic* makeup of hundreds of thousands of these groups all over the world by testing their blood. They ignored outer distinctions of racial factors such as skin color.

"The result? The whole world's population boiled down to four major ethnic groups: Africans, Caucasoids, Mongoloids, and Australians. Which category did the Indians fall into? Mongoloid! Where did the Mongoloids come from? Not from Jerusalem.

"All one has to do is look at the book's color-coded maps to see this. By comparing North and South America's color codes to that of the Holy Land's, one can see that there is no way Indians could have migrated from Jerusalem.

"This study backs up what the Smithsonian Institute has been saying all along—the Americas were populated by three migrations from Asia coming across the Bering Strait."[61] Science has never presented confirming evidence for the Book of Mormon.

"If only," I smiled, "Joseph Smith hadn't given the plates back to the angel. Because as it stands now, archaeological evidence is the only avenue through which the Book of Mormon can ever be substantiated.

"Class, let me ask you this: After today's lesson, could Mormon missionaries ever convince you, by archaeological claims, of the authenticity of the Book of Mormon?"

"No," the class said in unison.

"What are some irrefutable statements you could make to them?"

"Easy," Matt called out. "First, I'd tell them that according to Martin Harris, reformed Egyptian was a combination of four languages, half in script, half in symbols, which wouldn't even have been readable.

"Second, that it is illogical for Jewish Nephites to have spoken Egyptian or have had Old Testament Scriptures written in it. For proof," he said, referring to his notes, "I can quote the Smithsonian Institute: 'No Old World forms of writing have been shown to have occurred in any part of the Americas before 1492.'"[62]

"Very good, Matt. Tia?"

"Absolutely no cities with Book of Mormon names have been found," she stated. "Nothing Jewish, either. And, like Matt, I can quote the Smithsonian's statement that says 'no evidence has been found to corroborate any contact with ancient Egyptians, Hebrews, or the Near East.'"

"Ilya?"

"I don't see how new study on genetics can be ignored. If Jews are Caucasoids and American Indians are Mongoloids, de whole Book of Mormon claim is destroyed!"

"Robert?"

"I'd point out that the Book of Mormon has failed four major scientific tests: plant life, animal life, metallurgy, and script."

"Susan?" I asked, hoping her defensive attitude had changed, "how would you refute the white bearded God?"

"Well," she said slowly, offering a better answer than I expected, "myths about Quetzalcoatl date him seven hundred years too late to match the time frame of Jesus' visit to the Nephites."

"Good. How about you, Pastor Bob?"

"Well," he mused, "what all these archaeologists are saying is impressive. The ruins have produced no Egyptian or Hebrew hieroglyphics, plus no reformed Egyptian. Also, the carvings on the Tree of Life Stone do not translate into Lehi, Sarah, and Nephi. The BYU interpretation is not valid."

"Everyone of you have been great in class today," I said. "We also appreciate Pastor Bob's visit. Do you think we can persuade him to play a closing song for us?"

The students began clapping and Bobbycito, grinning, grabbed his accordion. He began a peppy-paced hymn, singing in both Spanish and English so everyone could sing along:

> *No puede estar triste el corazón que alaba Cristo.*
> *No puede estar triste el corazón que alaba Dios.*
>
> There's no room for sadness in a heart
>   that worships Jesus.
> There's no room for sadness in a heart
>   that worships God.
> I'm singing, rejoicing, I'm praising my Jesus!
>
> *¡Yo canto con gozo, alabo a mi Cristo!*
> *No puede estar triste el corazón que alaba Dios.*

The class sang along with him and it was a joy to watch their faces. I was sorry it had to end.

As he finished, I called out, "Remember, test tomorrow!"

While everyone groaned, I turned to again thank Bobbycito, assuring him I'd see him later.

Glancing at Susan, I wasn't sure what she was feeling. As she walked out the door, I saw Matt side in with her. Suddenly I felt relief—someone else was on the team!

Shoving papers into my briefcase, I headed out the door, trying to recall which lesson the Mormon Elders would be giving next.

Oh, yes—an episode in Christian history that they will claim validates Joseph Smith's first vision, his calling as a prophet, the gold plates, the Book of Mormon, the temple, priesthood, and every Mormon doctrine thereafter.

This episode was, according to the Elders, all part of God's plan. Well, I had another plan up my sleeve.

CHAPTER TEN

The Third Missionary Presentation

The great apostasy and the gates of hell

Y ou've been against the Mormon Elders all along!" Susan said with a huff. "All you do is talk about how wrong they are!"

As we pulled up in front of Ellen's house, I took a deep, but shaky, breath. Nothing was turning out like I'd planned. I had been praying all day for the opportunity to talk with Susan, and all we were doing was arguing.

"Susan, I'm going to be blunt," I said. "I started this venture with you thinking I could help. Each time we've met with the missionaries, I've made a point of showing you where the Elders have been deceptive and their beliefs unbiblical. But nothing seems to be registering.

"So, I'll tell you what I think. I believe the only reason you want to continue the lessons is not to convert Elder Black, but entice him into a romantic relationship!

"Susan," I then said more gently, "stop and consider what's at stake. Your faith in the Gospel of Christ is the most precious treasure you have. Are you willing to give all that up? Because that's exactly what will happen if you pursue this relationship. Instead of Elder Black giving up Mormonism, odds are that you'll be the one joining *his* church.

"And, what if you married him? Are you willing to give up the Gospel for a different one? Can you embrace the Book of Mormon, knowing the gold plates were a hoax? Can you stand in their congregation and sing, 'We Thank Thee Oh God for a Prophet,' knowing all along that Joseph Smith was *not* a prophet?"

Susan's lips tightened, her face drawn.

Finally, she whimpered, "But Elder Black really *loves* the Lord—that's got to count for something! The other night at the Ward basketball game, I spent twenty minutes witnessing to him about Jesus. He just listened, didn't talk Mormonism to me, and agreed that Jesus died on the cross for him."

"Susan, listen to me," I said gently. "If you continue seeing Elder Black after he's released, you'll be making a serious mistake. Take my word for it, Elder Black is *not* going to give up his religion for you."

Before I could continue, Wendy, spying us from the house, motioned for us to come in.

"C'mon," I said, patting her hand. "Let's go in. But, Susan, please be on guard. The Elders are going to use a lot of Bible verses in this lesson. The topic is the Great Apostasy—very important to Mormons. Their whole claim to a restored gospel rests on it.

"Mormons believe, contrary to what Jesus said, that the gates of hell *did* prevail against the church. Tonight, I intend to show that hell didn't."

Locking the car, we headed up the walk. Reaching the steps, Wendy held the door open, flashing a contagious smile. Ellen wasn't far behind.

"Come on in and join us on the patio," she invited. "We're having a few snacks first."

We followed her into the house and exited through the patio doors. *A few snacks?* I stopped short and gazed in wonderment.

A fuchsia tablecloth with a brilliant centerpiece of yellow daffodils displayed a dazzling array of delicacies. Tossed green salad; red cherry tomatoes; potato salad; coleslaw; colored Jello; a large plate of golden-fried chicken; olives, deviled eggs, pickles, chips, and a variety of desserts. I could scarcely take it all in.

"My," I said, "we weren't expecting this. . . ."

"After Elder Black gives the blessing," Ellen said, "you can both take a plate and start in."

Elder Black scooted off the edge of the chaise lounge, giving Susan a big smile. He folded his arms, and everyone else followed suit. In his prayer he included a lengthy request that the Lord bless Susan and me so that we might receive a testimony to the truthfulness of the "gospel."

Admittedly, I was moved over his prayer—but only because

Elder Black was so sincere about his calling. They were both so genuine. I had to keep reminding myself that sincerity of a belief doesn't constitute a truth.

Elder Barrett was also growing. Even though a greenie, I could see the change that had taken place. He was more sure of himself and bolder in his presentations. Soon, he'd be senior companion, taking Elder Black's place to tutor another greenie. Would Susan and I devastate him by refusing to be baptized? *How can I end this gracefully without hurting anyone?*

Ellen called to Isaac and Kimberly who were playing in the sprinkler. After drying them off with a towel and filling their plates, she sent them off to a smaller table to eat. We then scooted our lawn chairs into a semicircle and began eating with gusto.

Conversation soon gathered momentum. The Elders began sharing highlights of their families back home, describing blessings that had come to them for giving two years of their lives to preach the gospel. They then inquired about campus activities and agreed on how wonderful it was that our college had a missionary focus.

"We feel," Elder Black said, "that Protestant missionaries do an important work. They pave the way for our missionaries to present the *fullness* of the gospel."

As appealing as it was to debate over what *fullness* meant, I let it pass. I wanted to allow ample time at the end of the lesson to present my thoughts.

Ellen began collecting empty plates. "We decided," she explained, "to have the lesson out here since it's such a lovely evening."

Glancing over her shoulder, she said, "Wendy, you can take Isaac and Kimberly into the den now." Wendy nodded and they disappeared into the house.

Susan and I helped clear up while the missionaries arranged their lesson materials. Finally, as we all seated ourselves around the table, Elder Barrett placed his flip chart in its usual A-shaped position.

"Susan," he asked, "how did you *feel* as you read parts of the Book of Mormon?"

"Well," she responded slowly, "Many of the passages made me feel good because they sounded biblical."

Elder Barrett grinned. "That's exactly how you should *feel*. How did you *feel* when you prayed about the Book of Mormon and Joseph Smith?"

"I, uh, haven't really prayed about them yet," she answered weakly.

Turning to me, he asked, "How do you feel about following the Lord's example of being baptized?"

"I believe very firmly in following everything Christ taught," I quickly replied. "When I accepted the Lord, I was baptized."

"That's wonderful," he said enthusiastically. "Later tonight, we'll show you how important it is to be baptized by one holding proper authority."

Though tempted to argue his statement, I decided to let it ride. I needed all the extra time I could get.

Elder Barrett continued. "We know that our heavenly Father's truths are the same throughout all ages. Therefore, it's important that we learn about His laws and ordinances so we can prepare for eternal life.[1] That's why God sent Jesus Christ and why He chose apostles and prophets.

"After Jesus died," he explained, "the apostles continued to lead the church. As long as they were alive, teaching, writing, and giving continuous revelation, members were obedient, happy, and at peace.

"Susan," he said, "do you believe that *continuous revelation* to the church, given through the apostles and prophets, helped New Testament Christians find happiness and peace?"

Susan nodded.

"I testify to both of you," Elder Barrett began, "that my life has been enriched and blessed because I have followed the teachings of prophets God has called in these last days. The truth of their words has brought light into my life. It's through the light and truth of the gospel that we become sanctified."

At that point, he reached for his King James Version and began reading John 17:17, "Sanctify them through thy truth: thy word is truth." Then John 3:21, 'He that doeth truth cometh to the light.' The Book of Mormon also teaches that whatever persuades men to do good is of Christ, who is the light, life, and truth of the world.[2]

"It's very important to God's plan," he continued, "that He continue to guide His children in the same way. In view of the sad condition of our world, we need apostles and prophets more than ever. But God, as stated in Amos 3:7, will do nothing unless He first reveals His will to His prophets.

"Do you believe, Susan, that if we had apostles and prophets today, we could receive the same kind of blessings as the New Testament church?"

Susan nodded again.

"But," I said, jumping in before Susan got herself in deeper, "since the apostles *already* wrote God's Word down, there is no need for any more revelation."

"I understand what you're saying," said Elder Black gently. "But, Ephesians 4:12 says, 'And he gave some, apostles; and some, prophets; and some, evangelists; and some, pastors and teachers; for the perfecting of the saints, for the work of the ministry, for the edifying of the body of Christ.'

"The Scriptures are very plain" he continued, "that apostles and prophets are *necessary* to the church in order to *perfect* the saints. Remember Ephesians 2:20 says that the church is to be built on the foundation of apostles and prophets."

"But," I said, "you'll also recall how I noted last week that Paul didn't say the church was to be built on the foundation of *more* apostles and prophets. He said it is built on the foundation of *the* apostles and prophets, meaning the specific ones already called.

"The NIV clarifies Ephesians 4 even further. Do you mind if I read it?" I asked, opening my Bible before he could say no.

> It was he who gave some to be apostles, some to be prophets, some to be evangelists, and some to be pastors and teachers, to prepare God's people for works of service, so that the body of Christ may be built up until we all reach unity in the faith and in the knowledge of the Son of God and become mature, attaining to the whole measure of the fullness of Christ.

"It isn't saying that *future* apostles need to be raised up. Don't you think that if Jesus thought more apostles were necessary, He would have instructed the ones He had how to appoint a new one in case one should die?

"Neither does Ephesians 4 suggest that we need additional revelation. Even if one prefers the King James Version," I said, "the logic is plain. If the Bible was talking about perfecting the saints in *that* day, then that means the information they had was sufficient for that purpose.

"Further, Ephesians says that the saints are built upon the foundation of the apostles and prophets, Jesus Christ Himself being the chief corner stone. Your interpretation suggests that if we need new apostles and prophets, it means we also need a new Christ. He is the chief cornerstone but, like the apostles, also died."

"We appreciate your sharing what your Bible says," Elder Black mechanically responded. "But, the various Bible versions on the market today are really just opinions of men. By changing the Scriptures into everyday English, they have seriously changed the words. They're not inspired like the biblical writers in the King James Version."

"I think you have a misconception, Elder," I said. "You may not have thought about this, but the King James Version is also a translation by men. The difference, however, between the King James Version and more modern versions is that we are in a greater position today to fine-tune the meanings.[3] Did you know that there are twenty-five thousand biblical manuscripts and fragments in existence with the oldest dating back to A.D. 75–100?[4] Therefore, we have more advanced texts in Hebrew, Aramaic, and Greek to work from."

"Well," Elder Black said, slightly shifting the subject, "I believe by the time we get through with tonight's lesson, you'll better understand the need for apostles and prophets."

Reaching for a piece of paper, he drew a picture of a building. Drawing a horizontal line at the bottom to indicate a foundation, he wrote the words *apostles* and *prophets*.

"We believe the Scriptures," he said, "when they say Jesus Christ is the cornerstone of the church. Nevertheless, its foundation is built on the apostles and prophets.

"Now," he said, suddenly erasing the two words, "if the apostles and prophets are no longer there, what happens to a building when its foundation is taken away? Susan?"

"Well, it collapses," she replied.

"This is exactly what happened when the apostles and prophets died off. The church collapsed."

"Now, Elder," I interjected, "how could the church totally collapse when it had Jesus Christ as its cornerstone?"

"Nevertheless," Elder Black insisted, "history bears out that the church steadily began going downhill. When it finally entered the Dark Ages, God had to withdraw His church and priesthood from the earth. This left the church with no inspired leaders.

"But," he said smiling, "God always has a backup plan. Since there was no true church on the earth, He arranged for a restoration by raising up the prophet Joseph Smith."

"You're saying," I interrupted, "that there was no true church on earth up to the time of Joseph Smith?"

"That's right. While the people had enough truth to live good lives, they nevertheless did not have certain vital truths."

"So," I posed, "when Jesus promised in Matthew 16:18 that He would build His church and the gates of hell would *not* prevail against it, you're saying that the gates of hell *did*?"

Elder Black looked perplexed.

"Elder, what it sounds like you're saying is that Jesus was not capable of carrying out what He started."

"I'm not saying that exactly," he said hesitantly.

"But," I persisted, "that's also what your church teaches." I quickly pulled a piece of paper from my purse. "Your own Apostle Orson Pratt said:

> Jesus made his appearance on the earth in the meridian of time, and he established his kingdom on the earth. But to fulfill ancient prophecies, the Lord suffered that Kingdom to be uprooted . . . the kingdoms of this world made war against the kingdom of God, established eighteen centuries ago, *and they prevailed against it*, and *the kingdom ceased to exist* [emphasis mine].[5]

Elder Black, looking a little dismayed, was still quick to respond. "Jesus had good intentions and while God didn't plan on the apostasy, it happened. After all, individuals have their free agency and God doesn't force people to be righteous.

"It isn't our leaders' statement that makes the apostasy a fact," he said. "It was Jesus Himself." Elder Black quickly pointed to the flip chart.

THE APOSTASY
"For that day shall not
come, except there come a falling
away first."
2 Thessalonians 2:3

"There," he said, "you have your answer. Jesus Himself said a complete apostasy had to take place before He could come again. Therefore, the church ceased to exist."

"But, Elder, if you're saying that Jesus' promise failed and what He said in Matthew 16:18 isn't accurate, then we might as well toss out the Bible! If Jesus were talking about a complete apostasy in 2 Thessalonians, He'd be contradicting His earlier statement where He said His church *wouldn't* fail. I really believe Jesus is talking about a partial apostasy."

Elder Barrett, who had been thumbing through his Bible, quickly began reading:

"Isaiah 29:13 also foretells the apostasy. He says people will draw near to God with their mouths, but their hearts will be far from Him. Second Timothy 4:3–4 confirms this by saying that the people in the New Testament church would no longer 'endure sound doctrine.'"

"But, Elder Barrett," I said, "while 2 Timothy says apostasy was beginning in the church and would increase in the last days, *nowhere* does it say that there would be a *total* apostasy. Don't you think that if God, in His foreknowledge, saw the church would fail, He wouldn't have bothered with it in the first place? But, Paul assures us in Ephesians that there 'would be glory in the church and in Christ Jesus *throughout all generations, forever.*[6] That statement would be a lie if *total* apostasy had occurred. If Christ purchased the church with His blood and then the church fizzled out . . . what a waste!"

I watched their faces. Nothing was registering.

Elder Barrett continued.

"Matthew 24:9–11 and 2 Peter 2:1–2 say that false prophets and teachers arose in the church deceiving many. Paul repeats this in Galatians 1:6–8, 'I marvel that ye are so soon removed from him that called you into the grace of Christ unto another gospel.'"

Look who's talking, I thought.

"Jesus' apostles," he continued, "certainly tried to fulfill their calling. But, they were rejected, persecuted, and finally killed. Therefore, without their guidance, the saints fell deeper into error.

"Amos 8:11–12, referring to our time, said that in the last days God will send a famine of 'hearing the words of the Lord.' People will 'seek the word of the Lord, and shall not find it.' Why? Because God withdrew His church and priesthood from the earth and there were no more apostles and prophets."

Pointing to the flip chart, he said, "The bad news is that Jesus stated the Second Coming would not take place until the falling away occurred.

"The good news is that since an apostasy did occur, Jesus restored the church through Joseph Smith in 1820. He told Joseph there were no authorized Christian churches on the earth at that time and not to join any of them.

"God's purpose in appearing to Joseph Smith was to restore the primitive church and establish the Church of Jesus Christ of Latter-day Saints. The church, officially organized in 1830, was the stone Daniel prophesied of that would fill the whole earth and never again be destroyed.[7] Joseph Smith was the prophet God chose to fulfill that prophecy. The world once again had apostles and prophets!"

Elder Barrett then looked inquiringly at me.

"See if I have this right," I said. "The apostasy left the world without a true church from the time of the last apostle's death until Joseph Smith. Right?"

They both nodded.

"But, I still have a problem. As I see it, your whole church hangs upon the idea that there was a complete and total apostasy. However, I don't believe the church *totally* died out, and I believe history will bear this out. God says in Matthew 18:20 that where two or three are gathered together, there am I in the midst of them.[8] And there were at least *that* many down through history, regardless of how bad things got.

"I also believe that instead of Joseph Smith, God began His restoration through Martin Luther and the other Reformers."

Elder Black smiled. "We want you to understand that we acknowledge Luther and the Reformers as being inspired. We feel that God used them to bring the people out of Catholicism and prepare them for the Latter-day restoration."

"Elders," I said cautiously, "do you mind if I present some of my ideas?"

Both hesitated and looked at each other. Elder Barrett was the first to respond.

"We did have other things we wanted to cover but I suppose we could do it in our next session. Since you have a problem with the apostasy, perhaps it's best to get it ironed out before we move on. Also, we know you haven't received the same testimony of the restored gospel as we have, so we can understand why you might still have problems."

"Thank you." With that, I jumped right in.

"I'd like to take a look at history and see if the gates of hell completely prevailed or not.

"First, we need to understand what the Scriptures *really* mean when they talk about *church*.

"The word *church*, in Greek, means those who are 'called-out' of the world as born-again believers.[9] They, according to 1 Corinthians 12:27, are the ones who make up God's community, the church, also known as the body of Christ. Therefore, the church is not an institution or organization.[10] The church is the people.

"Now, I agree with you," I continued, "that as the New Testament church grew, men with power-seeking drives dominated. The bishops soon took over, controlling the churches. But, the question kept arising, 'who should control the bishops?' Influenced by an empire ruled by a single authority, the church followed the same pattern, which culminated in a pope.

"As time passed, rituals, Greek mysticism, and pagan rites for the dead, infiltrated the church by way of converts.[11] The clergy were elevated and the Gospel became distorted. No longer did salvation rest on the work done by God's grace at Calvary, but by specific works guaranteeing salvation. By A.D. 120 the church sank to the level of a *structural* church only . . . a hollow shell of an institution.

"But," I said, "even during this time of the second century, there were believers who constituted the *spiritual* church. Many people have the erroneous idea that Christianity's population was *small* making it inevitable for the church to cease.

"But, to the contrary, at the opening of the second century, church membership under the dominion of Rome alone, included several million people.[12] Believers were in every land and city from the Tiber to the Euphrates, from the Black Sea to northern Africa, and some think Christianity extended as far west as Spain and Britain.[13] 'The Christians were everywhere a multitude,' according to Pliny in an A.D. 112 letter to Emperor Trajan. Even at the close of the persecution period, the 'church was numerous enough to constitute the most powerful institution in the empire.'

"Now, common sense tells us that with its millions, there were bound to be some who still functioned as true believers, albeit in isolation or secret. Even if there were only two or three, God promised in Matthew 18:20 to be in their midst. If so, there was a true church.

"By A.D. 380, Christianity was recognized as the official religion of Rome. But, along with its prosperity came strong political involvements that hastened the structural church's deterioration, especially its hierarchy.

"Since members were not allowed to read the Scriptures, ignorance of the Bible prevailed. Most knew only what the clergy told them. Therefore, Amos 8:11, which you quoted earlier, was not predicting a hunger for the words of the Lord in our present day, but in *that* period: 'Behold, the days come, saith the Lord GOD, that I will send a famine in the land, not a famine of bread, nor a thirst for water, but of hearing the words of the LORD.'

"With the church's involvement in bribery, bloodshed, and immorality, it descended into the Dark Ages. Any who were able to remain faithful to Christ were admittedly few by comparison but, nevertheless, they existed. Overall, a restoration was needed."

"So," Elder Barrett interrupted, "even you are saying that the church disintegrated and needed to be restored."

"Yes," I replied, "the *structural* church. But, the *spiritual* church, albeit only a small number, *did* exist. Otherwise, it makes Jesus out to be a liar. Just because we don't hear about the spiritual church doesn't mean it wasn't there. The church was too populated for it to die out completely. Although there are no records to confirm this, we must base this idea on the fact that Jesus Himself declared that the gates of hell would not prevail against His *church*. And the church means any body of believers, no matter how small.

"Remember Elijah? When Jezebel said she was going to kill him, he escaped into the wilderness and bemoaned his lot to the Lord, telling Him all other believers were dead. 'I, even I only, am left,'[14] he despaired.

"But, he was wrong. The Lord told him there were seven thousand believers left in Israel who had not bowed to Baal.[15] Imagine, seven thousand that Elijah didn't even know about!

"Similarly, there were probably small groups or individuals during those dark ages who didn't know about other believers.

"Some of them, history records, tried to head movements but were unsuccessful. There were the Albigenses and the Waldensians in France (1170), John Wycliff in England (1376), Jerome Savonarola in Italy (1498), and many others, including John Huss in Bohemia (1415) who influenced Luther.

"Martin Luther, like Jeremiah, was chosen before he was born. *He* was the man God chose to set the stone loose from the mountain and start it rolling. He was such a key figure in God's plan, that one hundred years earlier John Huss, sentenced to be burned at the stake, prophesied of him.[16]

"I believe that the Reformation, started by Martin Luther, was *the* restoration of Christ's true church. It started that memorable day, October 31, 1517, when Martin Luther walked up to the Wittenberg cathedral and nailed his ninety-five theses to the door.

"The Holy Spirit then took hold and Christianity spread like wildfire. The Reformation broke out in Italy, France, the Netherlands, Switzerland, Denmark, Sweden, and Norway.

"Now, I don't mean to offend you Elders in any way," I said, "but, whenever God begins to restore His truths, they are always the *same* truths that Jesus and the apostles taught.[17] So, God's restoration, through Luther, brought back New Testament truths— repentance from dead works and salvation through faith in Christ and the grace of God.

"As the church rolled through the remaining centuries, God saw to it that His spiritual principles were kept alive through periodic revivals. Closer to our own time, in America, one such revival started in the 1700s and 1800s.

"Known as the Great Awakening, it revived New Testament truths, bringing mass conversions.

"Starting on the East Coast, it swept through New York and Philadelphia with converts numbering *three hundred thousand.*[18] It then spread southward. 'Five, ten or fifteen thousand would gather in . . . forest clearings,'[19] says one report.

"Polynesia and Hawaii were also affected. At a single church in Hilo, there were 1,705 saved in *one* day; 7,557 during the whole movement. Spreading even further to Britain and Wales, the Holy Spirit 'packed' churches, drawing 'crowds of many thousands in the open air.'[20] The Netherlands, Orient, and West Indies followed suit. It was," I said, "a wonderful move of God to keep His church alive.

"However, as is so often the case, after God does this, by the second and third generation everything dies down and believers often become apathetic. Lip service replaces heart service. Even Joseph Smith recognized this.

"So, God planned another revival. Not in 1820 with Joseph Smith, but in 1858! God moved so mightily—it was stupendous!

"This worldwide movement, known as the Second Great Awakening, surpassed all previous ones as far as its effects and lasting impact. It—"

Before I could continue, Elder Black interrupted.

"If you're saying that your stumbling block to a restoration through Joseph Smith is because you believe Martin Luther's 1517 reformation was the true restoration, why focus on 1858? That's *past* Joseph Smith's time."

"Yeah, I'm wondering, too," Susan added. "What's so significant about 1858?"

"Because," I said, "it's twenty-eight years *after* the Mormon Church was organized!

"If," I continued, "God intended His church to be restored through Joseph Smith's 1830 church, why would the Holy Spirit bother converting people within *Protestant* structures twenty-eight years later?

"Why, in 1858, didn't God move converts to be led to the Mormon Church?"

"Wow," Susan whispered. The Elders sat quietly.

"You don't need to answer," I said. "But, let me describe what happened. It was so exciting, it's almost unbelievable.

"When the 1858 Awakening hit with full force, it started in the United States. From there it spread to the United Kingdom, Australia, South Africa, and South India.

"While the numbers of conversions were small at first, they gradually grew. Christian newspapers reported it first, then the secular newspapers.

"Prayer meetings broke out everywhere. The masses were so desirous of prayer that in New York 'the striking of the five bells at twelve o'clock was 'known as the signal for the "hour of Prayer"'[21] Business houses closed just for the noon prayer meetings with more in demand.

"In Brooklyn, local merchants financed and organized a large theater to be thrown open for these meetings. Over six thousand people 'packed in every corner from the pit to the roof . . . no amount of elbowing could force an entrance. . . . The street in front was crowded with vehicles, and the excitement was 'tremendous.'[22] Buildings were packed, with hundreds left outside unable to get in. One report said prayer meetings 'were crowded and solemn, with the whole assembly sometimes in tears, under the melting power of the Spirit.'[23] In six months, fifty thousand New Yorkers converted to God. A letter from Chicago, dated March 21, 1858, stated:

> The Metropolitan Hall is crowded to suffocation. The interest in the First Baptist Church is beyond anything ever known in this city, and exceeds anything I have ever seen in my life. Some who have come to the city on business have become so distressed about their condition as sinners before God that they have entirely forgotten their business in the earnestness of their desire for salvation.[24]

"It was a move toward prayer that had never been witnessed before.

"But, the amazing thing was that there was no fanaticism, hysteria, or excitement—'simply an incredible movement of the people to pray.'[25] Neither did it have to do with denominationalism. Eight thousand Episcopalians, from all over America were converted in Methodist churches!

"As the Awakening spread to other states, the national press carried the news from coast to coast. A New York editor, in May of 1858, collected interdenominational figures showing over ninety-six thousand people converted in six months, with an average of fifty thousand a week.[26] A Baptist journal reported seventeen thousand converts. For a period of two years, there were ten thousand additions a week to church memberships.

"In Buffalo, two hundred towns reported six thousand conversions. Newark reported over two thousand in two months. A Washington newspaper reported that in New England there were ten thousand converts in two months.

"In Kentucky, churches were required to stay open day and night. Ohio's two hundred towns reported twelve thousand conversions in two months. In the Confederate and Union armies, converts numbered 150,000.

"At the sight of multitudes flocking to Protestant churches, it was reported that it left the 'Pope biting his nails.'[27] High church Anglicans couldn't understand why converts of the revival were entering other churches and not the '*true church.*' [emphasis mine].[28]

"Perhaps," I said, "LDS leaders were wondering the same thing?

"Then Europe began praying. In four months, Ireland estimated that ten thousand had been converted. Every denomination was packed and open-air meetings brought crowds as large as twenty thousand. Crime was reduced and prostitutes were seeking rehabilitation. Irish evangelist Grattan Guinness recalled in 1859:

> The predominating feature was the conversion of people of all ranks and positions, in ways sudden, startling, amazing. . . . Before that time, I had seen tens or scores brought to Christ under Gospel preaching; but this new movement of 1859 was something quite different. . . . Ministers were occupied until midnight, or even till two or three o'clock in the morning, conversing with crowds of inquirers who were crying: "What shall I do to be saved?"[29]

"Thousands continued to be converted and hundreds were turned away at church doors. In Wales, conversions 'did not fall short of a hundred thousand souls.'[30]

"England was next. On New Year's day in 1860, seven theaters opened with a nightly aggregate attendance of over twenty thousand. Seasonal aggregate attendances numbered over 250,000.[31]

"Australia, Switzerland, France, Belgium, Germany, and Russia were next. Amazingly, South Africa, with no link of communication with other countries to know what was happening, also went into revival. Then India:

> Old and young, men and women and children, suddenly seemed crushed by the agony of a deep conviction of sin, and then, as suddenly, seemed to believe in the forgiveness of sins. The people could hardly bear to leave the churches and came to them day after day.[32]

"This refreshing of God's remained effective for forty years, free of any sectarian spirit. More importantly, there was nothing new in the way of theology—only New Testament teachings.

"These souls were the *true* church—the spiritual body of Christ. When Jesus comes back, He is not coming back for an institution, but a *people*, made up of born-again Baptists, Methodists, Catholics, Pentecostals, Episcopalians—all believers wherever they may be found.

"Therefore, God restored His *true* church through Martin Luther and continued with periodic revivals to make sure the gates of hell would not prevail. There *was* a true church on the earth in 1820, despite what Joseph Smith claims Jesus told him.

"Elders, your leaders say that the purpose of the 1517 Reformation was to lead people out of Catholicism and into Mormonism. But, in 1858 twenty-eight years after the Mormon Church was organized, this is *not* what the Holy Spirit moved over two million people to do.

"Wouldn't you have thought that if the Church of Jesus Christ of Latter-day Saints was the only true church on the face of the earth, that God would have created a mass exodus to Utah?"

Silence.

"But, they were *not* led to Utah. Nor were they led to embrace teachings that taught that the Bible was not enough, or that God was too weak to preserve His church. Nor were they given a new revelation saying that to be saved one must receive temple ordinances, memorize passwords, do work for the dead, prepare for polygamy in heaven, or that the grace of God has no power to save believers in the highest heaven.

"So, Elders," I said, leaning back, "there's my problem. Your beliefs don't seem to square with history."

The missionaries sat motionless while Susan watched them expectantly. Even I studied their faces, hoping for some glimmer of light. When they spoke, I couldn't believe what I was hearing.

"Well," Elder Black finally said, "since we have a testimony that Joseph Smith was called as a prophet to restore the true church, we believe the Great Awakening could have been a plan of Satan to lead people away from the *fullness* of the gospel."

I was dumbfounded. "You mean," I said in amazement, "that Satan would bring over two million souls to God?" Even Susan appeared shocked.

With that, both Elders were at a loss for words.

Suddenly, I felt sorry for them. They were earnest young men trying so hard, but so blind.

"Elders," I said gently, "I wasn't saying all this to put you down or ridicule your beliefs. I'm simply presenting my viewpoint so that you can see the stumbling block that prevents me from joining your church. I invite you to offer anything that you think might change my mind."

I waited.

Finally Elder Black said, "We don't have the educational background to respond to everything you've said. All we have is the simple testimony given to us by the Holy Ghost. It tells us that what we preach and believe is true. The witness in my heart tells me that Joseph Smith is a prophet of God and that the Book of Mormon is true. I *know*," he suddenly declared with vigor, "that the Church of Jesus Christ of Latter-day Saints is the only true church on the face of the earth and that God has restored apostles and prophets in these last days to guide us!"

As I looked over at Susan, I finally saw an expression I hadn't seen before. Something was registering!

"Elders," I said, "I too have a testimony. I *know* that every statement and promise Jesus uttered is true. I *know* that if He said the gates of hell would not prevail against His church, then they didn't.

"I also *know* that God raised up Martin Luther to restore New Testament truths. I also *know* that God inspired periodic revivals throughout the world to keep His *true* church from dying out.

"My testimony is that I belong to the only true church—that spiritual body of called-out believers who claim Jesus as their Lord and Savior. I know I am saved by His good grace and I shall obtain heaven, however many levels, upon His promise."

Again, silence.

"Now, Elders," I said, "if both of us have testimonies, what determines which of our testimonies is the true one? There ought to be something we can use as a measuring stick to judge the truth of what each of us are declaring."

They stared blankly.

"Could that measuring stick," I posed, "possibly be the Bible, God's Word?"

After a few weak comments from the Elders, the evening ended on a somber note. Even Ellen was quiet. But much to my surprise, in spite of my presentation, the Elders asked if we still wanted to come to the next lesson. Such persistence! Susan, rather than jumping at the invitation this time, was gratifyingly quiet— but I could still see the struggle within her.

Elder Black looked intently at me. "There's at least one more lesson we'd like to present," he said. "It's entitled, 'Eternal Progression,' and answers important questions. It tells us where we came from, why we're here, and where we're going. It's a wonderful lesson on how families can stay together for eternity."

I knew exactly what the lesson covered—hadn't I given it enough times? The story of preexistence, the three degrees of glory, temple marriage for time and all eternity . . . that part would really appeal to Susan. I could just picture her imagining herself and Elder Black kneeling at the marriage altar.

How am I going to get us out of this? If I tell the elders no for myself, that might leave Susan coming alone to the lessons. On the other hand, I can't say no for her, that wouldn't be right. How can I end this whole thing? Lord, I need help—now!

The Elders waited for an answer. Then, surprisingly it came.

"Elders," I said, "how would you like to present your next lesson to my class?"

CHAPTER ELEVEN

The Fourth Missionary Presentation

Eternal progression and its destination

Is today it?" Susan asked.

"Yes, today is it," I responded.

Susan slumped further down on the bench, heaving a big sigh. Her eyes, red from lack of sleep, brimmed over with tears.

My heart went out to her, especially since receiving Tia's urgent call. She and Susan had talked until 4:30 that morning, with Susan finally becoming so distraught that she had run out of the dorm in tears. Tia thought Susan was wandering somewhere in the dark on campus. Concerned for her safety, Tia called me. I hurriedly dressed, jumped into the car, and sped to the college. After walking from one end to the other and calling her name, I finally found her on the campus hill overlooking San Antonio.

Sitting down beside her on the bench, neither of us spoke for a long time.

Finally, pointing off in the distance, Susan said, "You can see the Tower of the Americas from here. Matt took me there yesterday."

"That's nice," I said. "Matt's a fine young man. He'll make a good pastor—at least his sermons will never be boring." I tried to laugh.

"That's for sure," she responded in monotone.

"Do you like him?"

"Yeah, he's nice."

Finally we got down to the issue at hand.

"I guess," she said, "this is the day you expect me to break it off with the Elders."

"No, Susan. It's the day I want you to make a decision—the day you decide what *you* want. If you decide to continue the relationship with Elder Black after he's released and end up joining the Mormon Church, that's your choice. But, I've seen so many end up leaving Mormonism, then go through hell trying to undo everything." I patted her hand. "I just don't want you to go through that," I said.

"I've tried everything I know to help you," I continued, "but I don't know what more I can do. I asked the missionaries to present their lesson on campus instead of at Ellen's, feeling it would be easier for you to break it off. But, it's still your choice."

Susan, trying not to cry, then began to share in a more personal way. We continued talking until the sun came up.

"I know what I *ought* to do," Susan finally said. "After all, I've listened to everything you've presented in class and I know you're right. But, it's just that I like Elder Black so much . . ."

"I really sympathize, Susan. I know this decision is difficult. Do you still have any questions about Mormonism?"

"Yeah, I still have a few."

"Well," I said, noticing the campus starting to fill with students, "let's do this. Morning assembly will be starting pretty soon, so let's meet over lunch. We'll grab something from the cafeteria and go eat at one of the outdoor tables. I'm positive, Susan, that whatever your questions are, I can set your mind at ease. In the meantime, you have three classes before mine to mull over your decision. But, it *is* decision day. Okay?"

She nodded. I hated to leave her, but I had materials to prepare for first period. Besides, she needed space.

I quickly walked across campus toward my office. As I opened the door of the Ad building I glanced back. Matt was already sitting on the bench with her. *Now, where had he come from so fast?*

The students were excited, anticipating the arrival of the missionaries. I was relieved that Susan was there, looking better than when I left her earlier. I then turned my full attention to the class.

Concerned that some would challenge the missionaries too harshly, I began to brief them.

"Remember to show respect," I said, "and at least let them present their lesson. It'll provide good material for your notes.

"And, please, don't give them too bad a time. To come on to a Mormon with both barrels shooting from the hip isn't the right approach. Admittedly there are Christians who believe such conflict proves their zeal for God. However, I don't advocate it. If you've studied the facts and know your subject, you can present your case calmly and maturely without being insulting."

"Here de come!" Ilya shouted, pointing out the window.

Walking up the drive they were impressive in their dark suits, white shirts, ties, and lapel pins. They carried briefcases, a table easel, and a portfolio of visual aids. Pastor Donaldson was walking with them, pointing to our classroom.

"Class," I said quickly, "you should realize how brave they are to even show up. They already know what the Christian stance is toward them, but they're here anyway. They hope, of course, that one of you might be swayed." I couldn't help but look at Susan. I noticed Matt did too.

Entering the room, they both smiled nervously, obviously feeling out of place. Elder Black looked especially nice—I could see how Susan was drawn to him. But I wondered if he really cared for her as much as Susan thought. I had already heard about a Ward in another state that sanctioned their youth making boyfriend/girlfriend overtures to non-Mormons their own age until they were converted. After that, much to the devastation of the new convert, romantic relationships were dropped. It almost sounded like the "flirty-fishing" of the Children of God cult.

"Welcome to our class, Elders," I said, giving them a big smile. "Come on up front. The class is pretty well versed on LDS beliefs, so I don't think you need to explain any basics. Just go ahead and present your lesson." I then headed for a chair in the back of the room.

Facing the class, Elder Black began. "We're covering a subject today that I'm sure will interest all of you. Have any of you ever pondered the questions: Where did I come from? Why am I here? Where am I going after this life?"

"I came from Los Angeles," Matt jokingly quipped.

Tia gave him an exasperated look, then responded, "I never really questioned if I came from anywhere. However, I have to admit that I've wondered about the purpose of life—other than finding the Lord, that is."

Elder Black smiled. "Well, we're here to provide some answers. But, we need to start back at the beginning. Elder Barrett?"

Elder Barrett then stepped forward while Elder Black proceeded to put up the easel.

"Before we were born," he began, "we lived in a premortal world with our heavenly Father. He was our literal parent in that world."

Robert interrupted, "What do you mean by *literal?*"

"That means God was our father in the same way we have fathers here on earth."

"Does that mean what I think it means?" Robert queried further.

"Well, yes," Elder Black replied. "Acts 17:29 says, 'We are the offspring of God.' It's wonderful to know that He is our literal father. As His spirit children, we are very unique—our spirits are divine.

"When we were with Him in that world," he continued, "we noticed that our Father had one thing we didn't have—an immortal, glorified body. We wanted to become like Him and, like any earthly parent, He also wanted us to become like Him. Therefore, He formulated a plan whereby He would create an earth and send us down to grow and gain experience like He once did.

"From the Book of Abraham, we learn about the special council He convened . . ."

Then, stopping abruptly, Elder Black quickly asked, "Do all of you know about the Book of Abraham?"

The class, knowing it had already been proved to be an Egyptian funeral text rather than Abraham's writings, nodded politely. I was proud of them.

"Well, then you probably know," he continued, "that Abraham said that in the premortal world God gathered His spirit children together, which included Abraham and Jeremiah. From them He chose those who were to be leaders on earth.[1] This also included Jeremiah, for in 1:5 God says, 'Before I formed thee in the belly I knew thee . . . and I ordained thee a prophet.' The Book of Mormon also teaches that leaders were 'prepared from the foundation of the world.[2]

"In this premortal council, the question of salvation came up. Two plans were presented, one by Jesus, the other by Lucifer. Jesus' plan was chosen, which would allow individuals their free agency. Lucifer's plan, which would force everyone to be saved, was rejected. There was war, and Lucifer and his angels were expelled from heaven, as mentioned in Revelation 2:7–9.

"Plans then ensued to organize this world for us. I'm sure we were all excited. Mortality would give us a physical body, would be a testing ground to see if we would keep His commandments and, eventually, in the resurrection, we would have a glorified body like our heavenly Father's. Since birth would make us forget our preexistence, God promised that the Holy Ghost would guide us to the *true* church so we could find out about our premortal home.

"Now, before we move on, are there any questions?"

I quietly chuckled as I saw the hands shoot up.

Tia was first.

"You said that God had a physical body. Wouldn't that limit Him? How could He possibly be *omnipresent* if confined to a physical body?"

Elder Barrett responded with no hesitation. "When the Bible talks about God's being *omnipresent*, it is not really speaking about God Himself, but His Holy Spirit—the latter not to be confused with the Holy Ghost. Let me explain.

"While there is God the Father, God the Son, and God the Holy *Ghost*, there is also God the Holy *Spirit*. The latter a spiritual energy that proceeds from the throne of God and is diffused throughout the universe. This is what is omnipresent."

Tia didn't press the issue, but politely smiled and began writing in her notebook.

Matt, looking like he had something up his sleeve, raised his hand.

"Do you believe that God has certain laws that He is bound to comply with, or can He change them according to His whim?"

"We believe," Elder Barret responded, "that there are universal principles that God Himself cannot violate. They always existed and are coeternal with Him. He must abide by them or He would cease to be God."

A look of astonishment appeared on the students' faces.

"Well, then," Matt continued, "why did God violate the law of propagation?"

Both Elders looked baffled. But I was impressed.

"In Genesis," Matt continued, "God issued a universal law that each should multiply after its own kind. For example, the offspring of two squirrels will always be a baby squirrel. It will be just like its parents, fur and all. But, a donkey and an elephant can never produce a donkephant."

The class laughed as Matt, sober faced, continued. "Like must always produce like . . . right?"

"Of course," Elder Barrett responded.

"But," Matt continued, "you're saying that in the premortal world, God, who had a glorified, immortal body, literally beget children who were different. They were spirits, having no body like His! How come?"

Good question, Matt.

Elder Black looked a little taken back. "Of course, uh, we don't have all the answers. There are some mysteries that we aren't expected to know. That's one of them."

Matt leaned back looking rather proud of himself, then glanced at Susan with a look that said, *See—they're way out in left field!*

Ilya spoke up. "I tink vhen you say dat ve haf forgotten our premortal world, it sounds like Gnosticism. Do you know about dat?"

Both Elders looked blank.

"Gnostics," Ilya continued, "vas heretical group in Jesus' time. Dey, like Mormons, said salvation came by special knowledge. More especially, knowing vhere dey came from, vhy dey ver here, and vhere dey ver going. Dey also claimed der spirit vas divine, but mortality robbed dem of memory of der heavenly origin.[3] Salvation was finding out about der premortal glory. Dey also practiced baptism for dead."

I was impressed. I hadn't realized Ilya knew anything about the subject. But, she was right. Mormon beliefs were so Gnostic that BYU had, at one time, promoted the study of Gnosticism.[4]

Elder Barrett looked helpless. Elder Black, however, came to the rescue.

"I don't know anything about Gnosticism," he began, "but their belief that the spirits of men had a divine nature and that it was important to find out about their premortal world, doesn't surprise me at all. Many true doctrines were understood in Bible times. However, through the apostasy, those truths were lost. This necessitated God's restoring them through the prophet Joseph Smith."

I had to hand it to the Elders. Although the early Christian church had declared Gnosticism heretical, the apostasy was a convenient way to justify these beliefs.

"Well, let's move on," Elder Barrett said, suddenly renewed by Elder Black's answer.

"Earthly parents realize there comes a time when children must leave home, be on their own, and prove themselves. Similarly, our Father in heaven told us that we had to leave our premortal home and prove ourselves. We had to learn good from evil, which was the only way we could become more like Him. Genesis 3:5 says that one of the characteristics of God is to know good from evil.

"Therefore, the first purpose of life is to gain a body so that it can one day be immortalized and glorified. The second purpose is to learn good from evil through experience. The third, to prove faithful.

"I testify to you that our Father in heaven did indeed send us to this earth to learn about good and evil, so that we could work out our salvation. The choices we make will determine where we spend eternity. I'm grateful that I belong to the Church of Jesus Christ of Latter-day Saints and have apostles and prophets to guide me in those choices and restore knowledge about my premortal home."

Resuming his presentation, Elder Barrett said, "Since we don't remember our preexistent home, Philippians 2:12 says we must work out our salvation with fear and trembling. The Book of Mormon also says that 'this life [is] a probationary state; a time to prepare to meet God.'"[5] He then began reading other Mormon scriptures.[6]

At that point, Elder Barrett paused while Elder Black proceeded to place a large picture on the easel. Near the bottom, two globes were portrayed one above the other. The bottom globe was pure white, before which a white, spirit-like man stood, representing the premortal world and its inhabitants. The next one up, looking just like earth, had a mortal man standing before it, representing earth life.

Elder Black then placed another poster on the easel. This time, four more globes were depicted. A grayish one, directly above earth, entitled 'Spirit World.' Above that, a series of three globes in a row representing the Telestial, Terrestrial, and Celestial heavens.

"As much as people fear death," Elder Barrett continued, "we should understand that it's all part of the plan that God designed to bring us happiness. Only through this process can we gain an immortal body in the resurrection and become like our Father in heaven."

Matt raised his hand. "I'm curious about that gray globe you've labeled 'Spirit World.' Since it's between earth and the top three heavens, does that mean that after one dies, one must go there first, instead of directly to heaven—sorta' like purgatory?"

"That's right," came the response. "After death, our spirits go to the 'Spirit World,' which is divided into two sections. One section is Paradise, for those who accept the *true* gospel while on earth. The other is Spirit Prison, for those who did not."

"Oh, I see," Matt mused. "Sorta like Monopoly. Go straight to jail . . . do not pass Go . . . Is that right?"

The class snickered while the Elders looked momentarily stunned at his humor.

"Well, I don't know about that," Elder Barrett said, finally forcing a smile. "Let me explain.

"Prior to Jesus' death, there was a gulf that divided the Spirit World. But after Jesus' death, 1 Peter 3:19 tells us that He 'went and preached unto the spirits in prison.' So also does 1 Peter 4:6. He bridged the gulf between Paradise where the faithful spirits were, and Spirit Prison. Jesus opened the way so that later, LDS Elders, after they die, can go into the spirit prison, teach the fullness of the gospel, and set the prisoners free.

"However, since accepting the gospel is not only a spiritual act, but a physical one, those in prison must be baptized. Obviously, they have no body in which to perform this act. Therefore, we have holy temples where this is performed for them. This same ordinance of the Gospel was practiced by the early saints and acknowledged by Paul in 1 Corinthians 15:29, 'Else what shall they do which are baptized for the dead if the dead raise not at all?'

"This shows the wonderful mercy and justice God extends to His children. Certainly, those who died without knowledge of the gospel should not be consigned to hell for all eternity. They'll be given full opportunity to enter the kingdom of God through baptism."

"So," Robert interrupted, "how do you perform baptisms for dead people who died hundreds of years ago?"

"I'm glad you asked that," Elder Barrett said, smiling.

"Members of our church search out their genealogies in order to identify their dead ancestors. After recording birth, death, and marriage dates, they submit the names to the temple for vicarious baptism. In this labor of love, their diligent genealogical work proves that the hearts of the children have indeed turned to the fathers, fulfilling Malachi 4:5–6:

> Behold, I will send you Elijah the prophet before the coming of the great and dreadful day of the LORD; And he shall turn the heart of the fathers to the children, and the heart of the children to their fathers, lest I come and smite the earth with a curse.

"You mean," Robert said with shock, "that you believe Malachi was talking about *genealogy!*"

"Yes. In fact," Elder Barrett added, "this work for the dead is so important that the Lord will smite the earth with a curse if it isn't done.

"The reason it's so important," Elder Barrett continued, "is because, as Hebrews 11:40 states, we cannot be saved without our dead. I'm grateful to my heavenly Father Who has provided a plan whereby my dead ancestors can be saved."

"But," Ilya interrupted, "again dat is Gnostic. Dey also believed dey could not be redeemed until *all* ver redeemed."

Elder Barrett smiled. "They certainly understood the *gospel*, didn't they?"

Ilya glanced at me in wonderment then made notations on a piece of paper.

"You stated," Robert said, "that Malachi 4 means genealogy and work for the dead. But, it says that *Elijah* will initiate turning the hearts of the children to their fathers. Where does Elijah fit into the LDS picture?"

"Well, we don't usually cover that in this lesson, but we'll make an exception.

"In 1836, Elijah came to Joseph Smith and Oliver Cowdery and conferred upon them the necessary keys to begin this great latter-day work. In addition, Elias and Moses also appeared. Then, Jesus, adding His sanction."[7]

Robert looked puzzled. "I don't get it. You make it sound like Elias is a separate person from Elijah."

"That's right."

"But," Robert persisted, "didn't Joseph Smith know that *Elias* was simply the Greek word for *Elijah* and that John the Baptist fulfilled that Scripture? Let me read it, he insisted." Quickly opening his Bible, he turned to Luke 1:17 in his NIV Bible:

> And he [John the Baptist] will go on before the Lord, in the spirit and power of Elijah [Elias in the KJV], to turn the hearts of the fathers to their children and the disobedient to the wisdom of the righteous—to make ready a people prepared for the Lord.

Elder Barrett, without batting an eye, said, "Yes, John the Baptist would function in the *spirit* of an Elias, which simply means *forerunner*. But, the prophet Joseph Smith clarified the matter by stating that there was indeed a historical person named Elias.

"The reason the Bible doesn't mention him is because information about this individual was lost in the transmission of the Scriptures down through the centuries. Nevertheless, God through Elias and Elijah restored the keys for this work so that a way could be provided for those who never heard the Gospel."[8]

He then pointed to the three globes at the top of the chart. "Those who accept the *fullness* of the gospel and keep all the laws and ordinances of their heavenly Father as contained in the Church of Jesus Christ of Latter-day Saints will inherit the Celestial Kingdom. Paul knew about this kingdom and in 1 Corinthians 15:41, compared it to the glory of the sun."

Susan surprisingly jumped into the conversation. "Does that mean," she queried, "that only Mormons will go to the Celestial Kingdom and be married for time and all eternity?"

"Yes," he replied. "After all, our church is the one God Himself set up. Therefore, members of our church prepare themselves for exaltation in that kingdom.

"One of the ways we do that is by living the law of chastity. Since we were given the godly power of procreation so that we could participate in the creation of life, it is important that we don't misuse this sacred gift. If we are faithful, this gift will continue with us into the eternities.

"Another preparation we make is living the Word of Wisdom. This law teaches us to avoid alcohol, coffee, tea, tobacco, and injurious drugs so we won't damage our bodies or our spirits.

"On the other hand," he said, pointing to the chart's portrayal of the middle kingdom, "those who do not accept the fullness of the gospel will go to the Terrestrial Kingdom. This glory, Paul says, is comparable to the moon. Lastly, there is the lowest kingdom, the Telestial, comparable to the stars."

Then, as I expected, he began his programmed testimony.

"I am blessed to belong to the true church which provides all the laws and ordinances for me to follow so I can someday return to my Father in heaven. I'm also thankful that I belong to the Church of Jesus Christ of Latter-day Saints, the only true Church upon the face of the earth, which tells me about my premortal home and provides the means whereby I can be with my family forever."

With that, he took a picture from his wallet. "This," he said, holding it up to the class, "is my family back home. It would be devastating for me to think of eternity without them. I have grown to appreciate them even more since I've been away on my mission. The promise of life after death with them is a wonderful blessing I look forward to."

Glancing at my watch, I signaled to the Elders.

"Before we finish," Elder Barrett said, "we'd like to conclude by sharing a few Scriptures with you that back up everything we've said."

With those words, he and Elder Black took turns in quickly rattling off verses not mentioned previously. Since this was one of the lessons that quotes more LDS Scripture than Bible, it was not surprising that most of them were from the Book of Mormon and the Doctrine and Covenants.[9]

"Elders," I said, walking to the front, "thank you so much for coming. Class, did you enjoy their presentation?"

The class burst forth with a vigorous applause. The missionaries looked pleased and proceeded to fold up the easel and put their visual aids away.

Just as I called out, "Time for a break!" the intermission bell rang. Thanking the Elders again, we shook hands. They made no gesture to invite me to Ellen's again.

Everyone scrambled for the door except Susan, Matt, and four other students who, approaching the Elders, began besieging them with questions.

Noticing Susan hanging back, I decided she felt uncomfortable with me there. I left the classroom believing she would feel more free to tell the Elders of her decision. I hoped she knew that even if she ended up becoming a Mormon, I would still be her friend. Good grief! What was I thinking? *Of course she's going to cut it off with them!*

Sitting nervously on the bench, I watched the door until the four students left. Matt came out but stayed by the door. Susan was still inside. The minutes dragged. *Lord, give her courage!*

Just then, Susan and the Elders exited the building. Smiling, they shook hands. *That doesn't look like a final farewell to me,* I thought.

Waving to me, they set off down the walk. Susan and Matt ambled over to a bench, sat down, and began talking. *Now, why didn't she come over and at least tell me what she told them? Maybe she's agreed to continue the lessons with them and just doesn't want to tell me. Oh, Susan! But, at least good ol' Matt is helping out.* He was talking for all he was worth.

A series of three short bells signaled the end of the break. *Well,* I decided, *Susan and I are having lunch together—I'll find out what the score is then.*

I headed back into the room and everyone took their seats. Matt and Susan, however, were still outside.

Addressing the class, I said. "I think in the last few weeks we've covered Mormonism pretty well. So, Thursday, we'll be moving on to another religion.

"Are there any questions about the Elders' presentation?"

"I have one," Tia said. "What do you think about their salvation for the dead?"

"That doctrine," I said, "contradicts the Bible wherein Jesus said, 'the night is coming, when no one can work'[10] It doesn't say, 'don't worry about it—you'll get another chance after you're dead.' Interestingly, even the Book of Mormon confirms that only 'this life is the time for men to prepare to meet God [and] to perform their labors.' It even goes on to say that at death they can't say, 'I will repent.'[11]

"Then, that doesn't make sense," Tia interrupted. "Why would they teach something that contradicts what the Book of Mormon teaches?"

"Here's the reason," I said. "Originally, Smith didn't teach baptism for the dead. Giving the dead another chance in the spirit world was a gradual evolution in Mormon thinking.

"At the time Smith wrote, he was being influenced by the Presbyterians and Methodists of his time who were opposed to Universalism, which taught there was no hell and everyone would eventually be saved. Therefore, he incorporated the subject into the Book of Mormon, stating universal salvation to be false.[12]

"But, a year later Smith changed his mind and adopted the Catholic concept of purgatory, claiming universal salvation valid except for those committing the unpardonable sin.[13] But, this is no surprise. He changed his mind about a lot of things.[14] For example, the Book of Mormon teaches against a plurality of gods, polygamy, and secret societies, but Smith later embraced all three.[15]

"Genealogy and LDS ordinances for the dead, contradict 1 Timothy 1:4 and Titus 3:9. In particular, Mormons fail to understand 1 Peter 3:19–20 and 4:6, where Christ went and preached to the spirits in prison.

"Mormons would have you believe that the dead who didn't accept Christ in this world are kept in spirit prison until they can hear the Mormon gospel. After that, they can go to heaven where Jesus is.[16] There is absolutely nothing in the Bible to validate this.

"Does 1 Peter 3:19 say any spirits in prison repented and were saved as a result? Does it say any were baptized on behalf of them? No."

Tia interrupted. "Does it say who those people in Spirit Prison were?"

"Yes. They're identified in 1 Peter 3:20 as those who were disobedient in the days of Noah. Further, verses 20b and 21 confirm that they were *not* the ones who were saved—only those in the ark were. Mormonism teaches they will have a second chance to avoid hell and be saved in the Terrestial heaven where they will enjoy the presence of Jesus.[17]

"When Christ went to the Spirit Prison, He preached that part of the Gospel that explains about *judgment*. But," I said, "Mormons will argue that 1 Peter 4:6 says Christ preached the Gospel to the *dead*! It doesn't. The NIV says that the Gospel was preached 'even to those who are now dead.' In other words, the Gospel was preached to them *before* they died. Why? So that *after* death, which is what verse 6 is describing, they could be judged and 'give account to him who is ready to judge the living and the dead.' There is no second chance."

"I have another question," Robert called out, "but it's changing the subject."

"Go ahead."

"Ilya mentioned that Mormonism was like Gnosticism. What's that?"

"In brief," I said, "the Gnostics were a heretical group, active in some form during the New Testament period and in the following century.

"Like Mormons, they believed in a pantheon of gods and maintained that there was more than one heaven. They even declared that the ruler of the seventh heaven was the God of the Jews and the devil was his son—again, similar to what Mormonism teaches.[18]

"They also taught marriage in heaven and had secret passwords so they could pass by watchmen who guarded the heavenly gates.

"Salvation and redemption, for them, was gaining special knowledge through *gnōsis*—not the cross. It consisted of knowing that their real self albeit imprisoned in a body of evil matter, contained a divine spark, much like the Mormon's spirit being a divine offspring. Similarly, they believed that birth robbed them of recollecting their heavenly origin. Their confidence and salvation, therefore, consisted in knowing who they were, where they came from, why they were here, and where they were going—all of which the missionaries' lesson today was based upon.

"Infiltrating the church at Corinth, the Gnostics were, according to one scholar, the Christ party causing so much division."[19]

"How," Tia exclaimed, "did the Gnostics even get into the church?"

"First," I replied, "they were probably attracted to the Christ *principle*. Second, they were able to pass themselves off as Christians by professing a belief in Christ, using Christian terminology, and hiding their real beliefs.

"They believed that 'Christ' (not Jesus) was already within everyone. This is the divine spark I just mentioned. But only those who recognized this through self-realization, called *gnōsis*, or knowledge, could be saved and redeemed. While Paul taught that 'Christ in you' was a gift, Gnostics believed it was achieved through recognition of its inherent presence. They believed there was one Christ in heaven, and 'it' had already incarnated into many men and prophets in history, Jesus included. However, they did not believe Christ was incarnate in Jesus' flesh. Therefore, they taught that this 'Christ' left Jesus just before His resurrection.

"Soon, it became evident that the Gnostics had no reverence for Jesus the man since they believed all physical bodies were made up of evil matter. This is why later, when more was known about the Gnostics, John set forth a test so Christians could discern who were true believers: 'Every spirit that confesseth that Jesus Christ is *come in the flesh* is of God: And every spirit that confesseth *not* that Jesus Christ is come in the flesh is not of God' [emphasis mine].[20]

"Adding to problems at Corinth, Gnostics considered themselves more elite than the Corinthian saints. This was, of course, because they had achieved *gnōsis*, the special knowledge that their divine spirit had a heavenly origin and that their body was evil matter—thus of no consequence.

"Because they believed the spirit was the only thing good in man, their bodies could eat food sacrificed to idols and indulge in other immoralities. After all, since it would only be their spirit rising in the resurrection, it made no difference what they did in the flesh.

"They had great missionary zeal because, like Mormons, they realized they could only be redeemed when all were redeemed.[21] Therefore, they performed baptisms for the dead, believing this rite was a magical act that would free dead people's spirits and make them Gnostics. Without the ascension of all spirits, the body of Christ, which is scattered in pieces in all men, would be incomplete in heaven.

"They were, no doubt, the ones mentioned in 1 Corinthians

15:29.[22] At that time Paul did not pass judgment on their baptismal practice, probably for two reasons. First, he knew the true saints weren't the ones practicing it. Second, he didn't know as much about the Gnostics then as he obviously learned later.[23]

"So, Gnosticism and Mormonism are very much alike.

"But now, we need to summarize what the Mormon missionaries presented today." At that point, I was delighted to see Matt and Susan slipping into their seats.

"When Elder Barrett told us about the premortal world and the council, it was deceptive because he didn't tell all they believed. He only mentioned *one* God while we know they believe in a plurality of gods.[24] Orson Pratt confirms this teaching: 'If we should take a million of worlds like this and number their particles, we should find that there are more gods than there are particles of matter in those worlds.'[25]

"The Mormon Elders didn't reveal any of this. Neither did they make any mention of a mother in heaven, which they continually sing about in Ward meetings.[26]

At that point, I humorously cleared my voice, much to the delight of the class, and began squawking out one of the stanzas of *O My Father*:

> In the heav'ns are parents single?
> No; the tho't makes reason stare!
> Truth is reason, Truth eternal,
> Tells me I've a Mother there.

After the laughter and applause died down and taking my bows, I said, "Plus, they didn't tell us that God our heavenly Father has more than one wife.

"He also destroyed God's status of being omnipotent when he said that if God violated certain principles, He would cease to be God. This means that principles have superiority over Him.

"Another facet of this that they didn't mention is that heaven works on a democratic system. 'Intelligences,' or God's spirit children, according to a former BYU professor, could also dethrone Him:

> If He [God] should ever do anything to violate the confidence or "sense of justice" of these intelligences [spirit children], they would promptly withdraw their support, and the "power" of God would disintegrate . . . "He would cease to be God." Our

Heavenly Father can do only those things which the intelligences under Him are voluntarily willing to support Him in accomplishing.[27]

"There are Scriptures after Scriptures that declare that God cannot be what Mormons describe Him to be."[28]

"You would have thought," Matt interjected, "that Smith would have stuck with biblical concepts in order to gain more followers."

"He did, at first. In the Book of Mormon, he presented orthodox concepts of God. Mormon 9:9 says that there is 'no variableness neither shadow of changing' in God, refuting Smith's later teaching that God is progressing.

"As Smith's ideas changed, Book of Mormon passages were also changed. Specifically, they altered those verses that made a distinction between God the Father and God the Son.

"For example, in the original edition of the Book of Mormon, it stated that God is 'a Great Spirit,'[29] *not* a man. In 2 Nephi and Alma it declared that the Father, Son, and Holy Ghost are *one* God, not separate gods.[30]

"First Nephi 13:40 originally described the Lamb of God as 'the Eternal Father, and the Savior of the World.' But, now it reads, 'the Lamb of God is the *Son* of the Eternal Father.' They also changed verses that stated that the Virgin Mary is the 'mother of God' to read 'mother of the *son* of God.'[31] And, I could go on.

"If Smith was supposed to be a prophet, you would think he would have had God's message right the first time."

Robert raised his hand. "Could you clarify Elder Barrett's distinction between the Holy Ghost and the Holy Spirit."

"The specific distinction between the Holy Ghost and the Holy Spirit is this: The Holy Ghost, as defined by Bruce R. McConkie, 'can be in only one place at one time.'[32] His job is to come to a person and testify of the truth. Joseph Smith taught that the Holy Ghost is a man with a spiritual body. Like others in the premortal world, he is waiting to take on a physical body.[33]

"The Holy Spirit, on the other hand, as defined by Apostle John A. Widtsoe, 'is a universe-filling medium or influence.'[34] Apostle Parley Pratt further clarifies it by saying the Holy Spirit is 'a divine substance or fluid' and is 'the purest, most refined and subtle of all substances, and the one least understood, or even recognized, by the less informed among mankind.'"[35]

Susan raised her hand.

"The Elders quoted 1 Corinthians 15:40, which makes me wonder whether there might not be three heavens."

"Using that quote of Paul's to prove there are three heavens," I said, "is utter nonsense. First, Paul only mentions the words *terrestrial* and *celestial* and makes no mention of *telestial*. Second, Paul is talking about *bodies*, not heavens. He is explaining how our natural earthly body, which is terrestrial, will be changed in the resurrection to a spiritual, celestial body. Mormons are guilty of not studying the context of their quotes.[36]

"I truly feel sorry for the Elders," I added. "I can only hope they acquire a drive for truth that will lead them to investigate their beliefs. While they are very sincere," I said, "and like other Mormons may love the Lord Jesus Christ as I did, God wants them to get their theology straight and slough off the nonessentials.

"They also need to abandon the idea of belonging to the only true church. The true church, the body of Christ, is not an organization, upon which salvation rests. As Marvin W. Cowan states, [Jesus] never said, 'No man cometh unto the Father but through my Church.'"[37]

Just then the bell rang and the classroom quickly emptied. I surprisingly found myself slumping down in my chair. The last few weeks had exhausted me. However, I was pleased with the students. Robert, who looked at everything from an intellectual standpoint seemed to be grasping more of the spiritual aspect. Tia and Ilya were growing in their zeal for the truth. Matt, despite his humorous antics, was showing a serious side that I was beginning to appreciate. Then there was Susan . . . Susan! I jumped up from my chair. I'd forgotten about lunch!

Glancing out the window, I was relieved to see her still waiting. Grabbing my briefcase, I hurried out the door.

"C'mon," I said, grinning. "Let's go and fill up our plates with some of that delicious cafeteria food that the students don't seem to appreciate."

Susan smiled, but said nothing.

As we walked toward the cafeteria, I prayed. *Father, this is my last chance with Susan. You said no one could pluck Your children out of Your hand—You'd better do something!*

As we stood in line in the cafeteria, I wondered what our time together would bring. She still hadn't volunteered what she told the Elders.

Maybe, I thought dejectedly, *she's trying to get up enough courage to tell me what I don't want to hear. Maybe she's found the idea of being married for time and all eternity in a beautiful temple too appealing to resist.*

On the other hand, maybe she just needs questions answered. What on? The Book of Mormon? Quetzalcoatl? The apostasy? As I thought about her strong feelings for Elder Black, I wondered if anything I might say would make a difference.

CHAPTER TWELVE

The Witnesses of the Book of Mormon

What they really saw

Susan finally blurted it out, "What about the testimony of the Book of Mormon witnesses!"

At last I knew what was bothering her!

However, her question wasn't unusual. I'd heard it many times—even from ex-Mormons. But I still didn't know if she had ended it with the missionaries.

We carried our cafeteria trays to a picnic table beneath a huge willow tree. It was Friday, and a warm breeze wafted its way across campus. I could hear students talking about their plans for the weekend. Even I was thinking wistfully about driving down to the Gulf. But, I sighed, I needed to stick with Susan, however long it might take.

"Susan, before I answer, I need to know what you told the Elders."

"I . . . told them I'd call," she said hesitantly. "I'm sorry," she exclaimed, "I just couldn't do it!

"I know you probably think I'm crazy, in view of everything you've said in class. But I keep thinking about the testimonies of the witnesses printed in the front of the Book of Mormon.

"Three say they saw the plates and heard God's voice. Eight say they handled the plates and saw the engravings. That's pretty heavy-duty!

"And, since they're all dead, who can prove them wrong? Even if I prayed about it, I'm sure I'm not going to hear some booming voice say, 'No, Susan, they never saw the plates' or 'Yes, they did.'" She looked like she was on the verge of crying.

"Susan, what you need at this point," I said, "are more facts.

"So, let's look at the three witnesses—Martin Harris, Oliver Cowdery, and David Whitmer. First, however, we need to find out where that printed testimony came from.

"Did the three witnesses write it? No. It was Joseph Smith, himself, who drew it up. He spun it off from Doctrine and Covenants 17 where God supposedly told him he would provide him with witnesses.

"The significant point is that at the time he wrote it, he *knew* none of the witnesses had ever seen the plates with their *natural* eyes. Yet, when he worded it, he deliberately gave the impression they had.[1]

"Harris, himself, admitted that he never saw anything with his natural eyes. He said the plates were always covered by a cloth.[2] He further let the cat out of the bag when he revealed that neither had the other witnesses. On April 15, 1838, Harris stated publicly:

> He never saw the plates with his natural eyes only in vision or imagination, neither Oliver nor David & also that the eight witnesses never saw them & *hesitated to sign* that instrument for that reason, but were *persuaded* to do it. . . . [Harris later] said that he never should have told that the testimony of the eight was false, if it had not been picked out of (him) but should have let it passed [sic] as it was [emphasis mine].[3]

"So Susan, in reality, the three witnesses really saw nothing!"

"I don't know about that," Susan mused. "They had to have seen something . . ."

"What they saw," I said, "was a product of their own mind. Let me explain.

"Historical accounts suggest that the witnesses were effectively induced to see the plates in a vision because of Smith's mesmerizing methods.

"First, he persisted in badgering them by telling them that only the faithful could see them. That kind of remark would intimidate the best of men.

"Persuasion like that is similar to missionaries reading the promise at the end of the Book of Mormon to investigators. It says if, with a *sincere* heart, you ask God in the name of Christ, that the truth will be manifest to you by the Holy Ghost. This suggests that if you *don't* get an answer, you're *not* sincere.

"An investigator, therefore, is intimidated by the missionaries and fellowshippers who say they *have* received an answer. He or she then wonders what's wrong that God hasn't spoken. As a result of the intimidation, many keep praying *until* they get some kind of manifestation, which is usually produced by their own psyche.

"Similarly, Smith used the same psychology. Playing upon the witnesses' emotions, he engineered them into conjuring up a vision. In those kinds of circumstances, individuals will see exactly what they are expected to see.

"Here's an example," I said, opening my notebook. This is an account as told to the governor of Illinois, Thomas Ford, by more than one of Smith's key men. It tells how Smith manipulated all eight witnesses to see a vision:

> They [Smith's men] told Ford that the witnesses were "set to continual prayer, and other spiritual exercises." Then at last "he assembled them in a room, and produced a box which he said contained the precious treasure. The lid was opened; the witnesses peeped into it, but making no discovery, for the box was *empty,* they said, 'Brother Joseph, we do not see the plates.' The prophet answered them, 'O ye of little faith! how long will God bear with this wicked and perverse generation? Down on your knees, brethren, every one of you, and pray God for the forgiveness of your sins, and for a holy and living faith which cometh down from heaven.' The disciples dropped to their knees, and began to pray in the fervency of their spirit, supplicating God for *more than two hours* with fanatical earnestness; at the end of which time, looking again into the box, they were now persuaded that they saw the plates" [emphasis mine].[4]

"Each one conjured up, in their own minds, what they were expected to see—that is, if they wanted to be counted worthy. That they saw it with their spiritual eyes instead of natural, accounts for newspaper reports that said that all three witnesses told different versions. This 'makes it all the more likely,' author Fawn Brodie notes, 'that the men were not conspirators but *victims* of Joseph's unconscious but positive talent at hypnosis' [emphasis mine].[5]

"If the plates really existed, Susan, and God provided these men as witnesses, it makes no sense that they be subjected to accusations of guilt and unworthiness. Further, to be forced to pray until they conjured up a vision of plates in a box that was really empty—Why not let them see the actual plates?

"If all eleven witnesses had been shown the plates, if they existed, they would have had a stronger testimony about Mormonism being God's work. But, as it stood, all of them, with the exception of Smith's father, his two brothers, and two who died, left the church.[6] Not very impressive.

"The Mormon Church, of course, sticks to its story that none of the three witnesses ever denied their testimony. But, Oliver Cowdery, according to the Mormon publication *Times and Seasons,* did deny his.[7]

"Oliver Cowdery even joined the Methodist Church. He also said he was willing to make a public recantation and that he was 'sorry and ashamed of his connection with Mormonism.'[8]

"The LDS church, however, claims Cowdery came back to the church. But if he did, he must have left again, because when he died he was buried by a Methodist minister in Richmond, Missouri.

"The significant factor here, Susan, is if the witnesses didn't deny their testimony, then why did they turn against the church and embrace another faith?

"David Whitmer, although still believing in the Book of Mormon, became a member of the Church of Christ and died rejecting the LDS Church.

"Martin Harris joined Anna Lee's church, saying that his testimony of Shakerism was greater than that of the Book of Mormon.[9] Although later in life he came back to the Mormon Church and went through the temple ceremony, he said it was just to find out 'what was going on in there.'"[10]

"I guess," Susan said, "it isn't very logical that the three witnesses would turn their backs on Joseph Smith if they really believed he was God's prophet. Nor would they reject a church they felt God had restored."

"But, they did," I said. "However, suppose LDS leaders are correct and the witnesses never denied their testimony. Why would they still maintain that testimony and, at the same time, reject Smith's church?

"Yeah," Susan mused. "It doesn't make much sense."

"Well, I believe I know three reasons why. First, the witnesses surely wouldn't want to disillusion and destroy the faith of those who were converted to the Book of Mormon because of *their* testimony. I believe they retained a special feeling for the Book of Mormon because there were so many biblical concepts in it.

"Second, since their declaration is stated in the name of the Father, Son, and Holy Ghost, they would not only be guilty of perjury, but their credibility would be suspect the rest of their lives.

"Third, wouldn't they look pretty silly telling people that what they testified to and allowed to appear in print really didn't happen?

"Okay, that sounds reasonable," Susan said. "But, what about the eight witnesses saying they actually *hefted* the plates?"

"In the first place," I said, "there is no way they could have lifted them in the casual manner they describe. According to their reported size, the plates would have weighed nearly 230 pounds. Nevertheless, I do believe they hefted *something*.

"Whatever it was that they lifted, Smith persuaded them it was the plates. He may have duped them in the same way he duped two friends, William T. Hussey and Azel Vandruver.

"Showing them the supposed plates concealed beneath a canvas, Smith convinced them that they were so sacred that if they looked directly upon them they would die.

"One of the friends, however, was so anxious that he ripped off the canvas, saying, 'Egad, I'll see the critter, live or die!'"[11]

"What did he see," Susan asked excitedly.

"Nothing but 'a large tile brick,'"[12] I replied. "Smith was always pulling tricks like this. He evidently took great delight in fooling people about having gold plates."

"But," Susan asked, "how do we explain the fact that the witnesses said they saw *engravings* on the plates?"

"Many feel that Smith later concocted some kind of plates on his own. Oliver Cowdery could have made such a set, engravings and all, since he'd been a blacksmith in his youth.[13]

"By making some plates, Smith hoped to make money by exhibiting them. Joseph's father told Joseph Capron that 'when the book was published, they would be enabled, from the profits of the work, to carry into successful operation of [sic] the money digging business.'[14]

"In addition, John C. Bennett, a close associate, said that Smith asked him to go to New York and obtain some falsely engraved plates so that he could exhibit them at '25 cents a sight.'[15] While Bennett's story might be suspect, considering his dubious reputation, his story, nevertheless, was backed up by Apostle Orson Pratt's wife, Sarah.

"So, Susan, when one researches the facts, there is only one conclusion to reach. It was an elaborate hoax that snowballed from Smith's treasure-divining activities and tale-telling."

"Pretty impressive," Susan said soberly. "The more you tell me, the more I become convinced. But the Book of Mormon talks so much about Christ," she said wistfully.

"Susan, if the Mormon Church taught nothing else but what was in the Book of Mormon, it might not be so bad. But you know as well as I that, today, they teach doctrines completely foreign to the Book of Mormon—doctrines that the missionaries deliberately hide from investigators.

"In fact, I could also write a book that talks a lot about Christ. But, Susan, that doesn't make it God's Word. I could also read a passage from any cult's book of scripture and you wouldn't know whether I took it from the Bible or not. They all sound good. You can't go by how spiritual something sounds."

"Well," Susan lamented, "you have to admit that the idea of Quetzalcoatl being Jesus was intriguing."

"Yes. But, if Jesus were going to preach the Gospel by visiting other nations Himself, why bother giving the Great Commission to His disciples? Besides, if He did visit America after His resurrection, He wasn't very effective. The Lamanites didn't seem to derive any benefit from their scriptures and all the righteous Nephites were killed off in the end. When the descendants of the Lamanites, the Indians, finally did hear the Gospel, they had to hear it hundreds of years later from Christian missionaries. And remember, the Indian tradition of Quetzalcoatl doesn't fit the time frame of the A.D. 34 Book of Mormon account.

"Susan, has this helped you at all?"

"Yeah, it has . . . but . . ." Her voice trailed off.

"But, you're still thinking about Elder Black?"

She nodded.

"Susan, answer me this: If you became Elder Black's wife, would you like to share him with another woman?"

Looking startled, she gasped, "Of course not!"

"Well, that's exactly what you'd have to look forward to. If any future opportunity opens to make polygamy legal, the LDS Church will reinstate it. And, the way the country is going, this isn't impossible.

"Elder Black is looking forward to when he can become a god and people a new world with his offspring. But he knows he can't populate a planet waiting on just one wife to give birth to that many spirit children. If you refuse him more wives, whether now, in the Millennium, or in the hereafter, according to Mormon doctrine you will be holding him back and he'd be justified in divorcing you."

"I . . . I never thought of that," she mumbled.

"Of course," I said, "we're chasing bubbles in the air. Heaven isn't going to require polygamy. But if you were married to him, that's what you would be taught to anticipate—and, that may not be so pleasant.

"I'll never forget the wife of a counselor in the bishopric of my Ward sitting on my couch one day crying bitter tears. She said she knew that someday she would have to share her husband with other women and she could hardly stand it. She was so consumed with sadness and jealousy that it kept her in a constant state of misery."

"One last question," Susan said. "How can the Elders confidently challenge people to pray about the Book of Mormon, unless it *really* is true?"

"Susan, the answer is that the elders can safely give that challenge because they know most investigators will do only one thing—pray. A common mistake many make is believing it would be unspiritual to use any other method.

"But," I said, "they're wrong. Decision making must utilize every avenue at one's disposal. In other words, God gave us a brain to use. He doesn't expect us, as Josh McDowell says, to commit 'intellectual suicide.'"[16]

"But," Susan persisted, "what's wrong with just praying?"

"The problem is that many times we answer our own prayer. Investigators, impressed with Mormon ethics, youth programs, clean-cut missionaries, Family Home evening, welfare programs, plus the biblical tone of the Book of Mormon, unconsciously influence their own praying. In other words, deep down they are *hoping* the Lord will say yes, and this is bound to have an effect.

"Therefore, when they receive some kind of sensation, whether it be goose bumps or whatever, they attribute it to God. More often, it's from their own psyche."

"So, what else can you go by if praying doesn't always prove true?" Susan asked.

"You use a combination of four other methods. Here's a list I made," I said, pulling a paper from my briefcase:

Pray to initiate guidance in:
- researching the facts
- comparing the facts with God's Word

• receiving counsel from other Christians
Pray to confirm the above.

"When you start out with prayer first, it's *not* to ask if the Book of Mormon is true, but to guide you in pursuing the next four steps.

"Now, you may not be a researcher by nature—but, you can always buy a book and read someone else's research.

"For example, with the Book of Mormon you need to investigate particulars about geography, history, and archaeology. We've already shown in class that these subjects have proven Book of Mormon claims false. You also need to dig into the history of Joseph Smith.

"In addition, research includes talking with those who are well-versed on the subject—in this case, former Mormons. By acquiring information from the horse's mouth, so to speak, it helps to separate fact from any incorrect propaganda you may have read.

"Next, you compare the facts with the Bible—you may even want to write a list of the pros and cons. God's Word says to 'test everything. Hold on to the good.'[17] We've done this in class. Mormonism is definitely not biblical, Susan, and if you believe this, shouldn't this settle the matter?

"But, if it doesn't, you can take the next step, which is seeking counsel from other Christians including your pastor.

"After you've done all you can, you end with prayer, asking the Lord to give you wisdom in weighing all the information you've acquired. Then ask His Holy Spirit to help you make the right decision.

"Of course, at that point, one pretty well knows what the decision *ought* to be. In your case, Susan, I don't think there should be any question left in your mind.

"For example, in class we found that the Isaiah 29 reference to a sealed book did not mean the Book of Mormon but rather the closing of people's minds to the message of the prophets. Nor, was Isaiah's 'learned man' referring to some professor in New York City. Don't you think it illogical for God to tell his prophets to prophesy about a book in a land the Jews had never heard of and that had no possible relevance for them? The 'marvelous work and a wonder' was not Joseph Smith's work. It was God's work—the redemption of Jerusalem.

"In addition," I continued, "we saw that the Ezekiel 37 mention of the two sticks of Judah and Ephraim referred neither to the Book of Mormon nor the Bible. The two sticks were visual aids, telling of the eventual reuniting of the divided kingdoms of Judah and Ephraim.

"Joseph Smith was a deceiver, Susan. He pretended to translate nonexistent gold plates through a peep stone used for treasure divining. He claimed to have translated an Egyptian papyrus called the Book of Abraham, which was actually a funeral text.

"He also plagiarized ancient religious beliefs from books available in his time and palmed them off as revelation. He introduced extrabiblical scripture and doctrines foreign to the Bible. He usurped a priesthood reserved only for Christ by ordaining men to the Melchizedek priesthood. He taught an unbiblical god who is neither omniscient nor omnipotent, claiming he was a resurrected man who peopled this world by practicing polygamy.

"Smith was also a fabricator. He told three different versions of his first vision, changed the guardian spirit of his treasure from a bloody Spaniard to an angel whose name he couldn't decide on, and borrowed events surrounding the Book of Mormon from the Masonic Legend of Enoch.

"In addition, he fails the biblical test for a prophet because of his false prophecies. He was a necromancer, involved in the occult, magic circles, blood sacrifices, divining rods, and peep stones, all of which the Bible warns against.

"As for the three witnesses, historical accounts reveal that they never saw the gold plates with their natural eyes. They were pressured to conjure up their own personal vision after Smith intimidated them and hounded them over their lack of faith.

"To make matters worse, Smith printed a testimony of the witnesses, deliberately making it read like they had seen actual plates with their natural eyes. And, to top it all off, all three witnesses plus many of the other eight left the church and embraced another faith.

"The facts speak loud and clear, Susan. But, there are many who refuse to pay attention to them, believing everything must be solely a matter of faith. When one is asked to pray and told that a *good feeling* is the way God authenticates truth, that ought to sound an alarm!

"So, Susan, in trying to analyze whether Mormonism is right or wrong, you need to seriously consider the guidelines I suggested.

"You start with prayer for guidance, research the facts, compare your findings with God's Word and counsel with other Christians, then pray about what you've discerned."

Susan leaned forward, resting her elbows on the table. Covering her face with her hands she let out a deep sigh, but said nothing.

"Susan, I think the reason you're still confused is because of your feelings for Elder Black."

After a long moment of silence, Susan finally spoke. "I know the Book of Mormon can't be true. I also know you're right about my feelings for Elder Black. I'm . . . just *so* worn out," she said. With that, the flood gates opened and the tears came.

"Susan," I said, politely waiting a few minutes, "deep down, what do you feel you ought to do?"

"End it forever!" she said between sobs. "But," she moaned, "the Elders think I'm coming to next Tuesday's meeting, and I don't know how to say no to their face!"

Glancing at my watch I said, "I have an idea. Right now, I know the Elders are out tracting. Elder Barrett gave me the phone number at their apartment. If you call while they're out, all you have to do is leave a message on their recorder. But, remember, unless you're emphatic and stress that you don't want them to make any further contact with you, they'll persist."

"I'll do it," she stated firmly, sitting up straight. "I've got to get out from under this—it's taking over my whole life!"

"When?" I asked. "There's no time like the present as the saying goes." Rummaging through my purse, I said, "Here's a quarter and their phone number. You could use the phone booth over by the soft drink machine."

Susan slowly stood up.

"Have you noticed," I said, "what a beautiful day it is? Look at that clear blue sky! It's one of those days that reminds you of that poem by Browning, 'God's in his heavens and all's right with the world.'"

"Yeah," she said, taking a deep breath. "You know, now that I know I'm going to do it, I feel different—sorta' like, well, free. Of course, it might take me a while to get over Elder Black . . ."

As she scooted her chair out, Matt's voice called from the basketball court. "Hey Susan—a bunch of us are going down to the Alamo! Wanna' go?"

"You ought to," I suggested. "It'll be good to get your mind off things."

Susan hesitated for a moment, then called back. "Sure—I just have to make a telephone call first!"

As I watched Susan head for the phone booth, I slowly began

stacking our dishes onto the trays but still glanced after her. Yes, she was dialing. Now she was talking. A mixture of joy and relief poured through me—there, she hung up! *She did it! Thank you Lord!*

And, thank you, too, for Matt, as I observed him eagerly waiting for Susan to get through. *Thank you Lord for putting everyone in the right place at the right time.* I thought of 1 Samuel 2:9 "He will guard the feet of his saints"—*he certainly guarded Susan's.*

Balancing the trays on top of my briefcase, I headed back toward the cafeteria. Again I glanced back. Susan was walking with Matt toward his car. *Wouldn't that be something if she and Matt ended up getting married?*

Well, whether it meant marriage down the line or not, at least God had providentially placed him in her life—Susan needed a young man right now to take her mind off Elder Black.

The missionaries . . . I felt so sorry for them. They were such dedicated young men, firmly confident that they had the truth.

Nevertheless, despite their sincerity they had been deceptive in not telling, up front, everything Mormonism believed. They almost succeeded with Susan. I thought of the Scripture, "He thwarts the plans of the crafty, so that their hands achieve no success."[18]

After turning in the trays I walked toward my car, passing the basketball court. Four or five students were shooting baskets, spurred on by cheers from the sidelines. Robert and Tia were there along with a few others from my class.

Stopping for a moment, I watched them. These were tomorrow's missionaries, pastors, Sunday school superintendents, song leaders, pastor's wives . . . Who knew what path God would lead them in? They were here at Bible college to prepare themselves, and I was happy I was playing a small role.

I thought of Matt—someday he'd be a pastor. I chuckled, thinking of his special strut and humorous antics. His congregation would always be in stitches.

Finally reaching my car, I got in and started the engine. I sat for a few minutes, letting it idle.

And Susan? I could picture her as a pastor's wife. Maybe her experience with the Mormon missionaries was meant to be. Maybe some day she'd help a Mormon come out—or keep a Christian from going in. Maybe she'd write and tell me about it someday . . .

Rolling both windows down I let the warm crossbreeze move through the car. I took a deep breath and, smiling contentedly, gunned the motor and headed for home.

Chapter Notes

Chapter One

1. Josh McDowell, *Evidence That Demands a Verdict* rev. ed. (San Bernardino: Here's Life Publishers, 1979), 364.
2. Mike H. Reynolds "Preaching to the Choir," *The Inner Circle* 12, no. 3 (March 1995): 6.
3. John L. Smith, *Witnessing Effectively to Mormons* (Marlow, Okla.: Utah Missions, 1989), 29.
4. See Joseph Fielding Smith, *Doctrines of Salvation*, Bruce R. McConkie, comp. (Salt Lake City: Bookcraft, 1954), 49–50.

    Regarding the eternal nature of man, Joseph Smith said: "We say that God Himself is a self-existing being. . . . Who told you that man did not exist in like manner upon the same principles? Man does exist upon the same principles. . . . The mind or the intelligence which man possesses is *co-equal* with God himself. . . . The intelligence of spirits had no beginning, neither will it have an end. . . . The first principles of man are self-existent with God" [emphasis mine]. Sterling M. McMurrin, *The Theological Foundations of the Mormon Religion* (Salt Lake City: University of Utah Press, 1965), 50. Quoting Joseph Smith, *History of the Church of Jesus Christ of Latter-day Saints* rev. ed., B. H. Roberts, 7 vols. (Salt Lake City: Deseret Book, 1978), 6:310. See also Doctrine and Covenants 93:29.

    "The first principles of man are self-existent with God. God himself, finding he was in the midst of spirits and glory, because he was *more* intelligent, saw proper to institute laws whereby the rest could have a privilege to advance like himself" (Smith, *History of the Church*, 6:312) [emphasis mine].

    Regarding the rest of creation, McConkie explains that "Intelligence" and "spirit element" are synonymous. in *Mormon Doctrine* 2nd ed. (Salt Lake City, Bookcraft, 1979), 387. He also states: "It is an utterly false and uninspired notion to believe that the world or any other thing was created out of nothing or that any created thing can be destroyed in the sense of annihilation. *"The elements are eternal"* [quoting Doctrine and Covenants 93:33]. Ibid., 169. Emphasis McConkie's.

Joseph Smith said: "Hence we infer that God had materials to organize the world out of chaos—chaotic matter, which is element . . . *Element had an existence from the time he had. The pure principles of element are principles which can never be destroyed; they may be organized and reorganized, but not destroyed. They had no beginning and can have no end."* McConkie, *Mormon Doctrine*, 169. (emphasis author's). See also Smith, *History of the Church* 6:308.

B. H. Roberts, in *History of the Church* 6:310 n, goes further by quoting Robert Kennedy Duncan who explains that if man's intelligence is co-eternal with God, so is the element from which all of creation came, including a "pin head." Duncan, citing the law of the conservation of mass which states that "no particle of matter, however small, may be created or destroyed," concludes that this is why it is more logical to believe that God cannot create something out of nothing. Preexistent material is already in existence for everything in the universe.

5. Mosiah 15:1–4.
6. Alma 11:26–31.
7. Book of Mormon, 1830 ed., 25.
8. 1 Nephi 11:21.
9. No exact date is given in Mormon history. However, it is assumed that it was sometime between May 15, 1829 and April 1830.
10. Doctrine and Covenants, sec. 13.
11. Hebrews 7:14.
12. Smith, comp. *Teachings of the Prophet Joseph Smith* (Salt Lake City: Deseret Book, 1977), 172–73. Joseph Smith's preoccupation with animal sacrifice relates to his belief in sacrificing sheep to appease evil spirits who guarded buried treasure. For a living, Smith used a divining rod and seer stones to find buried treasure. He also made the statement that killing a lamb in the Temple was necessary to validate the ordination of Willard Richards as a member of the Quorum of the Twelve Apostles. This subject is discussed further in Chapter 7.
13. In numerous instances, revelations were made retroactive. That is, to validate a new policy or procedure in Smith's new church, they would go back to an old revelation and insert the necessary statement so as to give the impression the policy had come as revelation

at an earlier date. For details, see D. Michael Quinn, *Mormon Hierarchy: Origins of Power* (Salt Lake City, in association with Smith Research Associates: Signature Books, 1994), 9, 12, 15–16, 35–40.

14. Jerald and Sandra Tanner, *Mormonism: Shadow or Reality?* (Salt Lake City: Modern Microfilm, 1972), 179.

15. The LDS Church also believes the Melchizedek priesthood is needed to accomplish the resurrection. Brigham Young said, "If we ask who will stand at the head of the resurrection in this last dispensation, the answer is—Joseph Smith, Junior, the Prophet of God. He is the man who will be resurrected and receive the keys of the resurrection, and he will seal this authority upon others, and they will hunt up their friends and resurrect them." Thelma Geer, *Mormonism, Mama and Me*, 5th ed. (Chicago: Moody Press, 1986), 197, quoting Brigham Young in *Discourses of Brigham Young*, (Salt Lake City: Deseret Book, 1925), 116.

16. Marvin W. Cowan, *Mormon Claims Answered*, rev. ed. (Self-published, 1989), 78–79. Available through Utah Lighthouse Ministry, P.O. Box 1884, Salt Lake City, UT 84110.

17. Mormons also believe that the Holy Ghost can only be received by the laying on of hands by one holding the Melchizedek priesthood. This, however, discounts the day of Pentecost when the Holy Ghost fell upon many with *no* laying on of hands.

18. Cowan, *Mormon Claims Answered*, 79.

Chapter Two

1. Anson Shupe, *The Darker Side of Virtue* (Buffalo: Prometheus Books, 1991), 23.

2. The figure of 48,708 is the actual number stated in the May 1994 *Ensign*, official publication of the Mormon Church. (Cited in "From the Director," *Evangel* 41, no. 4 [May 1994]: 2). This figure does not include stake missionaries. Convert baptisms for 1993 numbered 304,808. Baptisms of members' children of record, 76,312.

3. As of April 1995, total church membership is 9 million. One million members were acquired since September 1991. The rate of growth since then "has been about 840 new members each day, the equivalent of two wards. The equivalent of a typical stake of 3,800 members was created every four and a half days" (*Ensign*, April 1995, 77). This also includes the newly baptized children of members. D. Michael Quinn, former LDS historian, states that the LDS Church doubles its population every ten to twelve years.

4. The actual figure is 284,419, according to the LDS 1995–1996 Church Almanac (Salt Lake City: Deseret News, 1994), 420.

5. *A Present Day Look at the Latter-day Saints* (General Assembly Presbyterian Church, 1990), 4.
6. Shupe, *The Darker Side of Virtue*, 24.
7. Ron Carlson and Ed Decker, *Fast Facts on False Teachings* (Eugene, Oreg.: Harvest House, 1994), 164.
8. Shupe, *The Darker Side of Virtue*, 20.
9. In *The Mormon Corporate Empire*, authors John Heinerman and Anson Shupe estimated the church's wealth at $8 billion (Boston: Beacon Press, 1985, 12). However, later Shupe notes: "We now know from additional information that we placed far too low a figure on its assets [in *Mormon Corporate Empire*]. In fact, the Church corporation's total wealth was likely somewhere near twice that amount at that time, and today even that estimate may be far too low" (*The Darker Side of Virtue*, 20).
10. Robert McKay "Just a Small Effort," *The Evangel* 42, no. 2 (March 1995): 3. McKay's figure was derived from calculating the tithing income of $4.3 billion per year, reported in a newspaper article entitled, "Church thrives on tithes," *Arizona Republic* (July 1, 1991), n.p.
11. Ron Rhodes, *The Culting of America* (Eugene: Harvest House, 1994), 15.
12. Rhodes, *The Culting of America*, 15.
13. Janis Hutchinson, "Project Family Night," *The Improvement Era*, September 1967, 36–40.

    _____ . "Mommy Likes Mud Too," *The Improvement Era*, May 1967, 84–86.

    _____ . "And Thanks for Those Neat Skippin' Rocks," *The Improvement Era*, December 1969, 21–24.

    _____ . "Lullabies and Warm Rice," *The Improvement Era*, March 1968, 24–26. The above articles were reprinted in various other magazines, Mormon and non-Mormon. Excerpts from "Project Family Night" were used in radio commercials on the family.
14. Michael H. Reynolds, "Quote of the Month," *The Inner Circle*, 11, no. 12 (December 1994): 8.
15. "LDS PR wins again," *The Inner Circle* 11, no. 11 (November 1994): 6.
16. Rhodes, *The Culting of America*, 15.
17. Shupe, *The Darker Side of Virtue*, 27.
18. Ibid.
19. In a conversation with two missionaries in Washington, they stated that they only spend a certain number of hours tracting. The majority of their time is spent contacting referrals given them by members of the Ward.

20. Shupe, *The Darker Side of Virtue*, 29.
21. Peg McEntee, "Number of LDS Spirits, But Problems Result," *The Salt Lake Tribune*, 2 April 1994, Religion section, D3.
22. Shupe, *The Darker Side of Virtue*, 37.
23. Ibid. See also, "Touring Groups Touch Hearts," *Church News* (June 20, 1981): 4.
24. Shupe, *The Darker Side of Virtue*, 36.
25. Ibid., 37.
26. Ibid., 37–38.
27. Ibid., 33.
28. Rhodes, *The Culting of America*, 16, quoting "What's New in the Headlines," *Christian Research Institute Newsletter* (November/December, 1991): 6.
29. Shupe, *The Darker Side of Virtue*, 23.
30. Rhodes, *The Culting of America*, 108.
31. Peter L. Berger *The Sacred Canopy* (New York: Doubleday, 1969), 21.
32. Ibid., 22.
33. Mircea Eliade, *Patterns in Comparative Religion* (New York: World Publishing, 1972), 62.
34. See Chapter 3.
35. Apostle and spokesman, Bruce R. McConkie stated: "The Church is a kingdom. The Lord Jesus Christ is the Eternal King, and the President of the Church, the mouthpiece of God on earth, is the earthly king. All things come to the Church from the King of the kingdom in heaven, through the king of the kingdom on earth." (Bruce R. McConkie, *Mormon Doctrine* 2d ed. (Salt Lake City: Bookcraft, 1979), 416.
36. Rhodes, *The Culting of America*, 15, 104.
37. Gal 1:9 (NIV)
38. Matthew 16:18.
39. Maurice C. Burrell *The Challenge of the Cults* (Grand Rapids: Baker Book House, 1981), 151.
40. "Three missionary milestones," *Church News* (April 21, 1985): 10.
41. "The Church & The World," *Bible Advocate* (November 1994): 13.
42. Deuteronomy 32:30.
43. Burrell, *The Challenge of the Cults*, 158.

Chapter Three

1. As of May 1994, worldwide membership was 8,696,224, according to the *Ensign*, official publication for the Mormon Church. In April 1995 they announced 9 million (p. 77).

2. John J. Stewart, *Joseph Smith the Mormon Prophet* (Salt Lake City: Mercury Pub., 1966), 204.

3. In a revelation given to Smith April 7, 1842, the full name of the political kingdom was given: "The Kingdom of God and His Laws, with Keys and power thereof, and judgment in the hands of his servants, Ahman Christ" (See also *The Mormon Hierarchy*: *Origins of Power* [Salt Lake City, in association with Smith Research Associates: Signature Books, 1994], 112).

4. John Heinerman and Anson Shupe state: "For them the prophecy [of Daniel] says that the Mormon people and the resources of their corporate empire will be the prime movers in a millennial overthrow of the United States government (*The Mormon Corporate Empire*, [Boston: Beacon Press], 19). Apostle Bruce R. McConkie states: "During the millennium . . . the Church . . . will have the rule and government of the world given to it." (Bruce R. McConkie, *Mormon Doctrine*, 2nd ed. (Salt Lake City: Bookcraft, 1979), 416; see also 338.

5. Dale Morgan, "The State of Deseret," *Utah Historical Quarterly*, 8 (1940): 139–140. See also, Heinerman and Shupe, *The Mormon Corporate Empire* (Boston: Beacon Press, 1985), 21.

6. *Journal of Discourses*, Joseph F. Smith, ed. (1854–1886; reprint, Salt Lake City: Brigham Young University Press, 1967), 18:341. Hereinafter the *Journal of Discourses* will be referred to as such with the volume and page number. (The *Journal of Discourses* is not a sole collection of Brigham Young's sermons. Other lectures by Mormon leaders are included.)

7. Klaus J. Hansen, "The Theory and Practice of the Political Kingdom of God in Mormon History, 1829–1890" (master's thesis, Brigham Young University, 1959), 15–16, quoted in Heinerman and Shupe, *The Mormon Corporate Empire,* 22.

8. They could also appoint a few non-Mormons. The council was sworn to secrecy about its existence under penalty of death. Later, it was made public. (See Quinn, *The Mormon Hierarchy*, 128.) Smith taught that the world should be governed by a "theo-democracy." This was to be achieved through the Council of Fifty and he was to be King over all the earth. Two of his apostles, Lyman Wight and Heber C. Kimball referred to Smith's title as, "President Pro tem of the world". (See D. Michael Quinn, *The Mormon Hierarchy*, 124.)

9. J. D. Williams, "The Separation of Church and State in Mormon Theory and Practice," *Dialogue: A Journal of Mormon Thought*, (Summer, 1966): 46–47. (Hereinafter, Williams, "Separation of Church and State.")

10. Jerald Tanner and Sandra Tanner, *Mormonism—Shadow or Reality?* (Salt Lake City: Modern Microfilm, 1972), 416.
11. Tanner and Tanner, *Mormonism—Shadow or Reality?*, 417.
12. Hyrum L. Andrus, *Joseph Smith & World Government* (Salt Lake City: Hawkes Pub., 1972), 21.
13. Apostle Bruce R. McConkie stated: "*The Church (or kingdom) is not a democracy*; legislation is not enacted by the body of people composing the organization; they do not make the laws governing themselves. The Church is a kingdom. The Lord Jesus Christ is the Eternal King, and the President of the Church, the mouthpiece of God on earth, is the earthly king. All things come to the Church from the King of the kingdom in heaven, through the king of the kingdom on earth. . . . During the millennium the *kingdom of God* will continue on earth, but in that day it will be both an *ecclesiastical* and a *political* kingdom. That is, the Church (which is the kingdom) will have the rule and government of the world given to it." (McConkie, *Mormon Doctrine* 2d ed. (Salt Lake City: Bookcraft, 1979), 416 (Emphasis in original).
14. Klaus J. Hansen, *Quest for Empire* (Lincoln: University of Nebraska Press, 1967), 127.
15. Andrus, *Joseph Smith and World Government*, 91.
16. Hansen, *Quest for Empire*, 128, 131–32.
17. Andrus, *Joseph Smith and World Government*, 20.
18. Susan M. Andersen and Philip G. Zimbardo, "Resisting Mind Control," *USA Today*, November 1980, 46.
19. Tanner and Tanner, *Mormonism—Shadow or Reality?*, 420, quoting Stanley S. Ivins, *Millennial Star*, 29, (date unknown): 746.
20. Tanner and Tanner, *Mormonism—Shadow or Reality?*, 423.
21. Ibid., 423.
22. Williams, "Separation of Church and State," 38.
23. Tanner and Tanner, *Mormonism—Shadow or Reality?*, 422, quoting Stanley S. Ivins, *The Moses Thatcher Case* (publisher and date unknown).
24. Andrus, *Joseph Smith and World Government*, 69, 85.
25. Ibid., 87.
26. Leland H. Creer, "The Evolution of Government in Early Utah," *Utah Historical Quarterly* (January 1958): 27, quoted in Andrus, *Joseph Smith and World Government*, 87.
27. Dale Morgan, "The State of Deseret," *Utah Historical Quarterly* 8 (April, July, October, 1940): 79, quoted in Andrus, *Joseph Smith and World Government*, 87.
28. Klaus J. Hansen, *Quest for Empire* (Lincoln: University of Nebraska Press, 1967), 65.

29. Andrus, *Joseph Smith and World Government*, 116.
30. Hansen, *Quest for Empire*, 67.
31. G. T. M. Davis in the St. Clair Banner, 17 September 1844, 2, quoted in Tanner and Tanner, *Mormonism—Shadow or Reality?*, 416. See also, Quinn, *Mormon Hierarchy*, 55, 124, 138, 643.
32. For John Taylor's anointing, see "Daily Journal of Abraham H. Cannon," 2 December, 1895, 198, quoted in Tanner and Tanner, *Mormonism—Shadow or Reality?*, 417–418. For Brigham Young's coronation, see Hansen, *Quest for Empire*, 66. For Wilford Woodruff and Lorenzo Snow's, see Heinerman and Shupe, *The Mormon Corporate Empire*, 20.
33. *Journal of Discourses*, 6:25.
34. *Journal of Discourses*, 2:182. Brigham Young attributes this teaching to Joseph Smith: "Will the Constitution be destroyed? . . . and as Joseph Smith said, 'the time will come when the destiny of the nation will hang upon a single thread.'" (Ibid., 7:15.) See also 2:182.
35. Andrus, *Joseph Smith and World Government*, 15–16.
36. *Journal of Discourses*, 6: 345–346.
37. *Journal of Discourses*, 7:57. Brigham Young made a blanket statement that anyone not joining the Mormon kingdom during the Millennium would be annihilated, suggesting they will become sons of perdition. However, present day leaders are more specific on who will be Sons of Perdition. It is not everyone who says "no" to Mormonism, but those who have actually had the truthfulness of Mormonism revealed to them by the Holy Ghost and then reject it (Bruce R. McConkie, *Mormon Doctrine*, 2d ed. [Salt Lake City: Bookcraft, 1979], 746). Non-Mormons who reject Mormonism who have not had this "revelation," will not become sons of perdition, but inherit either the Telestial or Terrestrial Kingdom. Two other doctrines will be reinstituted during the Millennium. Polygamy and the doctrine of blood atonement. The latter will be a civil necessity for murderers; that is, capital punishment. But, it will also be considered a necessity to handle Mormons who commit certain sins that Christ's blood cannot cover, "even though they repent". . . . Their only hope," says Joseph Fielding Smith, "is to have their own blood shed to atone as far as possible, in their behalf" (Joseph Fielding Smith, compiled by Bruce R. McConkie, *Doctrines of Salvation*, [Salt Lake City: Bookcraft, 1954], 1:135). "This doctrine, Bruce R. McConkie states, "can only be practiced in its fullness in a day when the civil and ecclesiastical laws are administered in the same hands" [meaning the Millennium] (McConkie, *Mormon Doctrine*, 93).
38. Apostle John Widtsoe confirms Brigham Young's teaching that the

ultimate punishment of the sons of perdition may be that they, having their spiritual bodies disorganized, must start over again, must begin anew the long journey of existence repeating the steps that they took in the eternities before the Great Council was held (*Evidences and* Reconciliations [Salt Lake City: Bookcraft, 1960], 214). Erastus Snow, in *Journal of Discourses,* 7:358-359, in speaking of the second death, also reiterated Brigham Young's teaching saying this is what was meant in Matthew 10:28, speaking of destroying both soul and body in hell.

39. Andrus, *Joseph Smith and World Government*, 29. See also *Doctrine and Covenants*, 57:1–4; Ether 13.

40. Orson Pratt, *The Seer* 2 (May 1854): 266. Both capitals will issue political as well as ecclesiastical mandates. Bruce R. McConkie, in *Mormon Doctrine*, says: "With the millennial advent, the kingdom of God on earth will step forth and exercise political jurisdiction over all the earth *as well as* ecclesiastical jurisdiction over its own citizens" (500) [emphasis mine]. Hyrum L. Andrus, in *Joseph Smith and World Government*, states: It was held that in some future day the Kingdom of God would have two great centers of world government-the City of Zion on our Western continent, and Jerusalem. . . . Jerusalem, though not so prominent in matters of government, was *also* to be established as a center of political law for the eastern hemisphere (29—30) [emphasis mine]. See also Joseph Fielding Smith *Doctrines of Salvation* 3:69–70.

41. Tanner and Tanner, *Mormonism—Shadow or Reality?,* 427. See also Tanner and Tanner, "Will Benson Be King?" 42 *Salt Lake City Messenger* (April 1980): 1–2.

42. Heinerman and Shupe, *The Mormon Corporate Empire*, 20.

43. Ibid.

44. In 1965, church leaders tried to influence Mormon congressmen. Pres. David O. McKay and his two counselors contacted eight congressmen and three senators, asking them to vote to repeal Section 14B of the Taft Hartley Act. One Congressman said he would vote that way, but only because he already felt so inclined. Five signed a letter saying they would not (Wallace Turner, *The Mormon Establishment* [Boston: Houghton Mifflin, 1966], 292–93). Although these particular Mormon politicians did not "obey," the Mormon Church can still sway a vote at the polls if they make their wishes known to the general membership.

45. Heinerman and Shupe, *The Mormon Corporate Empire*, 28.

46. Anson Shupe, *The Darker Side of Virtue* (Buffalo: Prometheus Books, 1991), 19.

47. Heinerman and Shupe, *The Mormon Corporate Empire,* 57.

48. Ibid., 81.
49. Hansen, "Theory and Practice," in *Quest for Empire*, quoted in Heinerman and Shupe, *The Mormon Corporate Empire*, 22.
50. Heinerman and Shupe, *The Mormon Corporate Empire*, 28.
51. Ibid.
52. The first, or general, endowment available to members today, only ordains members to *become* kings and queens, priests and priestesses. Modern members interpret the ritual as something which will materialize in heaven when they become gods over their own planets. However, there was a unique endowment in early Mormon history, called the "second" endowment, which actually ordained individuals as kings, on the spot. (Many believe this is secretly being practiced today, but only among the church hierarchy.) Today, leaders say it was a prerequisite to receiving the second Comforter (the first comforter is the Holy Ghost, the second is the Savior). This means that after one has this second ordinance, one can "see the face of the Lord and live, even though being in the flesh." (See *Journal of Discourses* 9:87.) If this should happen, the Lord would declare to the individual: "Your calling and election is made sure." If one's calling and election is made sure, one's salvation and exaltation in the Celestial Kingdom is then assured regardless of what sin one might commit in the future, with the *exception* of murder, adultery, and blasphemy against the Holy Ghost. Whether the second endowment is the same under which Joseph Smith was crowned king is not clear. Today, some Fundamentalist groups offer the ordinance of the second endowment and crown their leader as king, under which all male members achieve certain ranks of nobility. I received a letter some years ago from a Mormon I had known before he joined a fundamentalist group in Utah. His personality had completely changed since he acquired "nobility." He also wrote in King James English on stationery that had a coat of arms. See also Michael W. Homer, "'Similarity of Priesthood in Masonry': The Relationship between Freemasonry and Mormonism," 27, no. 3 *Dialogue: A Journal of Mormon Thought* (Fall 1994): 34.
53. David A. Reed and John R. Farkas, *Mormons Answered Verse by Verse* (Grand Rapids: Baker, 1993), 12. Reed and Farkas are referring to a statistical projection supposedly made by Brigham Young University. However, the *Salt Lake Tribune*, 2 April 1994, Religion section, said that sociologist Rodney Stark, in 1980, "predicted that the next century would see an enormous growth in the membership of the Mormon Church—to as many as 265 million by 2080." Therefore, BYU

may simply have been reiterating what Stark said. (Anson Shupe, *The Darker Side of Virtue*, 23). Elder Neal A. Maxwell, an LDS apostle predicted a more conservative figure of ninety million (See *The Salt Lake Tribune,* 2 April, 1994, Religion section).

Chapter Four

1. The words read from the Mormon handbook are paraphrases of the subjects covered in the lessons. They are not direct quotations from the books themselves. Nevertheless, it relays the same message. The use of the word "feel" is, however, an accurate one.

2. See, Janis Hutchinson, *Out of the Cults and Into the Church* (Grand Rapids: Kregel Publications, 1994) for a full presentation of the emotional problems experienced by ex-cultists attempting to convert to Christianity.

3. *Journal of Discourses*, Joseph F. Smith, ed. (1854–86; reprint, Salt Lake City: Brigham Young University Press, 1967), 7:289, quoted in *The Evangel,* 41, no. 7 (October 1994). Brigham Young also said, "So hear it all ye ends of the earth; if you ever enter into the kingdom of God, it is because Joseph Smith let you go there. . . . no man or woman in this generation will get a resurrection and be crowned without Joseph saying so" (Conference discourse on October 8, 1854). Recipients of the second heaven, the Terrestrial Kingdom, will consist of honorable men of the earth and traditional Christians. Also, those who died without the law, such as heathens. It will also include those Mormons who were "not valiant in the testimony of Jesus" (meaning the testimony of Mormonism). (See Doctrine and Covenants, 76:71–79.) Those in the first, or lowest, heaven, the Telestial Kingdom, consist of those who would not receive Christ and those thrust down to Hell but who later repent; that is, all those who cannot be redeemed from the devil until the last resurrection. (Doctrine and Covenants, 76:81–85.)

4. Mormons teach that Jesus was not perfect. He had to come "to earth to work out his own salvation" and "himself needed baptism." (Bruce R. McConkie, *The Promised Messiah* [Salt Lake City: Deseret Book, 1978], 482, 485, quoted in Thelma Geer, *Mormonism, Mama & Me* [Chicago: Moody, 1986), 187.

5. Orson Pratt declared: "If we should take a million of worlds like this and number their particles, we should find that there are more Gods than there are particles of matter in those worlds." (*Journal of Discourses*, 2:345).

6. In a Fireside (an informal group church meeting, usually youth), May 12, 1967, a Mormon speaker stated:

"Our God knows all things concerning us, but He has innumerable Gods who preside over him, and have their own creations who may know more than ten times as much as he does. As he lives on and creates, he will learn and gain more experience eternally. Each God has dominion over many other Gods, ten or a million, depending on his progression and experience. Kolob is the first of God's creations and is next to the throne of God. The God on Kolob is the Supreme God over all the planets and suns under his dominion. Under Kolob there are 12 governing suns, equal in size and under these, there are two-hundred million 'glorified suns' and around each of these, there are solar systems like ours. Upon each of these two-hundred million suns, there is a God. There are millions of Gods between our God and Kolob . . . but our God represents the Supreme God of Kolob and beyond, and is in constant communication with them."

The above quote was copied from a book many years ago while I was a member of Mormon Fundamentalism. Unfortunately, at that time, I was not diligent in noting references and only abbreviated names of sources. Therefore, the only reference I noted for the following quote was: RCA Book, May 12, 1967, Fireside taken by MDA. However, the information contained in this quote pertaining to Kolob and the 12 governing suns can be found in "The Egyptian Grammar of Joseph Smith." (See Smith, *History of the Church*, 2:238, 286.) In a lecture series given at Barratt Hall in Salt Lake City on August 26, 1953, entitled *The Pearl of Great Price Through Forty Centuries*, James R. Clark refers to Joseph Smith's Egyptian Grammar which he compiled as he was allegedly translating the records of Abraham and Joseph. The Grammar gives the Egyptian names for the stars and the fifteen moving planets. For example, *Kolob* for the eldest star; *Flosisis* for the sun; *Floesse* for the moon; and *Jahoheh* for the earth. He also attempts to describe how every planet is under the government of another. For example, Smith wrote: "The earth under the governing powers of Oliblish, Enish-go-on-dosh, and Kae-e-vanrash which are the three grand keys, or, in other words, the governing powers which govern the fifteen fixed stars—twelve under that which governs the earth, the sun, and the moon which have their power in one with the other twelve moving planets of this system" (Ibid., "The Pearl of Great Price and the Cosmography of the Universe," 56ff).

7. Lorenzo Snow's couplet is taken from one of his poems which appeared in print for the first time in an article written by his son, LeRoi C. Snow, "Devotion to a Divine Inspiration," *Improvement Era*, June 1919, 22:656, 660.

8. Early Mormonism also taught that Adam/God, in his previous world of mortality, was the savior of that world, comparable to Jesus Christ of this world. According to the *Deseret Weekly*, 29 December, 1888, 20–21, Joseph E. Taylor read a lecture in the Logan Temple on June 2, 1888. In that lecture, he says: "All that Father Adam did upon this earth, from the time that he took up his abode in the Garden of Eden, was done for his posterity's sake and the success of his former mission as *the savior of a world*, and afterwards, or now, as the father of a world only added to the glory which he already possessed."

   He further explains that the reason Adam had power to take up his life and not have his new mortal body go through death and a resurrection, is because "as the savior of a [previous] world, he had the power to lay down his life and take it up again."

9. Doctrine and Covenants, 132: 19, 22.

10. *Journal of Discourses*, 3:319.

11. *Journal of Discourses*, 1:50–51, quoted in Tanner and Tanner, *Mormonism—Shadow or Reality?*, 173. The idea of Adam being God could have resulted from Joseph Smith's study of the Kabbalah (Jewish mysticism, see Chapter 7). In Kabbalism, the Divine Image manifested itself in a variety of ways but was also visualized as having a human form called *Adam Kadmon*, the first man. Further, Kabbalism taught that Hebrew letters had a numerical value of which occult meanings could be extracted. Lance S. Owens explains: "This strange equation of Adam as God was supported by a Kabbalistic cipher: the numerical value in Hebrew of the names Adam and Jehovah (the Tetragrammaton Yod he vav he) was both 45. Thus in Kabbalistic exegesis Jehovah equaled Adam: Adam was God." (Lance S. Owens, "Joseph Smith and Kabbalah: The Occult Connection," *Dialogue*, 27, no. 3, [Fall 1994]: 127).

12. Francis Michael Darter, *The Origin of the Temple Veil* (Self-published, Salt Lake City: 1955), 8, quoting *Women of Mormondom* (175–200), taught that after Adam partook of the Tree of Life, "he returned to his throne on our sun." Brigham Young taught that God, after creating the spirit bodies of his children, began partaking of the "course materials that was (*sic*) organized and composed on this earth, until his system was charged with it" and was then able to produce physical children (*Journal of Discourses* 4:217–18). Brigham Young also taught that when individuals become gods and goddesses and eventually Adams and Eves on a future world, in order "to commence the work of generation . . . they will go into the garden, and continue to eat and drink of the fruits of the corporal world, until this

grosser matter is diffused sufficiently through their celestial bodies to enable them . . . to produce mortal tabernacles for their spiritual children" (*Journal of Discourses* 6:275. See also, 10:255). The original Lecture at the Veil, approved by Brigham Young and first presented at the St. George Temple, also presented the same information. L. John Nuttall assisted Brigham Young and others in the writing of this Lecture. (See *The Original Lecture at the Veil* with special introduction by Fred C. Collier, [reprint available through Pioneer Press, 3332 E. Ft. Union Blvd., Salt Lake City, Utah 84121]. See also Diary of L. John Nuttall, 7 February, 1877, Special Collections, BYU Library. Also, L. John Nuttall Papers, Letter Press Book No. 4, 290, Special Collections, BYU Library).

13. Mormon theology also teaches that the premortal Jesus, not God the Father, was Jehovah of the Old Testament. Bruce R. McConkie stated: "Christ is Jehovah; they are one and the same Person" (*Mormon Doctrine*, 392). See also Abraham 2:7–8.

14, *Journal of Discourses*, 1:50-51.

15. David A. Reed and John R. Farkas, *Mormons Answered Verse by Verse* (Grand Rapids: Baker Book House, 1993), 62, from Spencer W. Kimball [title unknown] *Church News*, 9 October, 1976.

16. Tanner and Tanner, *Mormonism—Shadow or Reality?*, 173. See also, David John Buerger, "The Adam-God Doctrine," *Dialogue: A Journal of Mormon Thought* 15 (Spring 1982). Also Doctrine and Covenants 27:11.

17. Romans 8:15.

Chapter Five

1. Rodney Stark and William Bainbridge, "Network of Faith: Interpersonal Bonds and Recruitment to Cults and Sects," *American Journal of* Sociology 85 (May 1980): 1386–1387. This study, however, is from 1978. Since there has been an improvement in the missionaries' approach and the use of videos, this statistic may be quite different now.

2. Ernest Eberhard, "How to Share the Gospel: A Step-by-Step Approach for You and Your Neighbors" *The Ensign* (June 1974): 6–11. (Ernest Eberhard was president of the Oregon Mission.) See also John Heinerman and Anson Shupe, *The Mormon Corporate Empire* (Boston: Beacon Press, 1985), 31.

3. Eberhard, "How to Share the Gospel," 10.

4. The missionaries' first discussion, entitled "The Plan of Our Heavenly Father" usually covers the Book of Mormon. However, the Book of Mormon will be examined in a later chapter.

5. The first lesson also includes an in-depth discussion on faith, repentance, baptism, and the gift of the Holy Ghost, concluding with an invitation to the investigator to commit to baptism. Since their presentation on these three subjects is carefully presented as "Christian," the author has chosen to exclude this segment of their lesson. However, the chapter contains a few statements by the elders to this effect.

6. The Four-in-one consists of the King James version of the Bible, the Book of Mormon, the Pearl of Great Price and the Doctrine and Covenants.

7. Doctrine and Covenants 131:22.

8. Investigators, depending on their knowledge of the Bible, may ask different questions, thus leading the discussion in another direction. The purpose of this particular question is for the reader to become aware of two things: (1) the missionaries lack of biblical understanding; and (2) what the Bible actually says about becoming a child of God.

9. Mormonism teaches that it is only by belonging to the Mormon Church that one will receive power to become a son of God. (See Marvin W. Cowan, *Mormon Claims Answered*, rev. ed. [Self-published, 1989], 106; available through Mormonism Research Ministry, P.O. Box 20705, El Cajon, CA 92021). The term *sons of God* refers to being exalted in the Celestial Kingdom where they will eventually become gods and goddesses. The power that accomplishes it, is the priesthood, contingent upon their keeping LDS rules and being married in the temple.

10. This supposedly occurs after baptism, when hands are laid upon members and the words, "Receive ye the Holy Ghost," are uttered. See Joseph Smith's statement in Joseph Smith, *History of the Church of Jesus Christ of Latter-day Saints* rev. ed., B. H. Roberts, 7 vols. (Salt Lake City: Deseret Book, 1978), 3:380 and Ed Decker, *Decker's Complete Handbook on Mormonism* (Eugene, Oreg.: Harvest House, 1995), 100.

11. Galatians 4:1.

12. Romans 3:28.

13. Cowan *Mormon Claims Answered*, 104–105.

14. Nephi 27:13–14.

15. Joseph Fielding Smith, *Doctrines of Salvation*, comp. Bruce R. McConkie (Salt Lake City: Bookcraft, 1954), 1:189.

16. Faith in Christ is not enough. One must be obedient to all the rules such as abstaining from tea, coffee, alcohol, and tobacco, attend meetings, upholding the authorities of the church, going through

the temple, being married by the priesthood, e.g., having one's marriage "sealed for time and all eternity" by one holding the Melchizedek priesthood. Those who have acquired general salvation only by faith in Jesus Christ will not be saved in the heaven where God and Christ dwell.

17. While I have chosen to use the phrase, *He chooses special witnesses,* the actual quote from the Missionary outline states, "He chooses witnesses."

18. "The Writings of Joseph Smith" is found in the Pearl of Great Price. The latter also contains the Book of Moses and the Book of Abraham.

19. "Writings of Joseph Smith," 2:16–17.

20. Doctrine and Covenants 35:17.

21. Joseph Smith taught that there are certain sins that are so bad that even though one repents, they place one beyond the atoning blood of Jesus Christ. They can never inherit the Celestial Kingdom, only a lower heaven. This includes murder. To be saved in a lower heaven, one would have to have their own blood spilled. See Smith, *Doctrines of Salvation,* 1:135–136. No person who has committed murder can be forgiven and inherit the Celestial Kingdom, even if he or she has paid their dues in prison. Neither can this person ever be baptized into the Mormon Church. However, they can inherit the Telestial Kingdom after paying the full penalty in hell for a thousand years (See Bruce R. McConkie, *Mormon Doctrine,* 2nd ed. [Salt Lake City: Bookcraft, 1979], 520, 758). Joseph Smith also taught the "two strikes you're out" principle for those who had been through the temple. If one commits adultery for the first time, he or she can be forgiven. The second time, there is no forgiveness. See Doctrine and Covenants 42:24–26. There are actually three situations regarding adultery. According to Mormon doctrine, (1) a man may be saved in the Celestial Kingdom if, after committing adultery *before* accepting Mormonism, he repents (McConkie, *Mormon Doctrine,* 24). (2) If after becoming a Mormon and before going through the temple, he commits adultery and repents, he will be forgiven; but, the second time, shall be cast out. (Doctrine and Covenants, 42:24–26; *Mormon Doctrine,* 24–25). (3) If a Mormon commits adultery after being sealed in the temple and has had his or her *calling and election made sure* (which is to have the Lord personally appear and assure one of their exaltation [see *Mormon Doctrine,* 109–10]), he can never be saved in the Celestial Kingdom (Ibid. 24–25).

22. Luke 24:39.

Chapter Six

1. Acts 16:31.
2. Joseph Fielding Smith, *Doctrines of Salvation*, comp. Bruce R. McConkie (Salt Lake City: Bookcraft, 1956), 3:91.
3. Joseph Field Smith said: "If Joseph Smith was verily a prophet . . . this knowledge is of the most vital importance to the entire world. *No man can reject that testimony without incurring the most dreadful consequences, for he cannot enter the kingdom of God.*" *Doctrines of Salvation*, 1:189–90 [emphasis in original]. Brigham Young said: "No man or woman in this dispensation will ever enter into the celestial kingdom of God *without the consent of Joseph Smith.* (*Journal of Discourses*, Joseph F. Smith, ed., (1854–86; reprint, Salt Lake City: Brigham Young Press, 1967), 7:289). He further said: "No man or woman in this generation will get a *resurrection* and be crowned *without Joseph saying so*" (Ibid., Conference discourse on October 8, 1854).
4. See note 21, Chapter 5. A very dear elderly friend of mine joined the Mormon Church and, believing that all his sins were washed away in baptism, did not tell Mormon leaders that in his younger days he had committed murder. At the time of the murder, he had been sentenced to a state prison but, while working on a chain gang, had escaped. After that he lived an exemplary life. I acted as proxy for his deceased wife in the temple marriage ceremony which allegedly sealed him to her for eternity. A few years later, after joining the Mormon Church, his story was discovered. He was told by Mormon leaders that he would never have been admitted to the Mormon Church had they known, and that Jesus' blood does not cover murder. However, due to his age, the many letters from friends and acquaintances to Mormon officials attesting to his changed character, mine included, the motion for his excommunication was set aside and he was only disfellowshipped. The Stake President (my uncle-in-law) explained to me that he would have to become an "outcast and a wanderer of the earth" until such time that God required him to "pay the uttermost farthing of suffering," meaning "being cast into hell for a thousand years." After that, he would be saved in the Telestial Kingdom. Although Doctrine and Covenants 42:79 states there is no forgiveness for murderers, section 76:81-88, 98–112 further expounds on this by clarifying that after murderers suffer in hell, spiritual death will no longer apply to them and they will be saved in the Telestial Kingdom (See *Mormon Doctrine*, 520 and 758).
5. Hebrews 9:15.
6. James B. Allen, "The Significance of Joseph Smith's 'First Vision'

in Mormon Thought," *Dialogue: A Journal of Mormon Thought* (Autumn 1966: 29.

7. "Mormonism's Self Destruct" (La Mesa, Calif.: Utah Christian Tract Society, n.d.), quoting from David O. McKay's *Gospel Ideals* [Salt Lake City: Deseret Book, 1953], 85).

8. Smith, *Doctrines of Salvation,* 1:188.

9. Cited in Tanner and Tanner, *Mormonism—Shadow or Reality?* (Salt Lake City: Modern Microfilm, 1972), 146. A copy of the 1832 account in Joseph Smith's own handwriting, can be obtained by writing to Utah Lighthouse Ministry, P.O. Box 1884, Salt Lake City, UT 84110.

10. Scott Faulring, ed., *An American Prophet's Record: The Diaries and Journals of Joseph Smith* (Salt Lake City: Signature Books, in association with Smith Research Associates, 1989), 59, quoted in "Joseph Smith's Vision," *Salt Lake City Messenger*, No. 87 (November 1994): 5. See also Tanner and Tanner, *Mormonism—Shadow or Reality?*, 143–13. Brigham Young verified the diary account by stating: *"The Lord did not come . . .* But He did send His *angel* to this same obscure person, Joseph Smith . . . and informed him that he should not join any of the religious sects of the day, for they were all wrong" (Wally Tope, "Honest Questions for Honest LDS," flyer). Mr. Tope's reference: *Journal of Discourses*, 2:171. Compare George Albert Smith, *Journal of Discourses*, 13:294.

11. Joseph Smith, *History of the Church of Jesus Christ of Latter-day Saints*, 2nd ed., B. H. Roberts, 7 vols. (Salt Lake City: Deseret Book, 1978), 2:312. [Hereinafter, Smith, *History of the Church.*] See also Tanner and Tanner, *Mormonism—Shadow or Reality?*, 143–153.

12. Preston Nibley, *Joseph Smith the Prophet* (Salt Lake City: Deseret News Press, 1944), 30, quoted in Tanner and Tanner, *Mormonism—Shadow or Reality?*, 145.

13. Marvin S. Hill, "First Vision Controversy: A Critique and Reconciliation," *Dialogue: A Journal of Mormon Thought* (Summer 1982): 39–41.

14. Smith, *History of the Church,* 2:380–1. See also, J. Edward Decker and William J. Schnoebelen, comp., *And It DIDN'T Come to Pass: The False Prophecies of Joseph Smith (Issaquah, Wash.: Saints Alive in Jesus),* 3–4. Available from Saints Alive in Jesus, P.O. Box 1076, Issaquah, Wash.: 98027.

15. Doctrine and Covenants, 84:40–41.

16. Smith, *History of the Church,* 2:188–91. According to Heber C.

Kimball, in *Times and Seasons*, 6:868, Joseph Smith confirmed these false blessings.

17. Smith, *History of the Church* 5:336.
18. Doctrine and Covenants, 84:2–5, 31, 114–15.
19. Doctrine and Covenants, 124:56–60.
20. 2 Nephi 30:6. This also appears in the original, handwritten manuscript of 2 Nephi 30 and in the original 1830 edition of the Book of Mormon. The change was made in 1981.
21. Joseph Smith first heard of this from a Mormon named Burgess who said that a treasure of money was buried in a cellar of a widow's house in Salem, Massachusetts (Tanner and Tanner, *Mormonism—Shadow or Reality?*, 49). After hearing the story, Joseph immediately produced a revelation (Doctrine and Covenants, 111) to the effect that they would be successful in obtaining it.
22. Doctrine and Covenants, 121:5–15.
23. Doctrine and Covenants, 132:54.
24. Decker and Schnoebelen, *And it DIDN'T Come to Pass*, 23. See also T. B. H. Stenhouse, *The Rocky Mountain Saints* (Salt Lake City: Shepard Books, 1904), 42.
25. *And it DIDN'T Come to Pass*, 26–27. See also Smith, *History of the Church*, 2:182.
26. Doctrine and Covenants, 87.
27. See Tanner and Tanner, *Mormonism—Shadow or Reality?*, 190ff.
28. Doctrine and Covenants, 87. Other prophecies concerning the Civil War were made in various letters and other statements of Joseph Smith. See Tanner and Tanner, *Mormonism—Shadow or Reality?*, 190ff.
29. A study of Tanners' book, *Mormonism—Shadow or Reality?*, reveals that the Museum, as well as some Mormons, were aware of its existence before 1967. Because the details of this and other facets of the case are too lengthy to include here, one is invited to study Tanners' book, *Mormonism—Shadow or Reality?*, which offers a more complete presentation.
30. Tanner and Tanner, *Mormonism—Shadow or Reality?*, 301–2.
31. Ibid., 320. Since Smith was heavily involved in the study of hermetic-Kabbalism which promoted the return "to the primal vision" and "encouraged a *creative* rereading of sacred texts" within the "prophetic consciousness," the Book of Abraham would not be expected to be a literal translation (See Lance S. Owens "Joseph Smith and Kabbalah: *Dialogue* 27, no. 3 [Fall 1994], 166) [emphasis mine].
32. In a new publication, Michael W. Hickenbotham (*Answering Challenging Mormon Questions* [Bountiful, Utah: Horizon Pub., 1995]),

says the Church now admits that papyri, formerly believed to be the Book of Abraham, is an Egyptian funerary text. LDS scholars now claim that none of the papyri in their possession contain the text of the Book of Abraham. This is based upon a statement of Joseph Smith's that the Book of Abraham papyri contained red ink, but the papyri now held by the church contains none (p. 212). Some LDS scholars are suggesting that the original papyri purchased by the Mormon Church in 1835 never did contain the Book of Abraham. Since no extant copy of the Book of Abraham exists, it cannot be used to challenge the accuracy of Mormon claims.

Hickenbotham also states that Smith's explanation of the facsimiles in the Book of Abraham "correspond closely to the interpretation of Egyptologists" (p. 213). This is false. Facsimile number 1, which Joseph Smith explains as an "idolatrous priest of Elkenah attempting to offer up Abraham as a sacrifice," has been refuted by Egyptologists. Their interpretation, backed up by similar facsimiles found in other Egyptian locations, is that it is Osiris lying upon his bier and the jackal-god, Anubis, embalming him. There is also evidence that the original facsimile in Joseph Smith's possession had been altered.

A charge of altering also holds true for the hypocephalus (circular sheet of stiffened papyrus), known as facsimile number 2. The original hypocephalus had missing parts that were obviously filled in later with pencil. Smith, however, drew a picture of the hypocephalus from the original papyrus, showing the missing parts (see *Joseph Smith's Egyptian Alphabet and Grammar*), and the Mormon Church suppressed the drawing for 130 years. Someone in the 19th century (Smith?) drew in the missing parts on this facsimile before it was published in the 1842 Mormon newspaper "Times and Seasons." (For an extensive treatment, as well as pictures of the facsimiles, see Tanner and Tanner, *Mormonism— Shadow or Reality?*, 294–369.)

33. Ibid., 294–369.
34. Smith, *History of the Church*, 5:372.
35. Ideographs "are graphic symbols representing an object or idea without expressing, as in a phonetic system, the sounds that form its name. A symbol representing an idea rather than a word. A pictorial representation of an idea of object" *(Webster's New Universal Unabridged Dictionary,* Deluxe 2nd ed., 1979, 902). For a more in-depth presentation, see Tanner and Tanner, *Mormonism—Shadow or Reality?*, 111–114.
36. A seer stone is comparable to a crystal ball used by fortune tellers.

However, since a seer stone is a rock, it is not "transparent" as portrayed in movies.

37. John L. Brooke, *The Refiner's Fire: The Making of Mormon Cosmology, 1644–1844* (Cambridge: Cambridge University Press, 1994), 5.

38. Ibid., 6.

39. "Although the texts made it seem that Trismegistus was a predecessor of Moses, he was a creation of second-and third-century pagan Gnostics, a fusion of the Greek Hermes with the Egyptian Thoth. Though the French scholar Isaac Casaubon demonstrated their second-century origin in 1614, occult philosophers continued to read the hermetic texts as ancient revelation until the end of the seventeenth century" (Ibid., 10).

40. Kabbalah was not a tradition of historical dogma in Judaism but of mysticism which claimed to be open-ended, a 'pathway to prophetic consciousness.' Claiming to be guardian of the original knowledge Adam received from God, any person who had access to Kabbalistic symbols and lore, qualified for further revelation and visions from God. Kabbalah's powerful influence was, according to some scholars, one of the main sources of the Renaissance. Lance S. Owens states that "[Frances A.] Yates suggests that the true origins of the Renaissance genius may be dated from two events: the arrival of the *Corpus Hermeticum* in Florence and the infusion of Kabbalism into Christian Europe by the Spanish expulsion of the Jews" (Owens, *Dialogue*, 130). See Frances A. Yates, *The Occult Philosophy in the Elizabethan Age* (London, Routledge & Kegan Paul, 1979), 3–4.

Therefore, "Christian Kabbalah" [or Hermeticism], as Owens explains, "was not a recapitulation of the Jewish tradition, but its creative remolding, a metamorphosis engendered by newly aroused religion-making vision. . . . Like early Christian Gnosticism, the tradition reborn had a dynamism which bred creative reinterpretation" (Owens, "Joseph Smith and Kabbalah," 131). Joseph Smith had extensive exposure to its teachings and was probably the basis for his claim to extra-Biblical revelation.

41. According to Brooke, Greco-Roman Egypt was where the Hermetic philosophy originated. It was a combination of Gnosticism, Platonism, Egyptian theology, and metallurgical traditions. It passed from Islamic sources at the end of the twelfth century, with portions ending up in medieval Europe as alchemy (See Ibid., 8).

42. Ibid., 7.

43. Ibid., 10. Alchemy also stressed, "that which is below is above." That is, matter was a reflection of the divine realm above. This led

Christian alchemists to insist that everything was created spiritually first, a teaching which Joseph Smith incorporated into Mormonism.

44. Brooke, *The Refiner's Fire*, 22, quoting John Saltmarsh's "Sparkles of Glory," that "history would break into three dispensations of Law, Gospel and Spirit, or of letter, graces and God, or of the first, second and third heavens" (Saltmarsh bibliographic information unavailable).

45. Brooke, *The Refiner's Fire*, 24.

46. Ibid., 25.

47. Ibid., 13.

48. *Doctrine and Covenants*, 110.

49. See Brooke, *The Refiner's Fire*, 14.

50. Ibid., 17, 192.

51. Brooke, *The Refiner's Fire*, 14, 44. Historically, baptism for the dead by proxy was practiced by the Gnostics, including the Marcionites, the Montanists and the Cerinthians, according to Irenaeus and Origen. The Marcionites, for example, would hide a living man under a dead man's bed. The officiator would then ask the dead man if he wished to receive baptism. With no answer from the corpse, the man under the bed then responded that he wished to be baptized in behalf of the dead person. In some instances, the actual corpse was baptized. There are also suggestions of a distant precedent in Greek religious practices (See C. K. Barrett, "The First Epistle to the Corinthians," in *Harper's New Testament Commentaries* [New York, Harper & Row, 1968], 363). Aside from Paul's reference in 1 Corinthians 15:29, there is no written evidence that this kind of rite was practiced much before the mid-first century. Although, as Barrett notes, this doesn't mean it didn't take place—especially in the bizarre city of Corinth. It has been suggested by some scholars that the "Christ" faction mentioned in 1 Corinthians 1:12, were the Gnostics. They had the ability to infiltrate a religion and deceptively take on its color, much like a chameleon. Their unique beliefs led to their baptizing for the dead. Gnostics believed the spirit was good, but the body was evil and by baptizing for the dead, the departed's spirit would be released to heaven. Because of their stance that only the spirit mattered, they felt they could bodily participate in incest or any other sin and it didn't matter as long as their spirit was saved. Salvation for one's spirit was acquired through special wisdom or knowledge. Once achieved, they considered themselves spiritually elite. Although believing in the "Christ" principle within one's spirit, they did not believe it had

anything to do with the body, which God would certainly not raise in any literal resurrection. Only the spirit would ascend to heaven at death. They probably saw Paul's willingness to be torn by wild beasts as a futile commitment demonstrating his lack of spiritual wisdom. Paul, in 1 Corinthians 15:29 asks, in speaking on the subject of the literal resurrection of the dead, "Else what shall they do which are baptized for the dead, if the dead rise not at all? Why are they then baptized for the dead?" (KJV). He may be referring to the Gnostic Christ faction within the Corinthian church. As a brief aside, Paul was mimicking their belief that if they believe the body is evil and will *not* be resurrected, what's the point of their being baptized for the dead if the dead aren't raised? Paul then goes on to logically explain that if the dead aren't raised and the body is of no value, why would he fight wild beasts in Ephesus for merely human reasons? Paul, after making his brief reference to this group, then continues his theme on the resurrection of the dead.

A simpler explanation is that Paul may be referring to new converts taking the place of deceased believers who were influential in bringing them to faith.

52. Brooke, *The Refiner's Fire*, 217. In the Hermetic-Kabbalistic tradition, Lance S. Owens says: "The image of [the] eternal, transformative union [of the primal form of God] was perhaps mirrored in Joseph Smith's ritual of [the New Covenant of] celestial marriage" (Owens, "Joseph Smith and Kabbalah," 150). In Alchemical philosophy the mystery of God was the unknowable God as a single unity emanating into both male and female, mother and father. Kabbalists used sexual metaphors to show how divine intercourse between the divine Mother and Father produced the rest of creation. Therefore, marriage and sex had a spiritual significance portrayed by the sacred royal wedding of alchemy's mythological characters, King and Queen Rex and Regina. They represented Adam and Eve as metaphors of the primal mystery. The Kabbalistic text *Zohar* teaches that one can only become one like God, through sexual union (Ibid., 185). Therefore, the union of man and woman in sex or a sacred wedding, represented this divine mystery and sexual rituals were practiced within some Masonic and Rosicrucian ceremonies (Ibid., 140, 145, 149, 190). Seventeenth and eighteenth-century Kabbalists also practiced polygamy to express this mystery. "In Talmudic tradition the cherubim [on the Arc of the Covenant] were male and female and were sometimes found in sexual embrace. . . . The Talmud states, 'When the Israelites came up on the pilgram [*sic*] Festivals the curtain would be removed for them and the cherubim

shown to them, their bodies interlocked with one another, and they would say to them, 'Look, you are beloved of God as the love between man and woman'" (Ibid., 126).

53. Brooke, *The Refiner's Fire*, 19.

54. Ibid., 38.

55. Puritans were against supernatural claims because they had been condemned in England. However, if occasional miracles happened, they considered them divine. Brooke says that in the fringe communities, folk magic made itself evident.

56. Alchemic principles are found in the poetry of Anne Bradstreet of Andover and Edward Taylor in Massachusetts. Cotton Mather also referred to prayer as a "spiritual alchemy" (Brooke, *The Refiner's Fire*, 37).

57. Brooke, *The Refiner's Fire*, 208, from David Whitmer, *An Address to All Believers in Christ* (Self-published, Richmond, Mo.: 1887; reprint, 1938), 35.

58. Brooke, *The Refiner's Fire*, 205.

59. See E. Robert Paul's, "Joseph Smith and the Plurality of Worlds Idea." *Dialogue*, 19 (Summer 1986): 15–36; "Joseph Smith and the Manchester New York) Library" *Brigham Young University Studies*, 22 (Summer 1982): 333–56. Erich Robert Paul, *Science, Religion, and Mormon Cosmology*, (Urbana: University of Illinois Press, 1992), 76–78.

60. Ibid., 379.

61. Ibid., 379.

62. Ibid., 207.

63. William Morgan's *Masonry Exposed* was first printed in 1827. According to John L. Brooke, Heber C. Kimball had a copy. Lucinda Morgan (widow of William Morgan) who was plural wife of Smith, had a copy of Stearns' *Inquiry into the Nature and Tendency of Speculative Freemasonr* and Brigham Young had a copy of Joshua Bradley's *Some Beauties of Freemasonry* (Brooke, *The Refiner's Fire*, 250). The Tanners' book, *Mormonism, Magic and Masonry*, 50, states that "both Masonic and anti-Masonic books were available at the bookstore in Palmyra." Also that Henry Dana Ward's anti-Masonic book, *Free Masonry*, printed in 1828, contained the Masonic myth, e.g., the Enoch legend of the gold plate, from which Joseph could have borrowed.

64. See Brooke, *The Refiner's Fire*, 98.

65. According to Brooke, *The Refiner's Fire*, 361, Oliver Cowdery may have assisted Ethan Smith in the printing of his book. Cowdery had experience as a printer and peddled his trade, according to the

Cleveland *Herald*, in the towns of eastern New York and Canada. Cowdery's home town was Poultney, the same town where Ethan Smith's book was published. No doubt he had a copy of it when he moved to western New York and met the Smith family. Cowdery's stepmother also belonged to Rev. Ethan Smith's congregation.

The idea of the Indians being Israelites was well known for years before Joseph Smith. Joseph Mede first stated, in 1634, that the devil led the Indians to America. But by 1650, Thomas Thorowgood insisted they were the Lost Tribes. This motivated John Eliot to do missionary work among the Natick Indians. James Adair and Elias Boudinot, the latter in *A Star in the West, or an Attempt to Discover the Lost Ten Tribes of Israel*, continued the idea in 1775 and 1816. Ethan Smith then tried, in his book, to reconcile the lack of confirming data (See Brooke, *The Refiner's Fire*, 163).

66. This book was in the Manchester rental library, five miles from Joseph Smith's home. Since it was repeatedly checked out, the book's subject was "common knowledge" (Wesley P. Walters, *The Human Origins of the* Book of Mormon, [1979, "The Origin of the Book of Mormon," n.p., Institute of Pastoral Studies of the Christian Counseling & Educational Foundation; reprint, Clearwater, F.L.: Ex-Mormons For Jesus, n.d.], 9). It also included the idea that the Indians were the Tribes of Israel. Josiah Priest later published *American Antiquities* (n.p.: Hoffman & White, 1833), three years after the Book of Mormon came out. It summarized material available before 1830, quoting at least forty writers having the idea that the American Indians were Israelites. B. H. Roberts, Mormon Historian, says the works of Josiah Priest and Ethan Smith "were either possessed by Joseph Smith or certainly known by him, for they were surely available to him" (Walters, *The Human Origins of the* Book of Mormon, 8). For similarities between Ethan Smith's book, *View of the Hebrews, or the Tribes of Israel in America* (1st ed. 1823, 2nd ed. 1825. Reprint 1977, n.p. Arne Press) and the Book of Mormon, see Walters, *The Human Origins of the* Book of Mormon, 11.

67. See Brooke, *The Refiner's Fire*, 204.

68 Many of these ideas were also incorporated into Masonry.

69. The alchemist philosophy of divinizing human beings was adopted into Masonry. In the *Royal Arch* degree, its lecture begins with the question: "Are you a Royal Arch Mason? Ans. I AM THAT I AM." Towards the end of the ceremony, the initiate enters the first, second and third veils of the holy tabernacle of God with the password, "I

AM THAT I AM" (Henry Dana Ward, *The Antimasonic Review* [1828]: 2:117–118, available through University Microfilms, Ann Arbor, Michigan, American Periodical Series 1800–1850, Reel 769).

Chapter Seven

1. Smith claimed that by putting his face into the darkness of a hat containing a seer stone, "spiritual light would shine. A piece of something resembling parchment would appear, and on that appeared the writing. One character at a time would appear, and beneath it was the interpretation in English. Brother Joseph would read off the English to Oliver Cowdery, who was his principal scribe, and when it was written down and repeated to Brother Joseph to see if it was correct, then it would disappear, and another character with the interpretation would appear" (David Whitmer, *An Address to All Believers in Christ* [Self-published, Richmond, Mo.: 1887; reprint 1938], 12), quoted in *Mormonism, Magic and Masonry* by Jerald Tanner and Sandra Tanner (Salt Lake City: Lighthouse Ministry, 1983), 26. [Hereinafter, *Magic*.]

2. According to Mormon scholars Steven C. Walker and Richard Van Wagoner the first 116 pages of the Book of Mormon claimed to have been translated by switching between the Urim and Thummin and the peep stone (Walker and Van Wagoner, "Joseph Smith: 'The Gift of Seeing,'" *Dialogue: A Journal of Mormon Thought* [Summer 1982]: 53). See also Tanner and Tanner, *Magic*, 27.) Smith's mother, Lucy Mack Smith, described the Urim and Thummin as consisting "of two smooth three-cornered diamonds set in glass, and the glasses were set in silver bows, which were connected with each other in much the same way as old fashioned spectacles" (*Biographical Sketches of Joseph Smith the Prophet and His Progenitors For Many Generations* [Liverpool: S. W. Richards, 1853], 101, quoted in Tanner and Tanner, *Magic*, 27).

3. Tanner and Tanner, *Magic*, 20. The Tanners note that Lucy Mack Smith's statement appears on page 77 of the preliminary draft of her history which is located in the Historical Department of the LDS Church.

4. Tanner and Tanner, *Magic*, 20–21. According to an article by John E. Thompson entitled, "The Faculte of Abrac," the faculy of Abrac dated to the 17th century and was known in Smith's time and neighborhood. (*The Philalethes* [December 1982], 9, 15.)

5. Acrostics were used by the Hebrews to aid in memorization. "Hebrew poem[s] of which the initial letters of the lines or stanzas formed the alphabet in order. Twelve of the Psalms are of this character, of

which Psalm cxix. is the best example" (*Webster's New Universal Unabridged Dictionary*, deluxe 2d ed. [Dorset & Baber, 1979], 19).

6. Robert Hendrickson, *Encyclopedia of Word and Phrase Origins* (New York: Facts on File Pub., 1987) 2–3.
7. Ibid. Masons claimed to be able to obtain the faculy of Abrac.
8. B. H. Roberts, *A Comprehensive History of the Church* 6 vols. (1930; reprint, Povo: Brigham Young University Press, 1965), 1:26–27, quoted in Tanner and Tanner, *Magic*, 18.
9. Tanner and Tanner, *Magic*, 18.
10. Eber D. Howe, *Mormonism Unveiled* (Painesville, Ohio: n.p., 1834), 249, quoted in Tanner and Tanner, *Magic*, 26.
11. When Smith translated the plates they were, at the time, in a location elsewhere—hidden in the woods (See David Persuitte, *Joseph Smith and the Origins of the* Book of Mormon [Jefferson, N.C.: McFarland & Co. 1985], 73). Therefore, he did not literally translate the plates, but divined their message, supernaturally.
12. *Mormon Answer to Skepticism* (author unknown), (Webster's Grove, MO.: n.p., 1980), 104. "He said he saw Captain Kidd sailing on the Susquehanna River during a freshet, and that he buried two pots of gold and silver. He claimed he saw writing cut on the rocks in an unknown language telling where Kidd buried it, and he translated it through his peep-stone," quoted in Tanner and Tanner, *Magic*, 27.
13. See H. Michael Marquardt and Wesley P. Walters, *Inventing Mormonism: Tradition and the Historical Record* (n.p., Smith Research Associates, 1994), 205–6, quoting Joel Tiffany, "Mormonism–No. II," *Tiffany's Monthly* 5 (August 1859): 163–70. See also Tanner and Tanner, *Magic*, 25. This (brown) stone was found in the well at a depth of "twenty four feet." After this, Joseph spent about two years looking into this stone, telling fortunes, where to find lost things, and where to dig for money and other hidden treasure" (Ibid., 24–25). Smith also had a *white* stone which is the one usually referred to as the Urim and Thummin. He claimed to have translated the Book of Abraham with this white seer stone, rather than the brown one (See D. Michael Quinn, *The Mormon Hierarchy: Origins of Power* [Salt Lake City, in association with Smith Research Associates: Signature Books, 1994], 616, 623). The brown stone used to translate the Book of Mormon was the stone Smith first used during his occupation as a money-digger (Ibid., 4). For a picture of Joseph Smith's "green seer-stone," see John L. Brooke, *The Refiner's Fire: The Making of Mormon Cosmology, 1644–1844* (Cambridge: Cambridge University Press, 1994), 153.

14. C. M. Stafford claimed that Joseph Smith studied the palm of his hand and told his fortune (Tanner and Tanner, *Magic*, 26. See also, Ibid., 18).
15. A Patriarchal blessing is pronounced by an authorized Patriarch. His job is to declare which tribe one descends from and often tells the individual's future.
16. Tanner and Tanner, *Magic*, 19.
17. Quinn, *The Mormon Hierarchy*, 645.
18. This revelation appeared in the 1833 *Book of Commandments* (Zion [Independence, Mo.:], 1833) predecessor to the Doctrine and Covenants.
19. Tanner and Tanner, *Magic*, 29. See actual photograph of the original revelation contained in the *Book of Commandments*, in Jerald Tanner and Sandra Tanner's *Mormonism—Shadow or Reality?*, (Salt Lake City: Modern Microfilm, 1972), 19. Joseph Smith's divining rod was given to Oliver Cowdery's brother-in-law, Phineas Young. Young was also brother to Brigham Young and gave it to the latter. The rod, or cane, Brigham Young was often seen with after arriving in the Salt Lake Valley and with which he pointed out where the Salt Lake Temple would be, was the same rod (See Tanner and Tanner, *Magic*, 30). Presently, Doctrine and Covenants 8:6 reads "gift of Aaron."
20. Tanner and Tanner, *Magic*, 29.
21. This instance was related by William Stafford, contemporary of Smith's (See Tanner and Tanner, *Magic*, 32). See also, Howe, *Mormonism Unveiled*, 237–239.
22. Howe, *Mormonism Unveiled*, 237–39.
23. Tanner and Tanner, *Magic*, 33.
24. Ibid., 32–33.
25. Ibid., *Magic*, 34.
26. A nephew of William Stafford testified: "Jo Smith, the prophet, told my uncle, William Stafford, he wanted a fat, black sheep. He said he wanted to cut its throat and make it walk in a circle three times around and it would prevent a pot of money from leaving" Tanner and Tanner, *Magic*, 33.
27. Wandle Mace records this event in his journal: "Joseph told them to go to Kirtland, and cleanse and purify a certain room in the Temple, that they must kill a lamb and offer a sacrifice unto the Lord which should prepare them to ordain Willard Richards a member of the Quorum of the Twelve Apostles" (Journal of Wandle Mace, 32, microfilmed copy at Brigham Young University). See also *Magic*, 34.
28. See Chapter 1, 22–23, for full quotation.

29. According to Dr. Reed C. Durham, Jr., Jupiter was known to the Egyptians as Ammon; Zeus to the Greeks. Jupiter, in the presence of his priest, supposedly performed the most ancient form of marriage for time and for eternity (See "Reed C. Durham, Jr.'s Astounding Research on the Masonic Influence on Mormonism," *Mormon Miscellaneous*, Mervin B. Hogan, ed. (Nauvoo: New Nauvoo Neighbor Press, 1, no. 1 (October 1975), 15. (Hereinafter, Hogan, *Mormon Miscellaneous*.) The Masonic Order also endorsed the magic Table of Jupiter.

30. One phrase was in Latin.

31. Dr. Durham was chastised by Mormon leaders after he revealed the Masonic and magic connection of Joseph Smith and was made to sign a "test oath," a statement swearing allegiance to the divine mission of Joseph Smith.

32. Francis Barrett, *The Magus* (Printed in England in 1801, published in America in 1804) it was available in Smith's time. Dr. Durham traced it to Manchester and to New York. See also Tanner and Tanner, *Magic*, 2.

33. Hogan, *Mormon Miscellaneous*, 14–15.

34. Ibid.

35. Ibid.

36. Ibid. For a picture of the talisman, see Tanner and Tanner, *Magic*, 3. Interestingly, in astrology, Thursday is Jupiter's day and for sixty years Mormon fast meetings were on Thursdays. So also were the Lodge meetings of the Mormon Masons.

37. Michael W. Homer, "'Similarity of Priesthood in Masonry:' The Relationship between Freemasonry and Mormonism," 27, no. 3 *Dialogue: A Journal of Mormon Thought* (Fall 1994): 24–25.

38. Pearson H. Corbett, *Hyrum Smith-Patriarch* (Provo: Deseret Book, 1963, 453), describes these objects. See Tanner and Tanner, *Magic*, 5ff.

39. Reginald Scot, *The Discovery of Witchcraft* (1584, Norwood, N.J: Walker J. Johnson; reprint 1971). See Tanner and Tanner, *Magic*, 12. (The Tanners' book also contains pictures.)

40. Steven C. Walker and Richard S. Van Wagoner, "Joseph Smith: 'The Gift of Seeing,'" *Dialogue: A Journal of Mormon Thought* (Summer 1982): 66.

41. See Quinn, *The Mormon Hierarchy*, 659. Also, Tanner and Tanner, *Magic*, 30.

42. Quinn, *Mormon Hierarchy*, 649. See also Dean C. Jesse, ed., "Nauvoo Diary of John Tayor," Brigham Young University Studies 23 (Summer 1983): 34. Illustrated in Lance S. Owens, "Joseph Smith and Kabbalah," *Dialogue*, 27, no. 3 (Fall 1994): 47.

43. Joseph Smith's use of the term "apostate endowment" meant that the Masons originally had the true temple ceremony but, through time, it degenerated and many truths were lost.
44. Witnesses say he used a stone to locate the box. Smith, upon looking into his stone, may have interpreted the psychic vision as a dream, making it sound more biblical.
45. The sequence of events is reminiscent of the Masonic Legend of Enoch. Although Joseph Smith was not inducted into the Masonic Lodge until March 15, 1842, after his Book of Mormon story, his knowledge of Masonic lore could have been acquired earlier from his brother Hyrum who was a Mason. Books were also in print containing Masonic stories.
46. Joseph and Hiel Lewis, *Amboy Journal*, 30 April 1879, quoted in Tanner and Tanner, *Magic*, 41.
47. Tanner and Tanner, *Magic*, 40.
48. The name of "Nephi" as the angel, appeared in the following publications: The 1851 edition of the Pearl of Great Price; *Millennial Star*, Lucy Mack Smith's biography, *Biographical Sketches of Joseph Smith the Prophet and His Progenitors For Many Generations*, and *Times and Seasons* 3 (April 15, 1842): 753. Joseph Smith was editor of the *Times and Seasons* at the time the account of his story was published. Therefore, if this were in error, he would have corrected it. The full quote of the angel appearing in Smith's room, can be found in Bill McKeever's *Answering Mormons' Questions* (Minneapolis: Bethany House, 1991), 96–97. For a more detailed account of the angel's name-change, see Tanner and Tanner, *Mormonism—Shadow or Reality?*, 136–137. It has also been suggested that Smith could have been influenced by a story contained in Draper's *Intellectual Development of Europe*, 382 which reads, "About the close of the twelfth century appeared among the mendicant friars that ominous work, which, under the title of 'The Everlasting Gospel,' struck terror into the Latin hierarchy. It was affirmed that an angel had brought it from heaven, engraven on copper plates, and had given it to a priest named Cyril, who delivered it to the Abbot Joachim."

    Quoted in James H. Snowden's *The Truth About Mormonism* (New York: George H. Doran, 1926), 108.
49 Derived from Kabbalistic lore.
50. According to Dr. Reed Durham, Jr., the Legend of Enoch was refined and incorporated into modern Masonry in France by 1740–60. By 1802, American Masonry had it in print and by Smith's time was available in bookstores. See Tanner and Tanner, *Magic*, 47.

51. Hogan, *Mormon Miscellaneous*, 15. This legend given in the thirteen, fourteenth, and twenty-first degree of Masonry.
52. Michael W. Homer, "'Similarity of Priesthood in Masonry:' The Relationship between Freemasonry and Mormonism," 27, no. 3 *Dialogue: A Journal of Mormon Thought* (Fall 1994): 17.
53. Thomas S. Webb, *The Freemason's Monitor or Illustrations of Masonry* (New York: Southwick and Crooker, 1802), 256.
54. See Doctrine and Covenants, 78, 92, 96 and 104.
55. The Book of Mormon index says: "contain[s] five books of Moses, history of Jews to reign of Zedekiah, genealogy. See *Plates, Brass*."
56. Wesley P. Walters, *The Human Origins of the* Book of Mormon (1979; reprint of "The Origin of the Book of Mormon," n.p., Institute of Pastoral Studies of the Christian Counseling & Educational Foundation; n.d., Clearwater, FL: Ex-Mormons for Jesus, n.d.), 24.
57. *Palmyra Reflector*, 28 February 1831. See also James H. Snowden, *The Truth About Mormonism* (New York: George H. Doran, 1926), 57, quoting an affidavit given in Howe, *Mormonism Unveiled*, 235–36.
58. Elias Boudinot and James Adair, *A Star in the West, or an Attempt to Discover the Lost Ten Tribes of Israel.*
59. *Palmyra Reflector*, 28 February 1831, as quoted in Tanner and Tanner, *Magic*, 2.
60. Owens, ("Joseph Smith and Kabbalah," 171) claims the letter could be a forgery. However, Reed C. Durham, Jr. did not believe this.
61. A letter of Joseph Smith to Mr. John Hull of Lempster, New Hampshire, as quoted in Hogan, *Mormon Miscellaneous*, 13. According to Reed C. Durham, Jr., Joseph makes it "clear in the letter that the Kingdom of God was thought to be the true masonry, which, when ultimately established with a king and a president, would abolish all earthly confusion and evil and usher in the Millennium." After a lengthy description of Masonic related descriptions, Joseph concludes, "This is my present survey of Masonry in this world" (Ibid., 13).
62. Hogan, *Mormon Miscellaneous*, 13. Dr. Durham admits that "the Kingdom of God doctrine was masonically inspired. The Masonic Constitution is called the *Ahiman Rezon*.
63. Hogan, *Mormon Miscellaneous*, 13.
64. The Cyclopean eye was adopted by the Hermeticists, transposing it into the Christian context as the eye of Jehovah. See Owens, "Joseph Smith and Kabbalah," 145.
65. The Beehive, used in earlier centuries by Christian Hermetics, did not represent physical industry as so many think. Metaphorically, it represented the "hive" of one's inner soul. The industry of the bee

was illustrative of the spiritual labor required for the alchemic transmutation of the individual, or dark matter, into gold. Those who interpreted industry as seeking for physical gold, called "vulgar gold"
were considered "drones." The Beehive was used later in Freemasonry and was one of the ten emblems given a Master Mason.
Brigham Young used this symbol for the Mormon State, the Kingdom of Deseret (Owens, "Joseph Smith and Kabbalah," 143, 145).

Of interest is the similarity between the Temple Mormon's "first
token of the Melchizedek Priesthood or sign of the nail," and that of
the Masonic honorary degree of *Secret Monitor*, the latter conferred
only upon approved Master Masons. Whereas other Masonic degrees
are based upon the story of Solomon, Hyrum Abiff, and Enoch's treasure, this degree revolves around 1 Samuel 20, David and Jonathan's
interview of concern about King Saul. A Masonic brother of this degree learns, through a special handgrip how to caution (or encourage) another brother in public. In the Mormon temple the token is
not a handgrip, per se. Rather, the individual receiving the token holds
his hand out in the attitude of preparing to shake hands. The person
giving the token, presses the point of his forefinger in the center of
the receiver's palm, with his thumb on the opposite side of the hand.
The *Secret Monitor* grip "is [also] given in the palm of the hand, with
one finger, or two, impressing the palm, according to the necessity
of caution, or to the occasion for encouragement." (Henry Dana Ward,
Antimasonic Review, and Magazine [1828], 2:67). In another order
of Masonry, a Knight of Malta is told to "force the first finger into
the centre of the [other's] palm" (*Richardson's Monitor of Free Masonry*, 126, quoted in Tanner and Tanner, *Mormonism—Shadow or
Reality?* [1972], 488).

66. Hogan, *Mormon Miscellaneous*, 12.

67. According to Madam Blavatsky's *Secret Doctrine*, the circle sitting
    on a straight horizontal line . . . "comes from the Aryans, Egyp-
    tians, and Chaldeans, representing hidden deity, creative power, and
    divine thought versus creation." In another place she says the circle's
    name is *Ru*; that "it sits upon the head of the vertical beam of the
    cross, across which is a horizontal beam, thus forming the cross,
    called the *Sau-Cross*." According to Blavatsky, this *Ru/Sau* cross
    was one time on the back of a Phoenician coin. This was also called
    "Venus' looking-glass," a symbol of human procreation (Helen
    Blavatsky, *The Secret Doctrine* [Wheaton, IL: Theosophical Pub.,
    1993], page unknown).

68. Brigham Young gave this purpose for the temple endowment: "Your
    endowment is to receive all those ordinances in the House of the

Lord, which are necessary for you, after you have departed this life, to enable you to walk back to the presence of the Father, passing the angels who stand as sentinels, being enabled to give them the key words, the signs and tokens, pertaining to the Holy Priesthood, and gain you eternal exaltation in spite of earth and hell" (*Journal of Discourses*, Joseph F. Smith, ed. [1854–86; reprint, Salt Lake City: Brigham Young University Press, 1967], 2:31–32).

Joseph Smith taught that the angels in heaven used Masonic handgrips. According to E. Cecil McGavin:

"There is best evidence for believing that Joseph taught that Masonic principles and practices operated among the gods as well as on earth. His followers in Utah were taught, that there is a sort of divine Masonry among the angels who hold the priesthood, by which they can detect those who do not belong to their order. Those who cannot give the signs correctly are supposed to be impostors." (E. Cecil McGavin, *Mormonism and Masonry* [Salt Lake City: Bookcraft, 1949], 6). See also, Homer, "Similarity of Priesthood in Masonry," 64.

The five points of fellowship given in the LDS Temple is never explained in detail. Members believe it is a ritualistic act which they must know to pass by the angels in heaven. Since Joseph Smith took it from Masonry, here is the Masonic understanding:

"Foot to foot (teaches) that we will not hesitate to go on foot and out of our way to aid and succor a needy Brother; knee to knee, that we will ever remember a Brother's welfare, in all our applications to Deity; breast to breast, that we will ever keep, in our breast, a Brother's secrets, when communicated to us as such, murder and treason excepted; hand to back, that we will ever be ready to stretch forth our hand to aid and support a falling Brother; cheek to cheek, or mouth to ear, that we will ever whisper good counsel in the ear of a Brother, and in the most tender manner remind him of his faults, and endeavor to aid his reformation . . ." (McGavin, *Mormonism and Masonry*, 11).

Early Mormons believed the "temple garment represented the 'white stone' or new name given to each candidate" (Homer, "Similarity of Priesthood in Masonry," 40). In the Doctrine and Covenants, 130:11, referring to the white stone mentioned in Revelation 2:17, Joseph Smith said: "And a white stone is given to each of those who come into the celestial kingdom, whereon is a new name written, which no man knoweth save he that receiveth it. The new name is the keyword" (Homer, "Similarity of Priesthood in Masonry," 44–45). The giving of a new name is part of the temple ceremony.

69. Hogan, *Mormon Miscellaneous*, 12.

70. Ibid., 16.

71. Tanner and Tanner, *Magic*, 50. The Tanners also note that the last part of the word "Cu-*morah*" reminds one of the hill, *Mo-riah*. For other examples, as well as biblical sources for the names of the books within the Book of Mormon, see Tanner and Tanner, *Mormonism—Shadow or Reality?*, 94–95.

72. Hogan, *Mormon Miscellaneous*, 5.

73. See Walter F. Prince, "Tests for the Authorship of the Book of Mormon," *American Journal of Psychology*, 28 (July, 1917), quoted in Jacob Adamson, "Is There No Help For the Widow's Son," *Mormon Miscellaneous*, 6.

74. In June 1837, the *Latter Day Saints' Messenger and Advocate*, along with the *Encyclopaedia Britannica*, mention that the Eleusianian mysteries were rituals passed down from the beginning of the world, but revealed only to special initiates and enumerated the various rituals, e.g., washings and anointings, a oaths and penalties, a new name, etc. The Mormon temple ceremony comprises the same. See *A Dictionary of Religion and Ethics*, ed. Shailer Mathews and Gerald Birney Smith, (New York: Macmillan, 1921), 300. See also Quinn, *Mormon Hierarchy*, 626.

75. Hogan, *Mormon Miscellaneous*, 14. *The Latter Day Saints' Messenger and Advocate*, in June of 1837 recognized this resemblance between the mystery religions of New Testament times. There were also books on these subjects.

76. "Freemasonry adopted portions of the Kabbalah into its third degree, the Royal Arch, and into some of the higher grades" (Homer, "Similarity of Priesthood in Masonry," 108).

77. Hogan, *Mormon Miscellaneous*, 14. Smith was unaware that Masonry did not actually have an ancient origin, but began in A.D. 1717. After the last leader of the Rosicrucians died, the Masons adopted their mystery teachings, then burned the written evidence so as to destroy any connection with Rosicrucianism and instigate the idea that the contents of their organization descended directly from the ancients. See Ward, *The Antimasonic Review and Magazine,* 1:194.

78. The availability of these sources were mentioned in June 1837 in the *Latter Day Saints' Messenger and Advocate*.

79. The idea of the drama was originally used in the Rosicrucian order, then incorporated into French Masonry in 1750. As allegorical "mystery plays," they taught rituals which were "fundamentally Hermetic-Kabbalistic" (Owens, "Joseph Smith and Kabbalah," 151).

Of further interests is the twenty-eighth Degree of the Scottish rite known as "the rite de Perfection." It was "to be administered in a room painted like a vast garden, with open fields, forests, and mountains" (Ibid.,168). Those familiar with the Garden room murals inside the Mormon Temple will recognize the similarity.

80. Joseph Smith said:

Now, I ask all who hear me, why the learned men who are preaching salvation, say that God created the heavens and the earth out of nothing? The reason is, that they are unlearned in the things of God, and have not the gift of the *Holy Ghost . . . But I am learned, and know more than all the world put together. The Holy Ghost does, anyhow, and he is within me,* and comprehends more than all the world; and I will associate myself with him." (Joseph Smith, *History of the Church of Jesus Christ of Latter-day Saints,* rev. ed. B. H. Roberts, 7 vols. [Salt Lake City: Deseret Book, 1978], 6:309) [emphasis mine].

81. Smith, *History of the Church,* 6:305–12. Smith claimed to translate this interpretation from Genesis in the "old Bible." Owens states that "he really means the *Zohar,* since in Kabbalistic lore, it was seen as such" (Owens, "Joseph Smith and Kabbalah," 183).

82. Neibauer published a Kabbalist treatise in a Mormon publication, covering the *Zohar,* a famous text for the Jewish Kabbalah. Joseph Smith's diary states he was studying with Neibauer in 1844. This is also confirmed by former LDS historian D. Michael Quinn in *Mormon Hierarchy,* 643. Included in Neibauer's library was the *Yalqut Khadash* a seventeenth-century Kabbalistic text which interestingly contained information "on the mystical and salvific intention of sexual union between male and female" (Owens, "Joseph Smith and Kabbalah," 191). Smith, in turn, taught this to his key people. This was evidenced in the *Millennial Star* where Orson Hyde drew an illustration of the Kingdom of God resembling the Kabbalistic Tree of Life which represented the "mystical shape of the Godhead." See Ibid., 186–87, which also includes an illustration in Fludd's 1621 Rosicrucian work.

83. Smith, *History of the Church,* 4:307. Smith said the German was the most correct translation because it corresponded closest to the revelations God had given him. He was, however, tutored by Alexander Neibauer who was fluent in French, German and Hebrew. Neibauer could also read Latin and Greek (Owens, "Joseph Smith and Kabbalah," 174).

84. His request to join the Methodist church is believed by some to be due to the death of his firstborn child.

85. Utah Christian Tract Society, newsletter (July–August, 1971),
    quoted in Tanner and Tanner, *Magic*, 54–55. See also, *Mormon
    Claims Answered* rev. ed. (Self-published, n.p., 1989), 9.
86. *The Amboy Journal*, 11 June, 1879, 1, quoted in Tanner and Tan-
    ner *Magic*, 55.
87. "Non-gold plates," *The Evangel*, (November 1994): 6. See also, "Jo-
    seph Smith's Gold Plates," *Utah Christian Tract Society* (La Mesa,
    Calif.: n.d.), 5.

Chapter Eight

1. Henry Dana Ward, *The Antimasonic Review, and Magazine* (New
   York: Vanderpool & Cole, 1830), 2:99.
2. Mosiah 2:16–17.
3. Mormons also believe a third testament will come forth—the sacred
   record possessed by the ten lost tribes of Israel. They believe, as Doctrine and Covenants 133:27–30 states, that the ice shall melt and they
   shall come out of the north on a highway that will rise up out of the
   ocean. They will come specifically to Zion so that they can receive
   the temple endowment and conferral of the higher priesthood. Joseph
   Smith stated that "John the Revelator was then among the ten tribes
   of Israel who had been led away by Shalmaneser, king of Assyria,
   to prepare them for their return from their long dispersion" (Joseph
   Smith, *History of the Church of Jesus Christ of Latter-day Saints*,
   rev. ed. B. H. Roberts, 7 vols. [Salt Lake City: Deseret Book, 1978],
   1:176). Quoted in Joseph Fielding Smith, comp. Bruce R. McConkie,
   Doctrines of Salvation, (Salt Lake City: Bookcraft, 1956), 3:253.
4. Dating to 170 B.C. and 60 B.C. Up until that time, the oldest dated
   to A.D. 980. "The documents (of the Dead Sea Scrolls) were written between about 250 B.C. and A.D. 68, when, according to its ex-
   cavator, the nearby settlement of Qumran was destroyed by the
   Roman army in anticipation of its attack on Jerusalem. Although
   that is when the documents were written, some may have been composed *much earlier*. Indeed, the earliest documents among the Dead
   Sea Scrolls were *actually written before the establishment of the
   nearby settlement with which they are often associated*" (Hershel
   Shanks, "Of Caves and Scholars: An Overview," *Understanding the
   Dead Sea Scrolls*, ed. Hershel Shanks [New York: Random House,
   1992], xix) [emphasis mine].
       "The Transmission of the Hebrew Text: Until the discovery of
   the Dead Sea Scrolls (DSS) in 1947, the Hebrew MSS [manuscripts]
   (other than the Nash Papyrus fragment) were *dated no earlier than
   the ninth century A.D. The discoveries at Qumran, however, have*

pushed the MS [manuscript] tradition of the Hebrew Bible back a thousand years (Harper's Bible Dictionary, Paul J. Achtemeier, Gen. Ed. [Francisco: Harper & Row, 1985], 1037) [emphasis mine].

"MSS [manuscripts] of the Hebrew Bible: Before the discovery of the DSS [Dead Sea Scrolls], the chief extant MSS of the Hebrew OT [Old Testament] were: the Cairo Codex of the Prophets (A.D. 894); the Aleppo Codex of the entire OT (ca. A.D. 930); the Leningrad Codex (ca. A.D. 1008), which formed the basis of Rudolf Kittel's third edition of the Hebrew Bible; the British Museum Codex of the Pentateuch (first five books of the OT = Torah) (ca. A.D. 950); the Leningrad Codex of the Prophets (A.D. 1016); and the Reuchlin Codex of the Prophets (ca. A.D. 1105), which, unlike the others mentioned here stands in the Ben Naphthali rather than the Ben Asher tradition. There are other MSS, some of them quite fragmentary, but these are the most important MSS of the OT in the Masoretic tradition. With the discovery of the DSS in the Judean desert in 1947 and following, we now have MSS a thousand years older than those just mentioned" (Ibid., 1038).

5. The Old Testament of the King James version is translated from the Hebrew Masoretic text.

6. Tanner and Tanner, *Mormonism—Shadow or Reality?* (Salt Lake City: Modern Microfilm, 1972), 377.

7. Tanner and Tanner, *Mormonism—Shadow or Reality?*, 378. See also, Wayne Ham, "A Textual Comparison of the Isaiah Passages in the Book of Mormon with the Same Passages in the St. Mark's Isaiah Scroll of the Dead Sea Community," (master's thesis, Brigham Young University, 1961).

8. Dr. Sperry said: "After reading the Scrolls very carefully, I come to the conclusion that there is not a line in them that suggests that their writers knew the Gospel as understood by Latter-day Saints. . . . The Isaiah scroll is of relatively little use to Latter-day Saints as showing the antiquity of the text of Isaiah in the Book of Mormon," quoted in Tanner and Tanner, *Mormonism—Shadow or Reality?*, 378.

9. Hugh Nibley, *An Approach to the* Book of Mormon (Salt Lake City: Deseret Book, 1957), 13, quoted in Tanner and Tanner, *Mormonism—Shadow or Reality?*, 63.

10. *Deseret News* 1993–94 *Church Almanac: The Church of Jesus Christ of Latter-day Saints* (Salt Lake City: Deseret News, 1992), 338. See also Orson Pratt's statement about David Whitmer's experience in Journal of Discourses, Joseph F. Smith, ed. (1854–86; reprint, Salt Lake City: Brigham Young University Press, 1967), 7:29. Also D. Michael Quinn, *Mormon Hierarchy: Origins of Power* (Salt Lake City, in association with Smith Research Associates, 1994), 10.

11. H. Michael Marquardt & Wesley P. Walters, *Inventing Mormonism* (n.p.: Smith Research Assoc., 1994), 216. See also David Persuitte, *Joseph Smith and the Origins of The* Book of Mormon, 2d ed. (Jefferson, N.C.: McFarland & Co., 1991), 96.

12. Fawn M. Brodie, *No Man Knows My History* (New York: Alfred A. Knopf, 1971), 78. The attorney was J. A. Clark who was in Palmyra.

13. Brodie suggests that Joseph built a makeshift set of plates. *No Man Knows*, 80. See also Tanner and Tanner, *Mormonism—Shadow or Reality?*, 59.

14. Brodie, *No Man Knows*, 78.

15. When Latter-day Saints use the phrase "the gospel," they mean Mormon beliefs. Therefore, the "gospel" includes Joseph Smith's calling as prophet, the authenticity of the Book of Mormon, the Church of Jesus Christ of Latter-day Saints, and the plan of salvation, which includes preexistence, temple marriage, and the three heavens.

16. 2 Nephi 3:5–11 (From the brass plates, Joseph of Egypt's prophecy that a choice seer would be raised up in the latter days); Doctrine and Covenants 1:17–18 (Joseph Smith called of God); Doctrine and Covenants 5:10 (The word of the Lord, to this generation, shall come through Joseph Smith); Doctrine and Covenants 35:17 (Joseph Smith was given the fullness of the gospel); title page of Book of Mormon, 2 Nephi 3:11–12 and Ezekiel 37:15–19 the Book of Mormon and the Bible will grow together to clarify false doctrines and promote peace); 2 Nephi 29:6–9 (the Lord gives His word to all men); 2 Nephi 33:10–12 (if you believe in Christ, one will have to believe these words); John 10:14–16 and 3 Nephi 15:16–24 (the visit of Christ to his other sheep).

17. Tanner and Tanner, *Mormonism—Shadow or Reality?*, 96.

18. Alma 10:3.

19. Professor Anthon, responding to an inquiry from an Ohio newspaper editor E. E. Howe, wrote a letter declaring that Harris' report of their encounter was false. He stated the characters were not Egyptian hieroglyphics, but "crooked characters disposed in columns, and had evidently been prepared by some person who had before him at the time a book containing various alphabets. Greek and Hebrew letters, crosses and flourishes, Roman letters inverted or placed sideways, were arranged in perpendicular columns, and the whole ended in a rude delineation of a circle divided into various compartments, decked with various strange marks, and evidently copied after the Mexican Calendar given by Humboldt, but copied in such a way as not to betray the source whence it was derived" ("Wresting the Scriptures" [La Mesa, Calif.: *Utah Christian Tract Society*, n.d.], 20).

20. E. H. Plumptre, in Charles John Ellicott's *Bible Commentary*, offers the following on Isaiah 29: [v.11] "**The vision of all** . . . [is]
the entire substance of Isaiah's teaching. . . . [v.13] "**Wherefore
the Lord said** . . . The blind stupor was the outcome of a long hypocrisy. Lip-homage and an estranged heart had been the notes of
the religious life of Israel, and they could bear no other fruit. . . .
[v. 14] "**a marvellous work** . . . The sure doom of hypocrisy would
come upon the hypocrites: not loving the light, they would lose the
light they had, and be left to their self-chosen blindness. . . . [v.
16] "**Shall be esteemed as the potter's clay** . . . The men whom
he condemns were invertin the relations of the Creator and the crea-
ture, the potter and the clay, acting practically as atheists, denying
that there was a Divine order of which they formed a part. . . . [v.
18] "**In that day shall the deaf hear the words of the book** . . .
The open vision of the future is contrasted with the self-chosen ignorance of verse 11. The "book" . . . is, perhaps, the prophet's own
message, or the book of the law of the Lord, which will then be
understood in all its spiritual fullness. The doom of the "closed
eyes" of chapter vi. 10 shall then be in force no more" (Charles
John Ellicott, ed., *A Bible Commentary for English Readers* [New
York: Cassell and Company, n.d.], 4: 496–97).

Chapter Nine

1. Gustave Niebuhr, "Mormons Making Big Latin Gains," *The Seattle
Times* (11 December 1994) reprinted from *New York Times*, A–14.
This figure includes children of members.
2. M. T. Lamb, *The Golden Bible* (Provo: Ward & Drummond, 1886),
89–91, quoted in Tanner and Tanner, *Mormonism—Shadow or Reality?* (Salt Lake City: Modern Microfilm, 1972), 104.
3. Anthony A. Hoekema, *The Four Major Cults* (Grand Rapids: William B. Eerdmans, 1963), 78.
4. See Tanner and Tanner, *Mormonism—Shadow or Reality?*, 104.
5. Hoekema, *The Four Major Cults*, 86.
6. Ibid., 86.
7. Wesley P. Walters, *The Human Origins of the* Book of Mormon (n.d.
reprint of "The Origin of the Book of Mormon," n.p., Institute of Pastoral Studies of the Christian Counseling and Educational Foundation; 1979, Clearwater, FL: Ex-Mormons for Jesus), 2. This is a
presentation of B. H. Robert's unpublished paper written in the early
1920's. The original manuscript is in possession of the Reorganized
Church of Jesus Christ of Latter-day Saints, Independence, Missouri.
8. See M. T. Lamb's, *The Golden Bible* (Provo: Ward & Drummond,

1886), 259.272, quoted in Tanner and Tanner, *Mormonism—Shadow or Reality?*, 106–7.

9. Letter from Richard A. Parker, Department of Egyptology at Brown University, to Marvin Cowan, dated March 22, 1966. Quoted in Tanner and Tanner, *Mormonism—Shadow or Reality?*, 108.

10. *Journal of Discourses*, Joseph F. Smith, ed. (1854–86; reprint, Salt Lake City: Brigham Young University Press, 1967), 13:130–31.

11. Mormon Apostle Orson Pratt cited one of its translated phrases as, 'May the Lord have mercy on me a *Nephel*.' Pratt interpreted *Nephel* as *Nephite*. However, *Nephel* in Hebrew, means *untimely* (as in the untimely birth in Job 3:16) not an individual's name.

12. Tanner and Tanner, *Mormonism—Shadow or Reality?*, 115–116.

13. This common motif can be seen in another stone carving of the *Tree of Life*, explored in 1901 and mentioned in a 1924 paper by Dr. Max Uhle, "Explorations at Chincha," *University of California Publications in American Archaeology and Ethnology*, 21, no. 2, (1924): 55–94. This stone was carved out of a mountainside at Paracas Bay on the south coast of Peru, measuring 128 m. long and 74 m. wide (approximately 419' x 242') and could be seen ten miles out to sea. Quoted in Ross T. Christensen, ed., *The Tree of Life in Ancient America* (Provo: Brigham Young University, May 1968; reprint of "Newsletter and Proceedings of the S.E.H.A."; Provo: *The Society for Early Historic Archaeology*, n.d.).

14. Dee F. Green, "Book of Mormon Archaeology: The Myths and the Alternatives," *Dialogue: A Journal of Mormon Thought*, (Summer 1969): 75.

15. Hartley Burr Alexander, *The Mythology of All Races* 13 vols. (Boston: Marshall Jones, 1920), 11:70.

16. Letter to the author, dated March 27, 1980 from Arlene Robinson, assistant to the Secretary and Treasurer at *The Society for Early Historic Archaeology, Inc.* Ms. Robinson's mention of Dr. Jakeman's explanation is referencing his publication: *Stela 5, Isapa Chiapas, Mexico: A Major Archaeological Discovery of the New World* (Bibliographic information unknown. Ms. Robinson infers it is a Brigham Young University publication).

17. Letter to the author, 15 October 1980.

18. No author cited. "Chiapas Find of Relevance to Document," *El Paso Times*, 4 July 1965, quoted in Tanner and Tanner, *Mormonism—Shadow or Reality?*, 116. The two missionaries have been identified as Robert Elder and Vaughn Byington. They apparently obtained their information from a printed sheet used by Maurice W. Connell of the University Archaeological Society who was lecturing in the area.

19. The Department of Anthropology, "Statement Regarding the Book of Mormon" (Washington D.C.: National Museum of Natural History, Smithsonian Institution, n.d.), 3. [Hereinafter, *Smithsonian.*]
20. Dr. John L. Sorenson, professor emeritus of anthropology at BYU, said: "As long as Mormons generally are willing to be fooled by (and pay for) the uninformed, uncritical drivel about archeology and the Scriptures which predominates, the few LDS experts are reluctant even to be identified with the topic (Review of "Papers of the Fifteenth Annual Symposium on the Archaeology of the Scriptures," ed. by Ross T. Christensen, *Dialogue, A Joural of Mormon Thought* no. 1 [Spring 1966]: 145–146).
21. Tanner and Tanner, *Mormonism—Shadow or Reality?*, 124.
22. Ibid.
23. Jerald Tanner and Sandra Tanner, *Ferguson's Manuscript Unveiled* (Salt Lake City: Utah Lighthouse Ministry, 1988), 39.
24. *Smithsonian*, 3.
25 Mosiah 2:7.
26. See Martin Raish, "All that Glitters: Uncovering Fool's Gold in Book of Mormon Archaeology." *Sunstone* 6, no. 1 (1981): 13.
27. This claim usually pertains to archaeological periods III–V. An earlier period I and II, the preclassic period does, however, coincide with the time claimed for the Jaredites or Nephites. But, there is no evidence to link anything with the Jaredites or Nephites.
28. *U.A.S. Newsletter,* no. 64 (30 January 1960). [U.A.S. stands for University Archaeological Society at Provo, Utah.] Quoted in Bill McKeever, *Answering Mormons' Questions* (Minneapolis: Bethany House, 1991).
29. Tanner and Tanner, *Mormonism—Shadow or Reality?*, 99.
30. E. Cecil McGavin, *Mormonism and Masonry* (Salt Lake City: Bookcraft, 1949), 74–76.
31. Fran H. H. Roberts of the *Smithsonian Institute*, a letter dated 10 October 1958, quoted in Tanner and Tanner, *Mormonism—Shadow or Reality?*, 108.
32. Left by the Sumerians (ca. 2800–2360 B.C.). An ancient civilization situated between the Tigris and Euphrates rivers, later known as Babylonia. The Sumerians invented cuneiform writing. A major city was Ur, the birthplace of Abraham. It is in the southern part of what is now Iraq.
33. 2 Nephi 25:24, 29–30.
34. Alma 30:3.
35. Lamb, *The Golden Bible*, 109–110, quoted in Tanner and Tanner, "No Passover," *Salt Lake City Messenger*, no. 74, (February 1990), 10.

36. While, admittedly, there is one 'burnt offering,' they perform it incorrectly. Mosiah 2:3 says, "And they also took of the *firstlings* of their flocks, that they might offer sacrifice and burnt offerings according to the law of Moses." The Tanners quote Lamb, *The Golden Bible*, 109–10:

    According to the law of Moses the firstlings of their flocks were never offered as burnt offerings or sacrifices. All firstlings belonged to the Lord, de jure, and could not be counted as a man's personal property—whereas, all burnt offerings, or sacrifices for sin of every kind, must be selected from the man's own personal property, or be purchased with his own money for that purpose, while all firstlings of the flock, as the Lord's property, came into the hands of the high priest, and by him could be offered up as a peace offering, not as a burnt offering or a sin offering, himself and family eating the flesh. . . . This one little blunder, then, proves beyond the chance of question that the Book of Mormon could not have been inspired by the Holy Spirit or by an angel of the Lord (Tanner and Tanner, "No Passover," 11).

37. "Iron, steel, glass, and silk were not used in the New World before 1492 (except for occasional use of unsmelted meteoric iron). Native copper was worked in various locations in pre-Columbian times, but true metallurgy was limited to southern Mexico and the Andean region, where its occurrence in late prehistoric times involved gold, silver, copper, and their alloys, but not iron." ("Statement Regarding the Book of Mormon," Department of Anthropology, Smithsonian Institute [Washington D.C.: n.d.], 3). [Hereinafter, *Smithsonian*].

38. The Tanners state: "He told us that he had spent twenty-five years trying to prove Mormonism, but had finally come to the conclusion that all his work in this regard had been in vain. He said that his training in law had taught him how to weigh evidence and that the case against Joseph Smith was absolutely devastating and could not be explained away." Quoted from Tanner and Tanner, *Fergson's Manuscript Unveiled*, 3.

39. Ibid., 16.

40. "Horses were in the Americas, along with the 'camel . . . bison, mammoth, and mastodon [but] all these animals became extinct around 10,000 B.C." (*Smithsonian*, 2).

41. Tanner and Taner,, *Ferguson's Manuscript Unveiled*, 30.

42. Bruce R. McConkie said the Jaredites did not speak Egyptian, but "retained a tongue patterned after that of Adam" *Mormon Doctrine* (Salt Lake City: Bookcraft, 1958), 393.

43. Tanner and Tanner, *Ferguson's Manuscript Unveiled*, 34.

44. *Smithsonian*, 3.
45. In the 1830 edition of the Book of Mormon, Smith has his characters using the name of Jesus Christ *before* arriving in the New World.
46. See Jacob 7:27.
47. 3 Nephi 9:18.
48. *Times and Seasons*, 4 (15 May 1843):194.
49. Tanner and Tanner, *Mormonism—Shadow or Reality?*, 79.
50. Anthony A. Hoekema, *The Four Major Cults* (Grand Rapids, Mich.: William B. Eerdmans, 1963), 85.
51. The Tanners use an excellent analogy as to what Smith does in the Book of Mormon:
    "Suppose, for instance, someone were to come forth with a book which purported to be written by Moses entitled, *The Only True Sayings of Moses,* and in this book the following words were attributed to him: "Consider the lilies how they grow: they toil not, they spin not; and yet I say unto you that Solomon in all his glory was not arrayed like one of these.
    "Or, having George Washington incorporate the following into his speech: 'Four score and seven years ago our fathers brought forth on this continent . . .' These are the kind of errors that soon make themselves evident" (*Salt Lake City Messenger*, no. 74 [February 1990], 4:13).
52. The "other sheep" had reference to the Gentiles. Paul, in Acts 9:15, received a commission to preach to them and once converted, there would be neither Jew nor gentile, but one fold of Christians.
53. Alexander, *The Mythology of All Races*, 11:67–68.
54. *Quetzal* means the long, green tail-plumes of Pharomacrus mocinno, and *Coatl*, means serpent. Altogether it means the Green-Feather Snake.
55. According to Aztec tradition.
56. One tradition tells how Quetzalcoatl decides to head for his ancient home, so he burns his houses, buries his treasure and changes the cacao-trees into mesquite. On his journey, he encounters magicians "who demanded of him, before they would let him pass, the arts of refining silver, of working in wood, stone, and feathers, and of painting; and as he crossed the sierra, all his companions, who were dwarfs and hump-backs, died of the cold" (Alexander, *The Mythology of All Races*, 11:70).
57. Alexander, *The Mythology of All Races*, 11:68. Other legends say Quetzalcoatl was defeated in a ball-play game by Tezcatlipoca. The latter "cast him out of the land into the east, where he encountered the sun and was burned. . . . a myth of the morning moon, driven

back by night (the dark Tezcatlipoca) to be consumed by the rising sun." Missionary priests tried to identify him with St. Thomas the Apostle (68–69).

58. Michael Jordan, *Encyclopedia of Gods* (New York: Facts On File, 1993), 214–15.
59. There was an historical figure, Topiltzin Quetzalcoatl, born about A.D. 935.
60. See Sribala Subramanian, "The Story in Our Genes" *Time*, (16 January 1995): 54–55.
61. The Book of Mormon also says there were *three* migrations. Some Mormons may take advantage of the coincidental number three, claiming it parallels the three migrations of the Jaredites, Nephites and Mulekites. However, the study shows that the migrations to the Americas were by three *genetically distinct* groups, from *Asia*, classified as *Mongoloid*. The Book of Mormon, on the other hand, claims the three migrations were Jews from Jerusalem. This would put them in the *Caucasoid* group.
62. The exception is a few mysterious carvings on Norse stones in Greenland.

Chapter Ten

1. The missionaries may also include the following: Psalm 117:2; Mosiah 2:22; Mormon 9:9; Proverbs 3:5–6; Isaiah 55:8–9; 1 Corinthians 2:14; Nephi 28:31.
2. Ether 4:12.
3. Over one hundred scholars worked diligently on the NIV to convey the exact meaning.
4. Mike Reynolds, "Manuscript evidence and the golden plates" *The Inner Circle* 12, no. 5 (May 1995): 5. The fragment of Chapter 26 on the resurrection, in the gospel of Matthew, is in possession of Magdalen College Library at Oxford University, and previously had been dated at A.D. 200. However, Carsten Thiede (scholar and papyrologist) says "the style and script used in the fragments clearly dates them a century earlier. This date supports the traditional view that the gospel was written by an eyewitness to the life of Christ.—Matthew the apostle" (7).
5. *Journal of Discourses*, Joseph F. Smith, ed. (1854–86; reprint, Salt Lake City Brigham Young University Press, 1967), 13:125.
6. Ephesians 3:21 (NIV).
7. Daniel 2:27–28, 34–35, 44.
8. Matthew 18:20.
9. The Greek word is *Ekklesia*. *Ek* means out and *kaleo* means to call.

10. Milton R. Hunter stated that in order to reach the highest heaven, one "must become a member and live the gospel principles and ordinances of the true church of the Master—which is The Church of Jesus Christ of Latter-day Saints," quoted in *Mormon Claims Answered*, rev. ed. (Self-published, 1989), 11. Available through Utah Lighthouse Ministry, P.O. Box 1884, Salt Lake City, UT 84110. Mr. Hunter's statement, however, contradicts 1 Timothy 2:5 which says "there is one God, and one Mediator between God and men, the man Christ Jesus." Mormons claim *three* mediators, the LDS Church, Christ, and Joseph Smith. But, since Jesus said He is the Way and that no man comes to the Father but by Him, He didn't say," as Marvin Cowan aptly notes, "'no man cometh unto the Father but through My Church.'"

11. John Chrysostom (A.D. 345–407) tells of Marcion in the first century, practicing baptism for the dead. It is understandable that the Greeks of Asia Minor, in their zeal for their newfound religion, especially upon the subject of baptism, would have a desire to baptize the dead. However, Chrysostom stated that it was the "practice of heretics." This is proved by the fact that this ordinance was never considered a legitimate practice of any of the other branches of the church, even in New Testament times. Although Paul mentioned some who were doing this at Corinth, it should not be looked at seriously in view of the background and character of the Corinthians.

12. Hurlbut states in *The Story of the Christian Church* (Grand Rapids: Zondervan, 1970), 54: "One remarkable line of evidence has been found in the catacombs of Rome. Underground quarries of vast extent, which for two centuries became the hiding places, the meeting-places, and the burial-places of the believers, where in the graves of Christians, as shown by the inscriptions and symbols upon them, are estimated by some to number in the millions. Add to these millions many not buried in the catacombs; and then consider how vast must have been the aggregate in the Roman empire."

13. Hurlbut, *The Story of the Christian Church*, 48–49.

14. 1 Kings 19:1.

15. 1 Kings 19:18.

16. His prophecy stated: "You are now roasting the goose (Huss means goose in Bohemian) but in a hundred years there will rise up a swan whom you shall not roast nor scorch. Him men will hear sing and God will allow him to live." Quoted in Bill Hamon, *The Eternal Church* (Phoenix, Ariz.: Christian International Publishers, n.d.), 126.

17. In any move of God, we do not find doctrines foreign to the New

Testament, such as polygamy in heaven, genealogy, work for the
dead, or salvation by works.
18. J. Edwin Orr, *The Fervent Prayer* (Chicago, Ill.: Moody Press,
    1974), xiv.
19. Ibid., xv.
20. Ibid., xii.
21. Ibid., 7.
22. Ibid., 8.
23. Ibid., 13.
24. Ibid., 24.
25. Ibid., 8
26. Ibid., 10–11.
27. Ibid., 38.
28. Ibid., 38.
29. Ibid., 118.
30. Ibid., 63.
31. Ibid., 70.
32. Ibid., 105.

Chapter Eleven

1. Abraham 3:22–25.
2. Alma 13:1–4. Mormon missionaries also use Doctrine and Covenants
   138:55–56. Many "received their first lessons in the world of spirits
   and were prepared to come forth" to labor in the vineyard.
3. See Walter Schmithas, *Gnosticism in Corinth* (New York: Abingdon
   Press, 1971), 146–49. From the gospel of Thomas we read: "Gnosticism teaches men to understand himself as a piece of divine substance. He will be sure to be liberated from demonic rulers because
   he possesses the awareness of his inalienable divine being"
   (Schmithals, *Gnosticism in Corinth*, 30). See also *The Gospel of
   Thomas: The Hidden Sayings of Jesus* (San Francisco: Harper,
   1992). See also, Schmithals, *Gnosticism in Corinth*, 32.
4. See "New Compilation of Gnostic Scriptures is now available," *Insights An Ancient Window*, newsletter, Foundation for Ancient Research & Mormon Studies, Brigham Young University (Summer
   1987): 1. In Utah, there was a prominent Mormon who traveled and
   presented lectures on the "marvelous similarities" between Gnosticism and Mormonism which, he said, proved Mormonism true.
5. Alma 12:24.
6. The missionaries may also quote the following: 2 Nephi 2:21; Alma
   34:31–35; Alma 42:4; Mormon 9:27.
7. See Doctrine and Covenants sec. 110.

8. Mormons believe that the keys that Elijah restored, were the "sealing" keys. The appropriateness of Elijah restoring these particular keys is evidenced, according to Joseph Smith, by the fact that he was able to seal up the heavens so it could not rain. Therefore, the possession of these keys confirm that temple work performed for the dead will be sealed in heaven.

9. The missionaries may use the following: (After death): 1 Nephi 15:33–36; 2 Nephi 9:6; 2 Nephi 9:14; Mosiah 2:38; Alma 12:12–15, 27–28; Alma 40:12–13; Alma 41:3–15; John 5:25–29; Doctrine and Covenants 76. (Work for the Dead): Malachi 4:5–6; 1 Corinthians 15:29–30; Doctrine and Covenants 2; Doctrine and *Covenants* 128; Doctrine and Covenants 137; Doctrine and Covenants 138. (The Eternal Family): 1 Corinthians 11:11; Doctrine and Covenants 130:2; Doctrine and Covenants 131:2; Doctrine and Covenants 132. (Chastity): Mosiah 13:22; Exodus 20:14; Alma 12:14, 39:5; 3 Nephi 12:27-30; Romans 1:26–32; Ephesians 5:3–5; Doctrine and Covenants 59:6; Doctrine and Covenants 63:16. (Word of Wisdom): Daniel 1:8–20; 1 Corinthians 3:16–17; Doctrine and Covenants 89.

10. John 9:4.

11. Alma 34:32–35.

12. Alma 1:3–4; 2 Nephi 28:22–23. See also Jerald Tanner and Sandra Tanner, *Mormonism—Shadow or Reality?*, (Salt Lake City: Modern Microfilm, 1972), 196ff.

13. The Unpardonable Sin is murder and also sinning against the Holy Ghost. The latter consists of denying the Mormon Gospel after receiving a testimony of its truthfulness from the Holy Ghost.

14. B. H. Roberts, *Outlines of Ecclesiastical History* (Salt Lake City: Deseret News, 1902), 408. Smith changes his idea in a revelation given to Martin Harris. See Tanner and Tanner, *Mormonism—Shadow or Reality?*, 197. See also Joseph Fielding Smith, comp. Bruce R. McConkie, Doctrines of Salvation (Salt Lake City: Bookcraft, 1955), 2:160 and Doctrine and Covenants 19:6.

15. See Tanner and Tanner, *Mormonism—Shadow or Reality?*, 198ff.

16. Spokesman and Apostle, Bruce R. McConkie, in *Mormon Doctrine* 2d ed. (Salt Lake City: Bookcraft, 1979) misleadingly states "There is no such thing as a second chance to gain salvation by accepting the gospel in the spirit world after spurning, declining, or refusing to accept it in this life" [emphasis mine]. ["Gospel" means the Mormon gospel.] The above is a generalized statement to pacify non-Mormon critics. But, what Mormonism really teaches is that there will indeed be a second chance for everyone, the difference being that some may

not inherit the highest heaven. McConkie explains: "Those who have a fair and just opportunity to accept the [Mormon] gospel in this life and who do not do it, but who then do accept it when they hear it in the spirit world will not go to the celestial, but to the terrestrial kingdom." In other words, they will have a second chance to avoid hell. They will be saved in the middle heaven, the terrestrial, where they will enjoy the presence of Jesus but not God the Father (685–87).

17. Bruce R. McConkie, *Mormon Doctrine*, 687.

18. Joseph Smith also claimed a seventh heaven: "Paul said he knew a man who was caught up to the third heaven. But," said [Smith], "I know a man who was caught up to the seventh heaven." (From a lecture prepared by Joseph E. Taylor, Counselor in the Presidency of Salt Lake Stake of Zion from 1876 to 1904 and read in the Logan Temple, June 2, 1888. This lecture also appeared as an article entitled "The Resurrection" in the *Deseret Weekly*, 38, no. 1, (29 December, 1888). Note: Smith was no doubt borrowing this insight from the Masonic order, *The Holy Royal Arch*, which mentions a seventh heaven or degree. (See Henry Dana Ward, *The Anti-Masonic Review and Magazine*, 1828, 1:88.)

19. See Schmithals, *Gnosticism in Corinth*, 78–79.

20. 1 John 4:2–3.

21. Joseph Smith stated, "Let me assure you that these are principles in relation to the dead and the living that cannot be lightly passed over, as pertaining to our salvation. For their salvation is necessary and essential to our salvation, as Paul says concerning the fathers— that they without us cannot be made perfect—neither can we without our dead be made perfect." (Doctrine and Covenants 128:15).

22. According to scholars, Baptism for the dead was also done by people who denied the resurrection. (Schmithals, *Gnosticism in Corinth*, 389).

23. Gnostics did not believe Paul had the Christ spirit in him because of his emphasis on the body, works and labor. They stated: "He who acquires virtue through effort is inferior to and less perfect than Moses, who without labor, received it from God." (Schmithals, *Gnosticism in Corinth*, 204). As Paul gained more information about the Gnostics, he deliberately made statements to combat their beliefs: "Christ in you, the hope of glory; "I live, yet not I, but Christ . . ."; Till Christ be formed in you," etc. He also made statements to compete against the mystery religions. His phrase, "put on Christ" (Galatians 3:27) was an attempt to refute their rituals which had initiates putting on their god by donning special garments.

24. Joseph Smith said that "In the beginning the head of the Gods called a council of the Gods." Joseph Fielding Smith, comp. *Teachings of*

the Prophet Joseph Smith (Salt Lake City: Deseret Book, 1977), 349.

25. *Journal of Discourses,* Joseph F. Smith, ed. (1854–86); reprint, Salt Lake City Brigham Young University Press, 1967), 2:345. An unidentified Mormon stated the following: "Our God knows all things concerning us, but He has innumerable Gods who preside over him, and have their own creations who may know more than ten times as much as he does. As He lives on and creates, He will learn and gain more experience eternally. Each God has dominion over many other Gods, ten or a million, depending on his progression and experience."

    This quote was copied from a book many years ago while I was a member of Mormon Fundamentalism. Unfortunately, at that time, I was not diligent in spelling out references and only abbreviated names of sources. Therefore, the only reference I noted for the above quote was the *RCA* book, May 12, 1967, Fireside taken by MDA. (A fireside is an informal gathering in a church facility.) However, the concept can be fond in *The Seer*, ed. Orson Pratt (1853–1854; reprint, Liverpool: Franklin D. Richards, n.d.)

26. James Talmage wrote in *A Study of the Articles of Faith*, (Salt Lake City: Church of Jesus Christ of Latter-day Saints, 1977), 443, "We are expressly told that God is the Father of spirits, and to apprehend the literalness of this solemn truth we must know that a Mother of spirits is an existent personality." For many other quotes on this subject, see Marvin W. Cowan's book, *Mormon Claims Answered* (Self-published, 1989) available through Utah Missions, Inc., Box 348, Marlow, OK 73055.

27. Cleon Skousen, *The First 2000 Years* (Salt Lake City: Bookcraft, 1953), 355–356, quoted in Marvin W. Cowan's *Mormon Claims Answered*, 15.

28. (The omnipresence of God): See Psalms 139; Proverbs 15:3; Jeremiah 23:24; Acts 17:27; John 1:3. (God is unchangeable and eternal): Deuteronomy 33:27; Psalms 41:13; 90:2; 106:48; Isaiah 40:28; Jeremiah 10:10; Malachi 3:6; Colossians 1:17; 1 Timothy. 1:17; Hebrews 13:8; James 1:17.

29. Alma 18:26–28.

30. 2 Nephi 31:21 and Alma 11:26–31.

31. 1 Nephi 11:18.

32. Bruce R. McConkie, *Mormon Doctrine*, 359. When a Mormon receives the gift of the Holy Ghost after baptism, Mormon doctrine does not interpret this to mean that the actual personage of the Holy

Ghost resides in that person; but, rather, his power and influence. See also N. B. Lundwall, comp., *Discourses on the Holy Ghost* (Salt Lake City: Bookcraft, 1959), 12–13.

33. "The Holy Ghost is yet a spiritual body and waiting to take to himself a body as the Savior did or as the gods before them took bodies" (N.B. Lundwall, comp., *Discourses on the Holy Ghost* [Salt Lake City: Bookcraft, 1959], 73).

34. John A. Widtsoe, *Evidences and Reconciliations* (Salt Lake City, Utah: Bookcraft, 1960), 62.

35. Parley P. Pratt, *Key to Theology* (Liverpool, 1855), 29, 39.

36. The Mormon logic, even if they understand that Paul is speaking of human bodies not heavens, is that if there are different kinds of bodies, celestial or terrestrial, there must certainly be corresponding heavens to contain those types of bodies.

37. Cowan, *Mormon Claims Answered*, 111.

Chapter Twelve

1. Evidently Smith had no qualms about altering revelations. According to Apostle William E. McLellin, the testimony of the Twelve Apostles contained in the Introduction to the Doctrine and Covenants, was a 'base forgery' and that Smith had seriously altered other revelations. See Jerald Tanner and Sandra Tanner, *Mormonism—Shadow or Reality?*, (Salt Lake City: Modern Microfilm, 1972), 31. David Whitmer, in *An Address To All Believers in Christ* (Self-published, Richmond, Mo.:, 1887; reprint 1938), 49, accused Joseph of the same thing.

2. See Chapter 8 for full quote. Martin Harris was well known for his religious instability and that he changed his religious affiliation at least thirteen times in his life. In addition, he gave false prophecies and became carried away with his own visions. In one vision he saw Jesus in the form of a deer. In another, he said the devil looked like a jackass and had short smooth hair like a mouse. (See Tanner and Tanner, *Mormonism—Shadow or Reality?*, 56.)

3. Letter from Stephen Burnett to Lyman E. Johnson. A copy of this letter is in the Joseph Smith Collection in the LDS Church Archives. Quoted in David Persuitte, *Joseph Smith and the Origins of The Book of Mormon* (Jefferson, N.C.: McFarland & Co, 1991), 96.

4. Thomas L. Ford, *History of Illinois* (Chicago, Ill.: 1854), 257, quoted in Fawn M. Brodie's *No Man Knows My History* (New York: Alfred A. Knopf, 1971), 79–80.

5. Brodie, *No Man Knows My History*, 77.

6. David Whitmer, in his *Address to All Believers in Christ*, 28, stated:

"All of the eight witnesses who were then living (except the three Smiths) came out [of the LDS Church]. Peter and Christian Whitmer were dead. Oliver Cowdery came out also" (28). Quoted in Marvin W. Cowan's *Mormon Claims Answered*, rev. ed. (Self-published, 1989), 57. Available through Utah Lighthouse Ministry, P.O. Box 1884, Salt Lake City, UT 84110.

7. The following is the last stanza in a poem published in 1841 in the Mormon publication, *Times and Seasons* (2:482):

　　Or prove that Christ was not the Lord
　　Because that Peter cursed and swore?
　　Or Book of Mormon not his word
　　Because denied, by Oliver?

8. Affidavit by G. J. Keen. See also, Tanner and Tanner *Mormonism—Shadow or Reality?*, 54.

9. Cowan, *Mormon Claims Answered*, 56.

10. Tanner and Tanner, *Mormonism—Shadow or Reality?*, 58.

11. James H. Snowden, *The Truth About Mormonism* (New York: George H. Doran, 1926), 60.

12. Ibid.

13. See Tanner and Tanner, *Mormonism—Shadow or Reality?*, 59. Fawn Brodie also suggests that Joseph built a makeshift set of plates; see *No Man Knows My History*, 80.

14. David Persuitte *Joseph Smith and the Origins of The* Book of Mormon (Jefferson, N.C.: McFarland & Co., 1985), 59. Joseph Capron also says that Joseph Smith, Sr. "gave me no intimation, at that time that the book was to be of a religious character, or that it had anything to do with revelation."

15. Brodie, *No Man Knows My History*, 316–17. It is thought by some that Bennett invented the story.

16. Josh McDowell, *Evidence that Demands a Verdict*, rev. ed. (San Bernardino: Here's Life Pub. 1979), 3.

17. 1 Thessalonians 5:21 (NIV).

18. Job 5:12.

Bibliography

Witnessing Tracts, Tapes, and Pamphlets

Carlson, Ron. *Understanding Mormonism.* Audiocassette. Presents a compassionate case. Available through Saints Alive in Jesus, P.O. Box 1076, Issaquah, WA 98027.

Cetnar, Bill. *How to Witness to a Jehovah's Witness.* Audiocassette. Lecture by former high-ranking Jehovah's Witness. Available through Personal Freedom Outreach, P.O. Box 26062, Saint Louis, MO 63136.

Cults Bibliography. Pamphlet. Lists available publications. Available through Christian Research Institute International, P.O. Box 500, San Juan Capistrano, CA 92693.

Decker, Ed. *Some Pointers on Witnessing to Your Mormon Friends.* Pamphlet. Available through Saints Alive in Jesus, P.O. Box 1076, Issaquah, WA 98027.

Decker, Ed. *Sharing Christ with Mormons.* Two audiocassettes. Workshop on sharing with Mormons. Available through Saints Alive in Jesus, P.O. Box 1076, Issaquah, WA 98027.

Decker, Ed. *To Moroni with Love.* Available through Saints Alive in Jesus, P.O. Box 1076, Issaquah, WA 98027.

Decker, Ed. *Ed Decker and Dave Hunt Debate the Mormons.* Two audiocassettes. Available through Saints Alive in Jesus, P.O. Box 1076, Issaquah, WA 98027.

Decker, Ed and Jim Spencer. *The Mormon Dilemma.* Video. Deals with the differences between Mormonism and orthodoxy. Available through Saints Alive in Jesus, P.O. Box 1076, Issaquah, WA 98027.

Divine Truths in the Book of Mormon. Witnessing tract. Concerns the contradiction between the Book of Mormon and current Mormon theology. Available through Personal Freedom Outreach, P.O. Box 26062, Saint Louis, MO 63136.

Enroth, Ronald M., ed., *Evangelizing the Cults.* Ann Arbor, Mich.: Servant Publications, n.d.

Gardner, Jim and Cindy Gardner. *Jim and Cindy Gardner: Classic Mormons discover Jesus!* Audiocassette. To share with Mormons. Available through Saints Alive in Jesus, P.O. Box 1076, Issaquah, WA 98027.

The God Makers, I. Video. Available through Saints Alive in Jesus, P.O. Box 1076, Issaquah, WA 98027.

Harrison, G. T. *That Mormon Book: Mormonism's Keystone Exposed or The Hoax Book.* Self-published. Believed to be out of print.

Hougey, Hal. *Latter-Day Saints: Where Did You Get Your Authority?* Valuable study of Mormon priesthood. Available through Utah Lighthouse Ministry, Box 1884, Salt Lake City, UT 84110.

Hunt, Dave. *Cults in the New Age.* Audiocassette. Deals with the New Age Movement. Available through Saints Alive in Jesus, P.O. Box 1076, Issaquah, WA 98027.

McConkie, Bruce R. *LDS Apostle Confesses Brigham Young Taught Adam-God Doctrine.* Photographic reproduction of ten-page letter written by Mormon leader Bruce R. McConkie. Available through Utah Lighthouse Ministry, Box 1884, Salt Lake City, UT 84110.

Lewis, Gordon R. *Confronting the Cults.* Grand Rapids: Baker, 1966.

Lingle, Wilbur. *Witnessing Effectively to the Jehovah's Witnesses.* Audiocassette #12. Available through Personal Freedom Outreach, P.O. Box 26062, Saint Louis, MO 63136.

MacGregor, Lorrie. *What You Need to Know about Jehovah's Witnesses.* Eugene, Ore.: Harvest House, 1992. Available through Saints Alive in Jesus, P.O. Box 1076, Issaquah, WA 98027.

_____. *The Witness at Your Door.* Video. Ex-Jehovah's Witness. Available through Saints Alive in Jesus, P.O. Box 1076, Issaquah, WA 98027.

Martin, Walter R. "The Dos and Don'ts of Witnessing to the Cults." In *Cults Reference Bible.* Available through Christian Research Institute International, P.O. Box 500, San Juan Capistrano, CA 92693.

The Mormon Plan for America. Two audiocassettes. LDS plans for a Mormon theocracy. Available through Saints Alive in Jesus, P.O. Box 1076, Issaquah, WA 98027.

"Reaching the Cults for Christ." Article. Available through Christian Research Institute International, P.O. Box 500, San Juan Capistrano, CA 92693.

"Sharing Christ with Mormons." Two audiocassettes. Available through Saints Alive in Jesus, P.O. Box 1076, Issaquah, WA 98027.

Smith, John L. *Witnessing Effectively to Mormons.* Marlow, Okla.: Utah Missions, Inc., 1991. Booklet. Available through Utah Missions, Inc., P.O. Box 348, Marlow, OK 73055.

_____. *So You Are Interested in a Ministry to Mormons?* Marlow, Okla.: Utah Missions, 1989. Booklet. Available through Utah Missions, Box 348, Marlow, OK 73055.

_____. *Hope or Despair: Mormonism—True or False.* Marlow, Okla.: Utah Missions, Inc., 1987. Booklet. Available through Utah Missions, Inc., P.O. Box 348, Marlow, OK 73055.

Spencer, Jim. *Witnessing to Mormons.* Video, also on audiocassette. Available through Saints Alive in Jesus, P.O. Box 1076, Issaquah, WA 98027.

Suggestions for Witnessing to Mormons. Witnessing tract. Available through Personal Freedom Outreach, P.O. Box 26062, Saint Louis, MO 63136.

Sundholm, Conrad and Sandra Sundholm. *Witnessing and the LDS Mindset.* Seminar audiocassette package. Available through Saints Alive in Jesus, P.O. Box 1076, Issaquah, WA 98027.

Tanner, Sandra. *Tape #1: Lectures Given at Trinity Evangelical Divinity School.* Helpful overview for those wanting to understand Mormonism. Available through Utah Lighthouse Ministry, P.O. Box 1884, Salt Lake City, UT 84110.

Tanner, Jerald. *Problems in Winning Mormons.* Audiocassette. Shows how to use a loving approach to win Mormons to the Lord. Available through Utah Lighthouse Ministry, P.O. Box 1884, Salt Lake City, UT 84110.

A True Christian Presentation to a Jehovah's Witness. Witnessing tract. Available through Personal Freedom Outreach, P.O. Box 26062, Saint Louis, MO 63136.

The Unification Church: The Christian View. Slides and cassette. Examines the history, doctrines, and indoctrination methods. Witnessing suggestions included in closing segment. Filmstrip version also available through Personal Freedom Outreach, P.O. Box 26062, Saint Louis, MO 63136.

Vlachos, Chris A. *Adam Is God?* Pamphlet. Well-researched pamphlet on the Adam-God doctrine. Available through Utah Lighthouse Ministry, P.O. Box 1884, Salt Lake City, UT 84110.

Walters, Wesley P. *Mormonism: The Christian View.* Video. Deals with Mormon history, doctrines, claim to authority, changes in doctrine, and witnessing suggestions. Available through Utah Lighthouse Ministry, P.O. Box 1884, Salt Lake City, UT 84110.

_____. *New Light on Mormon Origins: From the Palmyra (N.Y.) Revival.* Dispels credibility of Joseph Smith's First Vision. Available through Utah Lighthouse Ministry, P.O. Box 1884, Salt Lake City, UT 84110.

_____. *An Examination of B. H. Roberts' Secret Manuscript.* Article. Examines this Mormon historian's analysis showing that Joseph Smith could have written the Book of Mormon. Available through Utah Lighthouse Ministry, P.O. Box 1884, Salt Lake City, UT 84110.

The Way of Private Interpretation. Witnessing tract. For members of The Way International. Available through Personal Freedom Outreach, P.O. Box 26062, Saint Louis, MO 63136.

Whitmer, David. *An Address to All Believers in Christ.* Pamphlet. One of the three witnesses to the Book of Mormon explains why he left the Mormon Church. Available through Utah Lighthouse Ministry, P.O. Box 1884, Salt Lake City, UT 84110.

Who's That Knocking At My Door? Pamphlet. Deals with Mormons. Available through Saints Alive in Jesus, P.O. Box 1076, Issaquah, WA 98027.

"Witnessing Tips: A Jesus Style of Evangelism." Article. Available through Christian Research Institute International, P.O. Box 500, San Juan Capistrano, CA 92693.

Witnessing to Cultists. Pamphlet. Christian Research Institute International, P.O. Box 500, San Juan Capistrano, CA 92693.

Witnessing to Mormons. Video. Available through Utah Missions, Inc., P.O. Box 348, Marlow, OK 73055.

Witnessing to Your Mormon Friends. Tract. Available through Saints Alive in Jesus, P.O. Box 1076, Issaquah, WA 98027.

Books

Andrus, Hyrum L. *Joseph Smith and World Government.* Salt Lake City: Hawkes, 1972. Pro-Mormon book presents Joseph

Smith's concept of world government, called the kingdom of God.

Brodie, Fawn M. *No Man Knows My History*. New York: Knopf, 1945. Excellent coverage of the life of Joseph Smith. Available through Utah Lighthouse Ministry, P.O. Box 1884, Salt Lake City, UT 84110.

Brooke, John L. *The Refiner's Fire: The Making of Mormon Cosmology, 1644–1844*. Cambridge University Press, 1994. Brooke is associate professor in the Department of History at Tufts University. He analyzes Mormon theology and traces Smith's theological ideas to the European Hermeticists and subversive sectarians of the Radical Reformation and how they were transferred to early American culture and picked up by Joseph Smith.

Cares, Mark. *Speaking the Truth in Love to Mormons*. Available through Utah Lighthouse Ministry, P.O. Box 1884, Salt Lake City, UT 84110.

Carlson, Ron and Ed Decker. *Fast Facts on False Teachings*. Eugene, Oreg.: Harvest House, 1994.

Crane, Dr. *The Bible & Mormon Scriptures Compared*. Available through Saints Alive in Jesus, P.O. Box 1076, Issaquah, WA 98027.

Cowan, Marvin. *Mormon Claims Answered*. Self-published, 1989. Available through Utah Lighthouse Ministry, P.O. Box 1884, Salt Lake City, UT 84110.

Decker, Ed. *Decker's Complete Handbook on Mormonism*. Available through Saints Alive in Jesus, P.O. Box 1076, Issaquah, WA 98027.

Decker, Ed and Dave Hunt. *The God Makers*. Available through Saints Alive in Jesus, P.O. Box 1076, Issaquah, WA 98027.

Ferguson, Thomas Stuart. *Ferguson's Manuscript Unveiled*. A Mormon concludes that the Book of Mormon is fiction. Covers Book of Mormon archaeology and geography. Available through Utah Lighthouse Ministry, Box 1884, Salt Lake City, UT 84110.

Hansen, Klaus J. *Quest For Empire: The Political Kingdom of God and the Council of Fifty in Mormon History*. Lincoln, Nebr.: University of Nebraska Press, 1967.

Hinerman, John and Anson Shupe. *The Mormon Corporate Empire*. Boston: Beacon, 1985.

Hutchinson, Janis. *Out of the Cults and Into the Church: Understanding and Encouraging Ex-Cultists*. Grand Rapids:

Kregel, 1994. Describes the turmoils and adjustments ex-cultists experience as they come to terms with Biblical truth. Offers practical guidance and insights into the understanding Christians *must* provide if ex-cultists are ever to break free of the emotional and social bonds of a cult.

Lamb, M. T. *The Golden Bible*. Good analysis of internal problems in the Book of Mormon. Available through Utah Lighthouse Ministry, P.O. Box 1884, Salt Lake City, UT 84110.

Larson, Charles M. *By His Own Hand Upon Papyrus: A New Look at the Joseph Smith Papyri*. Demonstrates the authenticity of the Book of Abraham, showing it is a pagan document known as the Book of Breathings. Available through Utah Lighthouse Ministry, P.O. Box 1884, Salt Lake City, UT 84110.

McKeever, Bill. *Answering Mormons' Questions*. Available through Mormonism Research Ministry, P.O. Box 20705, El Cajon, CA 92021.

McKeever, Bill and Eric Johnson. *Questions to Ask Your Mormon Friend: Challenging the Claims of Latter-day Saints in a Constructive Manner*. Available through Mormonism Research Ministry, P.O. Box 20705, El Cajon, CA 92021.

Martin, Walter R. *The Kingdom of the Cults*. Minneapolis: Bethany House, 1985.

Passantino, Robert and Gretchen Passantino. *Answers to the Cultist at Your Door*. Eugene, Oreg.: Harvest House, 1981.

Quinn, D. Michael. *The Mormon Hierarchy*. Salt Lake City: Signature Books, 1994.

_____. *Early Mormonism and the Magic World View*. Salt Lake City: Signature Books, 1987.

Reed, David A. and John R. Farkas. *How to Rescue Your Loved One from Mormonism*. Available through Utah Lighthouse Ministry, P.O. Box 1884, Salt Lake City, UT 84110.

_____. *Mormons Answered Verse by Verse*. Available through Utah Lighthouse Ministry, P.O. Box 1884, Salt Lake City, UT 84110.

Roberts, B. H. *Studies of the* Book of Mormon. Secret manuscripts of Mormon leader B. H. Roberts in which he expresses his doubts about the validity of the Book of Mormon. Suppressed by the Mormon Church for many years. Available through Utah Lighthouse Ministry, P.O. Box 1884, Salt Lake City, UT 84110.

Scott, Latayne C. *The Mormon Mirage: A Former Mormon Tells*

Why She Left the Church. Grand Rapids: Zondervan, 1979. Available through Utah Lighthouse Ministry, P.O. Box 1884, Salt Lake City, UT 84110.

_____. *Ex-Mormons: Why We Left*. Grand Rapids: Baker, 1990. Testimonies of eight ex-Mormons. Available through Utah Lighthouse Ministry, Box 1884, Salt Lake City, UT 84110.

_____. *Why We Left a Cult*. Grand Rapids: Baker, 1993. Testimonies of six individuals who came out of Jehovah's Witnesses, Christian Science, New Age, and Herbert Armstrong's World Wide Church of God. (Note: Since the publication of this book, the World Wide Church of God has undergone a complete turnabout in their doctrines and is no longer considered a cult by many evangelicals.)

Shupe, Anson. *The Darker Side of Virtue: Corruption, Scandal, and the Mormon Empire*. Buffalo, N.Y.: Prometheus Books, 1991.

Spencer, Jim. *Have You Witnessed to a Mormon Lately?* Vienna, Va.: Chosen Books, 1986. Available through Saints Alive in Jesus, P.O. Box 1076, Issaquah, WA 98027.

Tanner, Jerald and Sandra Tanner. *The Mormon Purge*. A revealing account of how the Mormon Church silences its historians and others through threats of excommunication and other reprisals. Includes information from secret church documents on how the Church betrayed its historians. Available through Utah Lighthouse Ministry, P.O. Box 1884, Salt Lake City, UT 84110.

_____. *The Mormon Kingdom*. Vols. 1 and 2. Salt Lake City: Utah Lighthouse Ministry, 1969–71. Discusses the Temple ceremony, Masonry, doctrine of blood atonement, baptism for the dead, Council of Fifty, Joseph Smith's secret ordination as king, his candidacy for president of the United States, and other subjects. Available through Utah Lighthouse Ministry, P.O. Box 1884, Salt Lake City, UT 84110.

_____. *Falsification of Joseph Smith's History*. Salt Lake City: Modern Microfilm, 1971. Proves the Mormon Church made serious changes in Smith's history after his death. Available through Utah Lighthouse Ministry, Box 1884, Salt Lake City, UT 84110.

_____. *Flaws in the Pearl of Great Price*. Available through Utah Lighthouse Ministry, P.O. Box 1884, Salt Lake City, UT 84110.

_____. *Mormon Scriptures and the Bible.* Salt Lake City: Modern Microfilm, 1970. Available through Utah Lighthouse Ministry, P.O. Box 1884, Salt Lake City, UT 84110.

_____. *Mormonism, Magic and Masonry.* Salt Lake City: Utah Lighthouse Ministry, 1983. A study of the influence of magic and Masonry on Joseph Smith and his family. Available through Utah Lighthouse Ministry, P.O. Box 1884, Salt Lake City, UT 84110.

_____. *Joseph Smith and Money-Digging.* Salt Lake City: Modern Microfilm, 1970. Available through Utah Lighthouse Ministry, P.O. Box 1884, Salt Lake City, UT 84110.

_____. *Covering Up the Black Hole in the* Book of Mormon. Proof that the Book of Mormon was written by Joseph Smith and did not come from gold plates written by ancient Jews. Also proof that Smith plagiarized from the King James Version of the New Testament. Available through Utah Lighthouse Ministry, P.O. Box 1884, Salt Lake City, UT 84110.

_____. *Mormonism—Shadow or Reality?* Salt Lake City: Utah Lighthouse Ministry, 1972. Comprehensive and revealing work on Mormonism. Available through Utah Lighthouse Ministry, P.O. Box 1884, Salt Lake City, UT 84110. Well-documented, an excellent book to give a Mormon.

Tanner, Sandra. *The Bible and Mormon Doctrine.* Salt Lake City: Modern Microfilm, 1971. Available through Utah Lighthouse Ministry, P.O. Box 1884, Salt Lake City, UT 84110.

Walters, Wesley P. *The Use of the Old Testament in the* Book of Mormon. Available through Utah Lighthouse Ministry, P.O. Box 1884, Salt Lake City, UT 84110.

Resource Organizations

Many of the following organizations have newsletters with articles pertinent to cults, tips on witnessing, and other literature. You may contact them at the following addresses:

American Family Foundation, P.O. Box 2265, Bonita Springs, FL 33959.

Answers in Action, P.O. Box 2067, Costa Mesa, CA 92628.

Christian Research Institute International, P.O. Box 500, San Juan Capistrano, CA 92693.

Cult Awareness Network (CAN), 2421 W. Pratt Blvd., Suite 1173, Chicago, IL 60645.

Hope Ministries, P.O. Box 841256, Pembroke Pines, FL 33084.

International Cult Education Program, P.O. Box 1232, Gracie Station, New York, NY 10028. Focuses on preventive strategies, including young people exposed to cults on school campuses.

Outreach Australia, David M. Liptac, 21a Clement St., Guildford NSW 2161, Australia.

Personal Freedom Outreach, P.O. Box 26062, Saint Louis, MO 63136. Many tracts, videos, and cassettes available, as well as Newsletter.

reFOCUS, P.O. Box 2180, Flagler Beach, FL 32136. A part of the American Family Foundation, provides help and material on all cults.

Saints Alive in Jesus, P.O. Box 1076, Issaquah, WA 98027.

Spiritual Counterfeits Project, P.O. Box 4308, Berkeley, CA 94704.

Through the Maze Ministries, P.O. Box 3804, Idaho Falls, ID 83403. Mormon material.

Utah Lighthouse Ministries, P.O. Box 1884, Salt Lake City, UT 84110.

Utah Missions, Inc., P.O. Box 348, Marlow, OK 73055.

Watchman Fellowship, Inc., P.O. Box 19416, Birmingham, AL 35219. Publishes the "Expositor," a monthly newsletter with witnessing tips to cultists.

Wellspring Retreat and Resource Center, P.O. Box 67, Albany, OH 45710. Rehabilitation facility for ex-cultists.

Witness, Inc., P.O. Box 597, Clayton, CA 94517.

Index